D0335851

MEDIA, ECOLOGY AND CONSERVATION

MEDIA, ECOLOGY AND
CONSERVATION

Using the media to protect the world's wildlife
and ecosystems

John Blewitt

*The Converging World Series
from the Schumacher Institute*

green books

First published in the UK in 2010
by Green Books Ltd,
Foxhole, Dartington,
Totnes, Devon TQ9 6EB

The Converging World Series is a project of
The Schumacher Institute for Sustainable Systems
Bush House, 72 Prince Street, Bristol BS1 4QD
www.schumacherinstitute.org.uk

Text printed on 100% recycled paper

Printed by TJ International, Padstow, Cornwall, UK

ISBN 978 1 900322 63 8

Contents

Foreword

by Harriet Nimmo

I first met John at some worthy gathering of 'meedya' people – academics and artists – who were thrown together by a regional cultural agency to see what happened when our worlds collided. My wish from the event was "can anyone help me show whether films and photos really do make a difference trying to save our planet". Two years later, in 2010 – here's John's book!

Those of us working in the wildlife media industry constantly assert that wildlife films and photos are one of the most emotive and powerful conservation communication tools. But are they – do they really make a difference? As perhaps the greatest communicator of them all (and Wildscreen's Patron), Sir David Attenborough's mantra is that "You cannot value what you do not know, and with knowing comes caring, and with caring there is hope."

With more than 50% of the world's rapidly growing population now living in cities and urban environments, we are becoming more and more disconnected from nature – and instead are spending increasing time connected to computers, virtual networks and an ever-expanding variety of digital media platforms. And yet human beings are visual creatures, and much of today's modern culture is infused with animal imagery – from advertising bill boards and corporate branding to children's books and our own screensavers.

Media, Ecology and Conservation investigates the role of new digital and traditional media in bringing people together to understand, care about and protect the world's endangered species and protected habitats. This insightful book makes a fascinating and thought-provoking read, with poignant and engaging observations and research – as well as perceptive interviews with some of the most important, visionary and pioneering players in the wildlife film-making and photography industry.

Harriet Nimmo,
CEO, Wildscreen
Bristol, June 2010

Preface

Images can be a very effective way of enabling professional educators and ordinary citizens to learn more about the interconnectedness of life, its wonder and its precariousness. They can engage our emotions, our feelings and intuitions as well as our discursive thoughts; and our mediascape today is multi-faceted and, in many cultures, ubiquitous. New media technologies offer many ways in which images and sounds can be worked, reworked, transformed, produced, consumed and disseminated, and although much of this book is about 'film' and 'photography', these terms have themselves been rearticulated by the many possibilities offered by the new technologies.

Thus throughout the book the terms 'film' and 'video' are used interchangeably, as are 'photograph' and 'image' whether produced digitally or in some other way. Although there are philosophical distinctions between digital and analogue photography and film-making that have much to do with the ontology of the image, such intellectual excursions are kept to the minimum, relying instead on a process of thick description. A book such as this needs to turn pictures into words, which is not always an easy task, or even a wise one to undertake. What we see and what we say we see are not necessarily the same, but both words and images are forms of communication, signs and symbols, ways of giving voice, of seeing what is heard, felt, touched, smelt and thought. So, if art, film and photography hold a mirror to nature, what does it say about us? Until we know who we are, or are comfortable with who or what we are, we can never really be at ease in a world that is palpably more significant than its single dominant species. Images, still and moving, can help us find who we are because they can operate non-discursively, because they present feeling through form, understanding through intuitive knowing and, even if seeing is not always believing, this is probably because we have not yet quite learnt what and how to see. Film and photography can help us do that, as I hope the following chapters indicate.

Chapter One offers a brief discussion of conservation strategy in the context of the cultural history of animals and people. The idea that as human beings have become more urbanised they have lost touch with what is left of the natural world is related to the way human culture has imagined and imaged the 'animal kingdom'. Organisations such as the media-conservation charity Wildscreen have been instrumental in bringing together communication, conservation and ecology, and the rest of the book explores the importance of the still and moving image in this process.

Chapter Two seeks to explain the nature of visual communication and visual literacy in the context of the various representations of animals and wildlife found in the contemporary media. There are sections on advertising, public relations, and the circulation of stories and images via the internet and popular television. Attempts to harness the capacity of new and old media for education as well as entertainment purposes are identified, with particular references to zoos, animal parks and their representation in film and television. The extensive amount and range of animal imagery leads to a sense that images are as real as anything else.

Chapter Three takes a closer look at natural history and environmental film and television, exploring the nature and impact of blue chip documentaries produced especially by the BBC and National Geographic. The role of some conservation scientists who have had a major media presence for many years, such as the primatologist Dr Jane Goodall, is contrasted with that of more populist presenters such as the late Steve Irwin. Some award-winning films that explore the relationship between human beings, animal conservation and economic development in new and sometimes more personal ways are also examined. The popularity of blue chip films and their explicit messages about the beauty of the natural world is evaluated in terms of their cultural influence and possible impact on increasing awareness of conservation issues and motivations to act.

Chapter Four investigates a number of films that have been explicitly made to promote conservation measures or reinforce educational activities. Some of the sections take on an independent life expressive of the independent nature of their production and development. Many of these films have been made by film-makers working outside as well as within the major media networks, and their reception by Western and African audiences is discussed in the context of how culture is an important influence on how films are understood – and so how films made for a specific conservation purpose should be made. A number of films are described in detail, and the work of a selection of Indian film-makers is identified as offering an approach to wildlife and nature documentary that clearly addresses economic realities that are not always given their due prominence in many Western productions. The chapter ends with a brief discussion of China as an illustration of how cultural attitudes and conservation values may not always coincide.

Chapters Five and Six explore the relationship between truth and the image. Chapter Five looks at how image production has involved within a general politics of truth. A short discussion of film and photographic theory attempts to place the discussion of specific films and photographs that adhere to an ethic of investigative journalism in a sharper conceptual context. The issue of cross-cultural differences and the rights or otherwise of animals and people, corporations and the media industry once again emerge as closely interlinked. The idea that the species barrier is something that not only viruses can jump is also examined, and the role of new media technologies, of multi-platform media and particularly the internet are discussed as offering enhanced educative and campaigning opportunities. The issue of difficult and uncomfortable images that shock and appal but at the same time depict 'reality as it is on the ground' is explored in Chapter Six. The significance of the still photographic image to, and in, wildlife conservation and nature communication is analysed by exploring the work and ideas of some key photographic artists, some important photographic exhibitions and the affordances of digital imaging technologies that may be used to alter or enhance nature.

This short excursion into wildlife, environmental and nature film and photography has been a personal journey too. I frequently asked film-makers, photographers, conservation activists, teachers and others whether the media 'makes a difference'. The question invariably elicited a deep intake of breath, which preceded some deep thought. It is hard to say what difference the media, in general terms, does make to our understanding of nature and our concern (or otherwise) for it and all the creatures that share our planet. It is also hard to speak for others, so the many people who have contributed their time, generosity, thoughts and wisdom are given space to speak for themselves as they did during the many interviews I conducted during the research for this book. However, I can speak for myself. In researching this book I have learnt a great deal about the media and about the natural world, about so-called 'non-human others' and our responsibilities to them and to the Earth as a whole. Much of my own learning has been through the media, by looking at and looking into the images that pervade our culture: the films, television programmes and photographs that have been intended by their makers to variously inform, amuse, educate, horrify, make aware or entertain. So my thanks and gratitude extends to all those people whose have spoken to me and are named in the text of the book, to the staff at Wildscreen and particularly Harriet Nimmo without whose support this book and my learning would not have happened as it has done, or probably at all. My thanks also go to Ian Roderick of The Converging World for sponsoring this volume, and to John Elford and his staff at Green Books for publishing it. If anything symbolises the convergence of our world it is the anthropogenic destruction of natural habitats, the curtailing of lives and living spaces of those other creatures which so clearly enrich our lives but with whom we seem unable to live in harmony. My thanks also go to my wife Lorna whose commitment to animal welfare and to the preservation of the natural world inspired me to embark on this study. Her comments on an early draft of the text were invaluable and wise. This book, though, is dedicated to the memory of my father who, if I remember correctly, was not a nature or animal lover as such, but a man who believed in the need to share, to live and let live, and who recognised the emotional frailties and intellectual limitations of the human species.

John Blewitt
Malvern
May 2010

Chapter One

Animals in human culture

The world about us

There are many ways of understanding the world, just as there are many ways of ignoring what is becoming increasingly apparent to us all. Climate change, often referred to as global warming, has now been generally acknowledged as largely being the result of human activity – specifically of industrialization, economic growth and development, and consumer lifestyles that increasingly demand more resource and energy use without due regard to their overall ecological consequences. Our turbulent climate is leading to unseasonal and untypical weather patterns, 'natural' disasters and geographic shifts in both flora and fauna as desertification increases and the Arctic ice melts. In fact, by treating the world and all that is in and on it as the property of human civilization, we (that is, *homo sapiens*) have set ourselves apart from the world rather than being a part of it. The world is converging in many ways: climate change, resource depletion and species extinction will affect everyone, from the poorest to the richest, although the richest will probably fare much better. The ideology and practice of economic development is arguably the dominant global worldview, but human culture is neither uniform nor totally materialistic. Some cultures, philosophies and religions, such as Buddhism and Jainism, view *homo sapiens* as intimately connected with other life forms and global ecological processes that of themselves demand our humility. Respect for the sentience and life force of other creatures is a cultural thread that runs throughout human history. Vegetarianism was discovered by Western colonialists in their encounters with the ancient cultures of the Hindus, Jains and Buddhists in India, and although viewed as somewhat radical or eccentric for many years in Christian Britain, vegetarianism is no longer seen as either exotic or cranky (Stuart, 2006). Although other religions have also shown respect for other creatures and the natural world, many critics have frequently pointed out that sacred texts have sometimes been instrumental in shaping a mentality that holds the world as having value only in so far as its resources can be either directly used or can be transformed into some kind of commodity and exchange value. 'Progress' and 'development' have frequently ignored the traditional ecological wisdom of those 'ecosystem peoples' – indigenous or tribal peoples in India, South America and elsewhere who have been, and continue to be in many cases, sensitive stewards of the physical environment, articulating what are today recognised as sustainability values and living sustainable lifestyles often deeply informed by religious or spiritual values.

Given the current state of affairs, our planet undoubtedly needs us all to live, work and behave as if we were all ecosystem peoples even though it seems that most us in the developed and developing worlds are not – and remain most reluctant to change our ways in any radical sense. So, in using the world as a resource, by exploiting, killing and consuming other creatures for food, fashion, furniture or fun, we, *homo sapiens*, are also directly responsible for the extermination of other species at a rate that is as great if not greater than that of the last mass extinction, which occurred in prehistoric times. Current extinctions are generally running at about 1,000 times the natural or background rate that scientists would have expected. Indeed, it has often been remarked that wherever human society develops and, particularly where Western colonialists have intervened to develop or otherwise exploit new lands, the lives and habitats of other creatures are soon destroyed. After Captain James Cook had paved the way for the European settlement of Australia, much of the flora and fauna of that continent, including the Aboriginal peoples who were themselves categorised as fauna, were threatened and in some case eradicated. Alan Moorhead's classic history of the European invasions of the South Pacific between 1767 and 1840 is aptly named *The Fatal Impact*. Today, even iconic creatures that have become either official or unofficial national symbols, such as the Indian tiger, the American bald eagle and the African elephant, have shared the same experience and possibly the same fate. Many familiar creatures are likely soon to be as dead as a dodo – so much so that 'Lonesome George', the last surviving giant tortoise from Pinta Island in the Galapagos, has become an icon and subject of a number of television documentaries on modern conservation's struggles against the relentless pressure of human encroachment (Nicholls, 2007).

If we need reminding of how bad things have become, then a quick glance the latest edition of the International Union for Conservation of Nature's (IUCN) *Red List of Threatened Species* will provide us with much important and depressing information (IUCN, 2009). The headline results indicate that

21% of all known mammals, 30% of amphibians, 12% of birds, 28% of reptiles, 37% of freshwater fishes, 70% of plants, 35% of invertebrates are either critically endangered, endangered or vulnerable. In most categories the statistics for the years 1996 to 2009 reveal a worsening situation, although there are instances where conservation efforts have successfully brought a species back from the brink. Many ecological restoration projects and others designed to save or reintroduce endangered species or protect habitats are real but reactive attempts to remedy a dire situation that, somewhat ironically, displaces indigenous ecosystem peoples just as economic development has frequently done (Dowie, 2009). The United Nations proclaimed 2010 as the International Year of Biodiversity, and with the proclamation comes a range of targets aimed at reducing biodiversity loss. Unfortunately, according to the IUCN many of these targets are unlikely to be met and so species extinction and, more broadly, loss of biodiversity will mean fewer resources for us to exploit and a spiritually poorer, less interesting and less comforting place for ourselves to live in.

Quite simply, in killing other creatures we are killing ourselves, and in destroying their habitats though economic development, logging, urbanisation, human population expansion, pesticide use, pollution, industrial agriculture, beam or bottom trawling, over-harvesting, mining, quarrying and climate change, we are in danger that when the planet recovers, as James Lovelock's Gaia Theory tells us, it will do so without us (Lovelock, 2006). Biologist E.O. Wilson has argued a loss of 90% in the area of a given habitat leads to a reduction of 50% in the number of species that a habitat can support, and this has occurred in far too many areas that have concentrations of high biodiversity. We are destroying nature's capacity to bounce back. If artificial environments replace or crowd out natural ones, then the phenomenon known to biologists as 'the death of birth' will occur. We need other creatures and organisms for they provide useful ecosystem services: they colonise waste ground, cleanse water, enrich soil, provide us with food and even create the very air we need to breathe. Wilson (2001: 335) writes:

> We should judge every scrap of biodiversity as priceless while we learn to use it and come to understand what it means to humanity. We should not knowingly allow any species or race to go extinct. And let us go beyond mere salvage to begin the restoration of natural environments, in order to enlarge natural population and stanch the hemorrhaging of biological wealth. There can be no purpose more enspiriting than to begin the age of restoration, reweaving the wondrous diversity of life that still surrounds us.

Research undertaken for The Economics of Ecosystems and Biodiversity (TEEB) reports published by the United Nations uses economic tools to demonstrate just how important the natural world and other species are to human well-being. Markets fail to capture most ecosystem values because nature is perceived as a public or common good, that is, 'free'. This has led to over-exploitation, such as continuing deforestation and overfishing which are serious problems that demand strict control and sound economic husbandry. For example, established Marine Protected Areas cover just 0.5% of the world's oceans, but if they were extended to conserve between 20-30% it has been estimated that a million new jobs would be created and an annual marine catch worth up to US$80 billion could be sustained (TEEB, 2009). Pavan Sukhdev, the economist and banker who is leading the TEEB enquiry, has stated that the ratio of costs of conserving ecosystems or biodiversity to the anticipated benefits of conservation is in the region of 1:10 or 1:25. In some cases, the ratio may be as high as 1:100. An unpublished reported for the UN by the London-based consultancy Trucost estimated that the combined cost to the environment by the world's 3,000 most important corporations in 2008 was US$2.2 trillion (Jowit, 2010). Does money talk?

The World Conservation Strategy, first published in 1980, was a collaborative endeavour of the International Union for the Conservation of Nature and Natural Resources (IUCN), the WWF (World Wildlife Fund, now World Wide Fund for Nature) and the United Nations Environment Programme. It articulated many ideas and principles that have since been embraced by the term 'sustainable development'. That is, development is understood by The World Conservation Strategy (1980: 1) as "the modification of the biosphere and the application of human, financial, living and non-living resources to satisfy human needs and improve the quality of life" and conservation as "management of human use of the biosphere so that it may yield the greatest sustainable benefit to present generations while maintaining its potential to meet the needs of and aspirations of future generations". The 1980 strategy articulated three specific objectives:

- to maintain essential ecological processes and life support systems
- to preserve genetic diversity
- to ensure the sustainable utilization of species and ecosystems

As Beder (2006) writes, conservation has since been interpreted and practised in many different ways – not always successfully and not always presenting development and conservation/sustainability as equally valid or even necessary. There have been many debates as to what can and should be done. For some people, science and technology will solve issues of environmental degradation and species loss. For others, it will be the operation of the free market or efficient management practices by either private corporations or government or a combination of the two with a little help from their friends in the conservation movement. What is clearly the case is that animals and the natural world are variously perceived as a resource, as a source of significant commodity value and as possessing intrinsic moral or spiritual importance. A tiger is to be revered but also killed as a trophy or for its skin becoming a mark of social or gender-related status or because it has within it the ingredients for a medicinal cure to a variety of human ailments. Tigers are a source of national pride, of spiritual sustenance but also a source of income.

Animals and human history

Animals are part of human history; they have co-evolved with us, and have been domesticated and hunted by us for food and recreation. There have been menageries and zoos for centuries, animal worship and animal sacrifices for millennia, and real and imaginary communication between us and other species probably since time began. An animal's appearance may offer good or bad omens depending on where, when and who you are. Anthropologists such as Richard Nelson (1983) and Brian Morris (2000) have shown how animals have become integral parts of human culture and consciousness in the Arctic lands of North America and in the African state of Malawi. Nelson's anthropological research with the Koyukon people of Alaska in the 1970s documents a world and a people that have been significantly altered by development, but he was still able to see a qualitatively different world being lived. For the Koyukon, the human and natural worlds are closely linked through various shared spirits. Animals display human characteristics because animals were themselves humans in the 'Distant Time' – the time of myth and creation. The physical world has its own spirits but it is also sensate, conscious, alive, and as such requires respectful action and understanding that closely resembles practices of sensitive environmental, conservation and sustainability management. Neither animals or plants are over-exploited, and waste is avoided as being practically irresponsible and spiritually dangerous. Like other anthropologists and ethnographers, Nelson (1983: 239) concludes that "reality is not the world as it is perceived directly by the senses; reality is the world as it is perceived by the mind through the medium of the senses".

Given this, the problem here is that each society sees its own reality as absolute and bases its own regulations and methods of dealing with the environment and other creatures accordingly. Anthropologist Tim Ingold points out that the environmental conservation practices carried out by peoples such as the Koyukon fundamentally differ from the more scientific, rational and technological practices of Western agencies and governments. For the West, nature is separate from and subordinate to humanity, whereas for the hunter-gatherers and other indigenous peoples, conservation is based on a deep trust and sharing of nature. When control is exerted by these peoples, it is control over human relationships rather than over nature itself. Ingold believes that the scientific West views this notion of sharing as metaphorical rather than as literal, and in doing so the West is perhaps diminishing itself by its own intellectual relativism. He writes (2000:76):

> The distinction between the human and non-human no longer marks the outer limits of the social world, as against that of nature, but rather maps a domain within it whose boundary is both permeable and easily crossed. . . . For nature, we say, does not really share with man. When hunters assert the contrary it is because the image of sharing is so deeply ingrained in their thought that they can no longer tell the metaphor from the reality. But we can, and we insist – on these grounds – that the hunters have got it wrong. . . . I am suggesting that those who are 'with' animals in their day-to-day lives, most notably hunters and herdsmen, can offer us some of the best possible indications of how we might proceed.

For Bruce Rich (2008) there is a lot to learn from ancient civilisations. In India during the fourth and third centuries BCE, the political realist Kautilya and the emperor Ashoka (a once-fearsome warrior who converted to Buddhism following the appallingly bloody battle of Kalinga) initiated a series of edicts which were carved into pillars of rock. These laid the foundation for a new moral and legal system, articulating values of religious tolerance, social welfare, environmental justice and animal welfare. On the Fifth Pillar Edict can be read a list of protected species including bats, tortoises, ducks, swans, rhinos and deer; in fact all four-legged creatures that are not needed for food or for some other important use should be protected. A number of practical conservation measures were identified, including restrictions on the harvesting of certain flora and fauna such as fish ponds and elephant forests. Chaff should not be burnt in the field, in order to protect animals and insects that feed off it. Throughout the text runs a deep respect for the lives and sentience of other creatures, combined with a well reasoned and ecologically intuitive eco-pragmatism: "Forests must not be burned in order to kill living things or without any good reason. An animal must not be fed with another animal." As Bruce notes, if the latter injunction had been adhered more recently, 'Mad Cow Disease' would not have occurred.

Historians such as Keith Thomas (1984), Harriet Ritvo (1989) and Keith Tester (1991) have shown how attitudes towards animals and the natural world have been altered in the West as the more ancient habits, customs, rituals, superstitions, knowledge and understanding have been replaced by a modernist sensibility. The development of the scientific mind led to the classification and categorisation of the natural world, the growth of hunting (killing) for fun and for sport, the exposition of various theories and interpretations of evolution and natural selection and a parallel emergence of a desensitised utilitarian and a morally conscientious appreciation of the putative rights and welfare of animals. It can be argued that the way we treat animals is an indication of how civilised and culturally mature we actually are, and it is salutary to relate this to the experience of increased urbanisation, industrialisation and the distancing of the human social world, of everyday life, from the natural environment. Animal rights, conservation and eco-system welfare are linked to how human societies understand themselves. The modern period has seen the slow decline of anthropocentrism as animals have become no longer simply an extension of the human world, no longer needed for transport or power. And even if animals are still eaten, the abattoirs have become discretely hidden from public view, the meat placed in plastic packages and even presented as a ready pre-cooked feast just waiting for the microwave. Thus concern for animals, either in terms of the welfare of individual non-human beings or for the future of whole species and the ecologies upon which they and we depend, relates to not only the world as we have shaped it but, reflexively, to how the world has in turn shaped us. Whether we support the policies and campaigns of animal rights organisations, put a bird box in our suburban garden, cuddle the dog or perceive the natural world through the spectacles of Animal Planet, National Geographic, Disney Nature or the BBC Natural History Unit, we do so primarily for social reasons. If we see the lion as king of the jungle or a creature under threat, 'an endangered species', then we are invariably saying something about ourselves as well as that non-human other. We apply schemas, conceptual frameworks, to our experience of the world, enabling us to cognitively organise and make sense of our experiences which are themselves formative elements of our culture facilitating communication, cultural transmission and patterns of social conduct (Bloch, 2005). In time, these cultural experiences may even shape the neural connections and networks in our brains. Finally, it should be remembered that animals are frequently perceived as a social problem or economic threats. Wolves have been systematically eradicated from many areas of the world because of the threats they pose to domesticated livestock, and the North American bison was driven to near-extinction in the nineteenth century as much to feed the growing industrial machine in America as to destroy the livelihood and culture of America's indigenous peoples (MacIntyre, 1995; Barclay, 2002; Isenberg, 2002). Animals are also a factor in human illness, as clearly documented in the Hans Zinsser's classic 1935 study *Rats, Lice and History* (Zinsser, 2000); although now, as viruses increasingly seem easily to jump the species barrier, progress in biotechnology and genetic engineering clearly has a more risky side than many corporations care to admit. Feral pigeons in urban areas are often environmental health hazards. In the UK, badgers are considered by many farmers to be the cause of bovine TB, and dogs are so numerous in countries like the USA and UK that dog litter has become a serious health concern. However, it is perhaps Zinsser's suggestive comparison of rats with humans that has the most bearing on the struggle to bring about effective animal and habitat conservation. Zinsser writes (2000: 208)

> Neither rat nor man has achieved social, commercial, or economic stability. This has been either perfectly or to some extent, achieved by ants and by bees, by some birds, and by fishes in the sea. Man and the rat are merely, so far, the most successful animals of prey. They are utterly destructive of other forms of life. Neither of them is the slightest earthly use to any other species of living things. . . . All that nature offers is taken for their own purposes, plant or beast.

Animals, imaging and the culture of everyday life

Our attitudes to animals and the natural world continue to evolve, but our direct connection and contact with other creatures is also becoming increasingly mediated, limited, contradictory and not a little confused. Franklin's (1999) sociological analysis of the role and perception of animals in modern culture explores the increasing sensitivity exhibited to the needs and welfare of animals, the use of animals in zoos for entertainment, the close relationships between many human beings and their pets, and the mass industrialised production, slaughter and processing of animals for burgers and other convenience foods. Increasingly, scientific and popular literature, television documentaries and feature films suggest that animals are an integral part of human culture and that increasingly human beings are attempting to both communicate with non-human creatures and for them. Public animal welfare and anti-hunting campaigns, together with popular TV programmes about companion animals and their owners, are clear examples of this. Documentary features such as *The End of the Line* (2009), about over-fishing, and *The Cove* (2009), about the slaughter of dolphins in Japan, integrate compassion with human self-interest, concern for human survival and worries over the moral integrity of human life on earth. Attitudes to animals, and what is understood as 'natural', vary between national cultures and within them. Many societies are multicultural, with many urban areas playing host to a wide range of different ethnic groups, religious traditions, assumptions, ideologies, systems or theories of knowing (epistemes), customs, superstitions and prejudices. Each community will agree, or at least largely agree, on how they see, or socially construct, the world around them.

Over thirty years ago Stephen R. Kellert (1979, 1980) conducted a survey of Americans' attitudes to animals for the Department of the Interior, Fish and Wildlife Service. His reports noted that attitudes fell into basically nine categories:

Naturalistic: an interest and affection for wildlife and the outdoors.

Ecologistic: a concern for the environment as a system, with close interrelationships between wildlife and natural habitats.

Humanistic: a strong affection for individual animals, usually companion animals or pets.

Moralistic: a moral concern regarding the treatment of animals, opposing their exploitation or any action considered cruel.

Scientistic: an interest in the physical attributes and biological functioning of animals.

Aesthetic: artistic and/or symbolic characteristics of animals.

Utilitarian: the practical, commercial and material value of animals and their habitats.

Dominionistic: the concern to master or control of animals, as in sporting events.

Negativistic: the active avoidance of animals as a result of indifference, dislike or fear.

However, life is never so simple or straightforward. Arluke and Sanders (1996) in their ethnographic studies of human-animal relationships have described how the relationships between human attitudes and actions, beliefs and behaviours, are not always straightforward, are often in conflict and sometimes intentionally and sometimes unintentionally compartmentalised. 'Animal lovers' may work in animal research labs; caretakers in animal shelters euthanise many of their charges; and dog owners present themselves to others as their pet's 'mommy' or 'daddy' but may also simply abandon them when the routine of day-to-day care becomes too inconvenient, too costly or just boring. A somewhat extreme form of the parental relationship to pet animals is the phenomena explored in Lynn Alleyway's documentary *My Monkey Baby* (2009), which showed a number of couples and individual women in America adopting monkeys as surrogate children, dressing them in nappies and frilly dresses and putting them in cots at night. This apparently bizarre human behaviour that on one level is about love is on another unconscionably selfish and cruel. It is said that 15,000 monkeys are kept as pets in the USA, and although it is illegal it is likely that the practice also exists in the UK. Many toys take the form of cute and cuddly animals, such as those made by the Furreal company whose website includes animations of a 'newborn' honey bear, a chimp and a panda sucking a baby bottle. Another company, the Electronic Pet Shop, offers a "personalised adoption package" for those contemplating purchasing something "small 'n' furry", allowing the customer to select the name of the animal to be entered on the adoption certificate together with its vital statistics. Zambi, a baby elephant, has multiple sensors and just loves to play with you. Its ears are made by African children and 50% of the profits go to a charity helping African children orphaned by AIDS.

In Japan, pet owners frequently exhibit photographs, often no more than snapshots, and sometimes stone sculptures, of their deceased companion animal at its graveside. This may be to reinforce fond memories of their animal companions, to enable the owners to feel they are still with them, or may be a means of communicating with their deceased loved one, believing that their pet still exists somewhere. Chalfen's (2003) study of Jindaiji Pet Cemetery in Tokyo suggests that elements of traditional Japanese culture are being articulated through this seemingly very contemporary visual practice – showing gratitude and indebtedness to creatures that gave happiness to their owners, ratifying a sense of individual and group belonging, acknowledging the primary importance of the household, maintaining orderly and pleasant relationships and fostering a good afterlife existence. Some popular animals such as dogs and ponies are increasingly used in care situations for therapeutic and other reasons.

Arluke and Sanders use the term 'sociozoologic scale' to explain the sociological rather than the individual psychological relationship to these animals. Societies, they say, tend to rank both people and animals according to their assumed natural worth. Those at the bottom can be mistreated and exploited, and those at the top cared for or even pampered. Anomalies and inconsistencies inevitably occur, but these rank orders are really about a system of social control that can, and frequently is, applied and adapted to the control of people. Thus, there are good animals – not so much pets but 'companion animals' which, for Mark Rowlands (2009) in his highly moving book *The Philosopher and the Wolf*, means that people are actually the guardians or stewards of their animals rather than their owners. Other animals are mainly useful as tools, and these may include creatures involved in laboratory experimentation, often justified as an essential means of advancing knowledge of human diseases and their possible cures. Occasionally, modern history has witnessed certain minority populations being ascribed a similar status by their masters and used as 'lab rats'. There are also bad animals – the dirty, the vicious, the stupid, the sub-human and the degenerate – and when classified as such there is only a short step to the mass extermination of the Nazi gas chambers.

As Clifton Bryant (Bryant, 1979) noted, we rarely bother to spend time reflecting on how significant animals are in our everyday culture, even though animals invariably inform the verbal and visual metaphors we use in everyday life. They are often good to think with: they generate political communication, religious parables or literary analogies. Rhetorical conventions often elide any supposed boundaries between the real, the representational and the symbolic. Animals are frequently anthropo-morphised in natural history films and entertainment television, in education, advertising and everyday life. Individuals are sometimes given animal characteristics. A lawyer who is a shark, a soldier who has the bravery of a lion, the enemy who is a vulture or animalistic demon, or the man who is a mouse. Animals may become symbols, icons, signs, conceptions of something other than themselves. The presentational forms adopted may articulate feelings that are not adequately expressed discursively. Pictures, music and sound effects convey meanings that words fail to do. Many television natural history programmes have explored characteristics and qualities that humans share with animals. Some are scientifically verifiable, some are speculative, some are fanciful and some are just good TV: chimps using cameras, elephants painting pictures, dolphins talking, elephants giving lessons on loyalty and family togetherness, and so on. Animals figure prominently in the language we use or, as Lakoff and Johnson (1980) show in the metaphors we live by – 'eat like a horse', 'looks ratty', 'barking up the wrong tree', 'cry wolf', 'blind as a bat', 'pig-headed', 'sick as a parrot'; and of course students are sometimes said to be studying 'Mickey Mouse' courses at university. Animal labels and metaphors are applied to products such as the Fiat Panda or the Jaguar car. The uses of animals, their discursive inscription or presentational re-articulation, are elements in an active and ongoing cultural process subject to political change, intellectual critique and emotional development.

Environmental, wildlife and nature film and photography has documented and influenced this process. For instance, in the 1940s the Humane Society of America released a short colour film entitled *Animals in the Service of Man* – a promotional picture for the work of the Society and its various sister organisations. In the age of the machine the narrator Lowell Thomas, the broadcaster and voice of Fox Movietone News, explains over a series of sequences featuring cows, sheep, pigs, horses and dogs that human civilisation is as dependent on animals as machines. The viewer is shown a man dressed in his hat and suit standing on the sidewalk of a busy urban street. His hat is made of animal fibre, so is his suit and shirt, his shoes are made of leather as is his watch strap. They all disappear as their provenance is made known. To save everyone's embarrassment, the film quickly cuts to a scene of the man dressed in a barrel walking along a street with his dog, as it is revealed that the cotton in his undergarments has been harvested by using the power and energy of horses. The viewer is later reminded that we humans tend to neglect and treat quite badly the animals we depend on. The film offers a shot of a car dump with the camera slowly panning to a carthorse struggling with his heavy load up a slight incline; and a cut to a close-up shot of a nail sticking out of the side of a cattle car that will tear the side of the cow rendering part of the meat unsuitable for human consumption.

The second half of *Animals in the Service of Man* argues that the lobbying for humane animal welfare laws make good economic sense – ensuring that cows and pigs are watered while in transit keeps them healthy and economically valuable. Animal welfare laws prevent unnecessary cruelty, indifference and neglect of domestic pets. Shots of a starving and diseased dog walking through a garbage dump strikes a dissonant chord as these images follow on quickly from those of the fun-loving and healthy dogs depicted only a few minutes earlier. Caring for animals therefore makes good civil sense, and the prevention of diseased animals for human food is a simple matter of human self-interest. Indeed, humans can learn from animals too. For some people, these other creatures may be presented as models of loyalty and devotion. The underlying message of this short promotional film is that kindness to animals could also influence how we treat other people, which in a time of war is clearly of the utmost importance. For the Humane Society, animals have many uses but are also intrinsically valuable.

The film does not mention race or ethnicity in any form, even though the use of animals in racial stereotyping and racial attacks was once a commonplace and is not unknown today. Unfortunately, as Dora Apel (2009), writes in her discussion of chimps, stereotypes and President Obama, America has not yet entered a 'post-racial' age, with the circulation of a number of racist jokes mocking the presidential candidacy of Barack Obama. Stereotypical racist images from the nineteenth century were dredged from the archives to be reused in the twenty-first. In February 2009 the *New York Post* published a cartoon satirising the President's financial stimulus bill. Building on a current news item about the shooting of a violent chimpanzee in Connecticut, the cartoon by Sean Delonas shows a dead and bleeding chimp lying face up on a sidewalk with three bullet holes in his chest. Looking over the animal, one cop says to another holding a smoking gun, "They'll have to find someone else to write the next stimulus plan." Apologists of the cartoon said there was no racist intent, for the stimulus package was so bad only a chimp, that is a Democrat, could have written it. Apel (2009: 134) comments:

> Those who find the image racist counter these arguments by pointing out that the bill is identified with President Obama and that the caricature of a black man through the image of a chimp is a resurgence of one of the oldest racist images in the United States.

Images of animals, in whatever form, are consequently elements of a society's cultural mentalité which, as Baker (2001) has effectively argued, can only be properly appreciated historically and sociologically and, given the contemporary cultural salience of the photographic still and moving image, visually too.

We eat animals, farm them and breed them in factories, shoot them, poison them and torture them in laboratories. Many creatures have frequently experienced intentional and sometimes thoughtless cruelty in legal, quasi-legal and illegal sports in the workplace and indeed in the home. It has been going on, probably for ever, but the nineteenth century saw the formation of organisations such as the RSPCA (Royal Society for the Prevention of Cruelty to Animals), and today the CIWF (Compassion in World Farming), PETA (People for the Ethical Treatment of Animals), IFAW (International Fund for

Animal Welfare) and others promote animal well-being, animal liberation or the rights of non-human others through a range of diffuse and diverse public communication and education campaigns. Terry Spamer, a former undercover operative with the RSPCA, has written about the widespread market for and sometimes ingenious nature of cruelty to animals. At the bottom of it, he says, is always the desire to make money out of the suffering of another (Spamer and Thorburn, 2007). As Bryant (1979: 412-13) remarks:

> Animals can be the perpetrators of crime, and the victims of crime. They may also be the object of crime, the motivation for crime, the instrument of or for crime, and even the mechanisms for the punishment of crime. . . . Animal-related crime may well be among the oldest forms of sanctioned social norm violation.

Encroachment on fishing rights or game hunting by poachers are for some simply ways of making a living. Poaching for elephant ivory, tiger skins or primate, turtle or tuna meat, or breeding and skinning animals (sometimes while still alive) for their fur is both a lucrative and growing business. Many iconic species are endangered or critically endangered, and for many conservationists poaching is a wildly irresponsible crime against the Earth's ecology. Roughly edited and raw footage of animal cruelty, the bushmeat trade or the killing of tigers or elephants for their skin or tusks can make the national news in the USA, UK and India. The trade in wildlife often means many deaths and incredible cruelty – animals chained, beaten, confined and so on. Academic, ethical and political debates over the extent, justification and nature of animal suffering has gone on for many years. Fortunately animals are no longer considered to be insensitive machines incapable of feelings or experiencing, although many animal abusers seem oblivious to this. As the philosopher Mark Rowlands (2002: 15) puts it succinctly in his measured but nonetheless impassioned discussion of animal suffering in *Animals Like Us*:

> When people claim that animals don't suffer 'in the same way as we do', what they are saying is probably right. But, unfortunately, they then tend to slide from this to the claim that animals 'suffer less than we do'. And that is almost certainly wrong. Not only do we have no evidence for the claim that animals, because of their lesser cognitive, imaginative, and speculative abilities, suffer less, in general, than we do, what evidence we do have tends to go the other way: animals suffer more.

Occasionally a hoax can reveal many complex and confusing attitudes regards human-animal relationships, as well as the nature of human sensitivities and gullibilities. In 2000 a student at the prestigious American University MIT produced the Bonsai Kitten website, complete with images and instructions on how to place a kitten in a small jar, feed it through holes and so be trained to grow into the shape of its container. The online reaction was quite vitriolic, with some protesters contacting the Humane Society of the United States which condemned the website, the presumed practice and the FBI for allowing it to happen. Eventually, the hoax was exposed, and some disturbing facts about the power of the image, the internet and their combined role in the construction of social reality were revealed. These lessons are perhaps best expressed in the following three comments:

YOU PEOPLE ARE DISGUSTING! YOU SHOULD BE ASHAMED OF TREATING LITTLE HELPLESS ANIMALS LIKE THAT. . . . HOW WOULD YOU LIKE TO BE STUCK IN A GLASS BOX. . . . HOW CAN YOU BE SO SICK AND TWISTED. . . . YOUR GONNA GO TO HELL AND BURN THERE BUT THAT ISN'T EVEN A GOOD ENOUGH PUN-ISHMENT. I DON'T KNOW WHAT ELSE TO SAY BUT THAT ITS SICK AND TWISTED. SHAME. RETARDS!
8th December 2003 at 14:51:26

what the f***, how could ppl do that to animals?? its f***ed up, it pisses me off as an animal lover the ppl would treat animals like that, if i could id per-sonally shoot em all
Jessi, 22nd September 2003 at 18:42:18

When I first got to this site, I assumed the entries had been manipulated in order to have the most insane, ridiculous one posted at the top – how else to explain the 'bonsai kittens are just like jews in the holocaust' post? I agree with others who have posted – the original site is somewhat funny, but these follow-up posts are much funnier, and really much more disturbing.
Brenda, 7th September 2003 at 11:28:12

Animals also take starring roles in feature films, animations, magazines and books such as *Free Willy* and its sequels, *Lassie* and its sequels, *Flipper*, *Black Beauty*, *The Horse Whisperer*, *Groundhog Day*, *Babe*, *Watership Down*, *Marley and Me*, *Grizzly Man*, etc. The list is practically endless. Some stories have become important political allegories. George Orwell's *Animal Farm* – the 1954 animation partly funded by the CIA – articulated Cold War values (Wells, 2009), while others have become eco-commentaries on the impact of human civilisation on the planet's natural ecosystems or the incarceration of wild animals in zoos. Wells argues that animations have a special ability to articulate values and issues that live action or photorealistic ciné narrations would find it very difficult to do. The very plasticity of the image becomes combined with the plasticity of the animators' imagination, the writer's ethical purpose and the production company's attempt to differentiate their product from those of others. He shows how some of Tex Avery's films for Warner Brothers incorporated visual jokes that encode and disrupt dominant assumptions about human relationships with animals. In *A Day at the Zoo* (1939), for example, Avery is able to subvert and parody the natural order of animal human relations that were, and are, constantly being legitimised, naturalised and aestheticised in films produced by the rival Disney corporation. Avery's cartoon films offer strong lines, vibrant colours, uncomplicated designs, brash sounds and funny voices that parallel the visual simplicity of the animation's narrative style. In one short sequence introduced with a "no zoo would be complete without a monkey cage" comment, the spectator sees a caged monkey and a man observing each other carefully, noting their similarities and eventually swapping locations. The sequence ends with the man in the cage and monkey looking at him from outside. The Darwinian inference that humans are descended from the apes was expressed at a time (just fourteen years after the Stopes monkey trial in Dayton Ohio) when evolutionary theory was being hotly disputed in many parts of the US. Indeed, it still is. Other animated films, such as *Madagascar* (2005), reveal a tension between the way many people perceive animals and the way they are in real life, in the wild. In anthropomorphising animals we tend to sentimentalise them, forgetting that, just as the animals in Madagascar did when they escaped from the confines of their urban zoo, they can do fairly unpalatable things when it comes to eating or even reproducing the species. Wells calls this the 'Madagascar problem', which has proved problematic for some animated adventures made for children and many natural history and wildlife programmes made for the 'family' audience. However, in Japan, Studio Ghibli's artistically exquisite and highly praised animations such as *Princess Mononoke, Spirited Away, Pom Poko* and especially *My Neighbour Totoro* convey a firm environmentalist message along with a powerful critique of industrial development. These films, like the use of photographs in the Tokyo pet cemetery, offer a re-presentation of traditional values, of Buddhist and Shinto symbolism and an ecological literacy through both the narrative and the detailed and intricate rendering of the natural world in the drawing and subtle use of colour. The natural world is 'seen' in a different way to that of human society. Human beings are more simply drawn indicating that we are just part of nature, not above it or more important than it (Stibbe, 2007).

Annabelle Sabloff (2001: 8) argues that in our modern world "most people in urban society are not usually aware of animals as a central or serious personal or societal concern". Most urban dwellers' interactions with animals are primarily social in nature, although the idea of the wild, as being somewhere away from the city, remains in a desire to connect with nature and natural life forms. As E.O. Wilson (1984) argues, the biophilic urge remains intense, even if highly mediated and somewhat muted. In discussing the pet phenomenon in New York City, a 'Petropolis', Olson and Hulser (2003) have shown how companion animals have led to civic and social changes which have sometimes led to conflict but have also, in some measure, led to a reassessment of human relationships with animals. We have become closer to them, recognising similarities that go beyond crass anthropomorphism or saccharine sentimentality. Olson and Hulser write (2003: 142):

New York City has become a petocracy – one boasting 1.5 million canine and 1.8 million feline inhabitants – in which the lines between pets and humans have blurred. The complex bonds that exist between humans and animal companions extend to an increasingly exotic menagerie including rats, snakes, miniature ponies and ferrets, as well as bunnies and fish. Cities are lonely places, and the need for unqualified love and the sharing of daily existence has led to a rise in pet ownership, especially after the September 11 disaster. The phenomena of the high-rise pet as surrogate human companion finds expression in the signs commonly sold at pet stores "Dogs are just children with fur". This section of 'Petropolis' features not only a video of Tillamook Cheddar, a Jack Russell terrier, in the act of painting, but also two of her scratch canvases (including *Go to Ground*) not in a 2001 exhibition at the National Arts Club ('Collaborations') in which she participated. Photographer William Wegman's nearly mythical Wiemaraners also make an appearance, in urban character portraits as well as in the artist's Weimaraner alphabet wallpaper border. Keeping them company is a photograph documenting Jeff Koons's gigantic Puppy that was displayed in Rockefeller Square in 2000, together with Sandy Skoglund's Revenge of the Goldfish and Radioactive Cats, whose commentary raises some darker social issues about animal companions.

This in turn has led to the loss of a "shared totemic imagination, that is, our ability collectively to name and experience the world as natural-beings-in-habitat, as animals, sharing the world in relationship with other beings" (Sabloff, 2001: 9). The implications are profound for our understanding, our conduct, our capacity and willingness to intelligently apprehend the complexities of the Earth's ecosystems and our impact on them. It also means that it is becoming increasingly important to recognise and understand how our urban geographies are influencing our relationships with and treatment of animals (Philo, 1995). For Sabloff, nature and the environment is little more than a backdrop to human culture and human activity. The labelling of animals as either largely good or bad, better or worse, restricts our cultural, social and spiritual development. Rowlands writes that even if we are unable to objectively judge animals in this way, we can admire them because they have attributes we lack and perhaps envy – their speed, their grace, their beauty, their strength, their sight, their hearing, their endurance, their power, their loyalty, their trust, 'sixth' sense and so on. Rowlands writes (2009:109) of his wolf:

> There was, of course, a certain sort of beauty that I couldn't possibly emulate. The wolf is art of the highest form and you cannot be in its presence without this lifting your spirits. No matter what sort of foul mood I was in when we began our daily run, bearing witness to that kind of silent, gliding beauty always made me feel better. It made me feel alive. More importantly, it is difficult to be around such beauty without wanting to be more like it.

For some, like the animal scientist Dr Temple Grandin (Grandin and Johnson, 2006) whose own form of high-functioning autism has enabled her to, as the title of a 2006 BBC television documentary put it, "think like a cow", the issue of understanding animals is related to being able to experience the world as animals experience it. For Grandin, this experience is emphatically visual, and being autistic, Grandin, like the animals, thinks primarily in mental images which have the capacity to be far more generative of fear and panic than words, verbal descriptions and verbal memory. 'Normal' people tend to 'see' their conceptions of things rather than the things themselves. People see things as symbols, merging things into something that is culturally meaningful. For animals and for Grandin, things are seen as discrete details making up the world in various ways which depend on the physical construction and location of their eyes in relation to their other senses and to the environment which they inhabit. Grandin (2009) develops ideas and concepts by storing and categorising the photo-realist images that accumulate in her mind. When she reads she converts text to images, as if making a movie for her own particular form of autistic intelligence enables her to develop conceptual meaning and articulate conceptual arguments imagistically. Whether some animals can do something similar or not is an intriguing question, but from the earliest times human beings have certainly created images of animals and other elements of their environment as tools for thinking, experiencing, hoping, projecting, worshipping and probably much more. Lewis-Williams and Dowson (1988) in an influential paper in *Current Anthropology*, and Lewis-Williams in the prize-winning book *The Mind in the Cave* (Lewis-Williams, 2002), have speculated on the mental processes involved. An image in the mind's eye conjured up from memory or from an altered state such as fatigue or one induced through shamanistic ritual could have been traced by the early *homo sapiens* of the Upper Paleolithic period onto the rocks of dark caves in what is now France or South Africa. These images may have represented 'real' animals but, whatever the case, "the images must have acquired significance that caused people to reach out to touch and fix them" (Lewis-Williams & Dowson, 1988: 215).

These images of 30,000 years ago elude definitive interpretation, but like today's images and symbols in film, on television, in advertising, in the zoo, museum, textbook, or internet they are undoubtedly redolent with culturally-based associations. The anthropologist Tim Ingold, in his discussion of totemic and animic[1] image creation, believes that the images created by aboriginal peoples in Australia and the far north of Canada and Alaska are not representational in any direct sense of their everyday material world. The totemic art of the Australian aboriginals focuses largely on the land, and the preferred medium tends to be painting, whereas the animic image creation of the Inuit looks towards the behaviour of animals and the preferred medium is sculpture. Each approach articulates the nature of their environmental dependencies and relationships. He writes (Ingold, 2000: 130):

> Whether their primary concern be with the land or its non-human inhabitants, their purpose is not to represent but to reveal, to penetrate beneath the surface of things so as to reach deeper levels of knowledge and understanding. It is at these levels that meaning is found. There is no division, here, between 'ecology' and 'art', as though hunting were merely a matter of organic provisioning and carving or painting gave vent to the free play of the symbolic imagination. This division, along with the dualism of nature and culture on which it rests, is of modern provenance, and it lies behind the conventional notion of the work of art as proof of a uniquely human capacity for creative thought and expression.

---

1. Ingold suggests that within a totemic theory of reality (of being) the forms life takes are already present in the features, textures and contours of the land. The vital life forces of plants, animals and people are in fact derived from the land. By contrast, within an animic theory of reality (of being) life itself creates form, for the vital force is not encased within a solid medium but is like the wind, forever flowing freely and circulating widely. It is this that animates the living world.

These peoples, like those who produced images in Lascaux or Chauvet, in all probability did not rank themselves above nature or value their productions as an expression of their intellectual superiority. Art and nature is one and the same; human beings are part of nature and more or less in tune with it, for if it were otherwise then serious problems could easily erupt. Thousands of years later it is interesting to note when reading the history of wildlife film, nature photography, environmental documentary and the other imaging of humanity and the natural world, that it is only very recently that clear attempts have been made to abolish the division between 'art' and 'ecology', the 'developed' and the 'developing' worlds, and even perhaps of 'culture' and 'nature'.

Conservation education and the media

Nature tourism, leisure attractions such as SeaWorld and ZooAmerica, the late Steve Irwin's Australia Zoo in Queensland, and animal parks such as Longleat in the UK or the African Lion Safari in Ontario, Canada, are big commercial ventures that, like many natural history film-makers and television producers, encode within their entertainments a range of conservation messages. The degree to which they actually make a positive difference to creatures in the wild is highly debatable, and has exercised the consciences of many professional conservationists and media practitioners for many years. The writer Alexander Walker sees natural history movies and animal attractions as primarily revealing human being's power over the natural world. In many ways, animals on film or in tourist venues perform for the spectator. They may be seen to 'act' naturally, but it remains a type of acting nonetheless. For Walker (1991: 154) many films, particularly those Disney ones that overtly anthropomorphise do, at the very least, allow "animals to be addressed as social beings, and nature as a social realm" suggesting "a breach in the species-barrrier between human and animal". Wildlife films and television programming in the 1970s and 1980s helped cultivate more sophisticated and informed audiences that no longer felt comfortable watching animals perform tricks in circuses, or captive lions in zoos pace dementedly up and down in their iron cages, or accepting the legitimacy of whale hunting, wearing fur or the clubbing of arctic seal pups in the interests of conservation. Conservation, education and entertainment have segued into an inarticulate sense of cultural responsibility for the natural world which is no longer natural, and for wild animals that are losing their battle to remain wild. Established by Christopher Parsons, one of the founding members of the BBC's Natural History Unit, Wildscreen@Bristol (later renamed

Wildwalk@Bristol) was originally envisaged as the UK Millennium Project '@Bristol', encompassing a visitor attraction, botanical house, IMAX cinema, news gallery and a little later an electronic arc or zoo which would exploit the most update digital imaging technologies to collect still and moving images of the world's most endangered and threatened species (Davies, 2000; Parsons, 2001). The IMAX cinema and Wildwalk closed in March 2007 largely because they failed to attract sufficient numbers of visitors and consequently income.

Wildwalk@Bristol, part of the original Wildscreen Millennium Project, seemed more radical and more ambitious. I visited in July 2004 as part of a small research project looking at sustainability education and visitor attractions (Blewitt, 2006). My impressions were that it was absolutely stunning, integrating touch-screen facilities, moving image clips, computer graphics and still photography with real world aquaria, greenhouses growing all manner of plants, live creatures such as birds and insects (mainly introduced to add interest to an otherwise quite technocentric attraction), with a clear and distinct message about the need for a more sustainable world and for responsible actions to attain this. Wildwalk offered a strong narrative combined with what I felt to be (borrowing a term developed by the Russian film-maker Sergei Eisenstein) a montage of attractions offering multiple ways into the conservation story. Each approach was as exciting as the other, but different, enabling it to capture a range of cultural interests and personal predispositions. It used popular cultural forms derived from television, film and to an extent video gaming to convey the message, mission and purpose of Wildwalk. The visitor, on entry, was presented with a series of graphics designed to shape his/her understanding of the world around them both within Wildwalk and beyond. There were powerful, dynamic and colourful messages about evolution, the increase in species over time followed by periodic extinctions, until when arriving at the present day the visitor was invited to see that contemporary phenomena are, in comparison, frightening and extraordinary. Backlit photographic images of evolving species, replicas of important fossils and short videos narrating key story lines projected onto a huge screen immersed the visitor in a sound and imagescape of growing plants, mixing media technologies, animate and animated materials. As well as being woven into the story, there were points where the visitor was confronted with calculated shocks and jolts. These 'disorientating dilemmas' were particularly apparent in the final scenario, where human culpability for the degradation of the planet was assertively presented. An electronic population counter whizzed by as visitors were invited to watch a video loop of urban living, famines in Africa, multi-lane highways, car junkyards, pollution of the land, sea and air, smoke and filth. This acted as a visual counterpoint to and commentary on the relentless numerical additions of the population calculator. The message was obvious, and there was little attempt to show alternative viewpoints, to provide balance or due impartiality, to offer feelgood solutions, escapist fantasies or just information for the visitor to to make up his or her own mind.

My impression was that this visitor attraction was in campaigning mode and was overtly and politically educative. Implicitly, and explicitly, much of the blame for this state of affairs was attributed to the big corporations using the suitably vague but overarching term 'industry'. Wildwalk appeared to be very different from the Eden Project which, built within a disused china clay quarry in Cornwall, had also been established as a Millennium Project to show visitors via its two large iconic biomes and later an educational and exhibition centre, how dependent they were on plants. The political and sustainability messages at the Eden Project were far more modest, politically cautious and conservative than those at Wildwalk (Blewitt, 2004). The politics at Wildwalk, though, dominated the entertainment, so much so that some visitors were perhaps reluctant to engage in what they may have expected to have been a fun visit. For others, a digital representation of an animal or wildlife habitat does not have the same entertainment attraction as an actual one or a simulated one in an animal park or zoo. As one education worker at Bristol Zoo said during an interview I conducted in 2009, "What worked was when they brought in live leafcutter ants and such like; what didn't work was the technology, however well designed the exhibits." The site was reopened in 2009 as the Blue Reef Aquarium, boasting 40 different marine habitats and a wide range of entertainments, underwater safaris, educational talks and conservation actions resembling less a political statement and more a real life Animal Planet or Disney Nature TV show.

A similar media-focused venture is the Bristol-based media-conservation charitable organisation Wildscreen (not to be confused with Wildscreen@Bristol), which is a valuable resource enabling teachers, students, conservationists and anyone else with an interest in conservation, film and photography to learn more. Wildscreen's stated mission is to promote an appreciation "of biodiversity and nature through the power of wildlife imagery". It currently comprises five initiatives or interrelated projects:

ARKive: a flagship digital library of still and moving images, audio recording and educational material.

Wildscreen Film Festival: held every two years since 1984 in Bristol bringing together wildlife film-makers from across the world, media executives and equipment manufacturers. It is the largest festival of its kind in the world.

WildPhotos: a photography symposium hosting its own annual wildlife photographic competition.

WildFilmHistory: encompassing oral history recordings and transcripts conducted with film-makers and television producers, and detailed information and links to a wide range of films dating back to the late nineteenth century.

Wildscreen Outreach: a touring programme of award-winning film screenings and masterclasses aiming to reach new audiences and potential new film-makers in the developing world.

Although Wildscreen has links with campaigning organisations and conservation NGOs, it is not itself a campaigning body but rather an education resource, as Harriet Nimmo, Wildscreen's Chief Executive, makes clear:

> We are really providing the resources for the campaigning organisations, but we will never be saying 'don't use ivory or don't eat fish or whatever'. In order to make people care about elephants or care about life in the sea we just show them what lives there. We operate in what we see as being in the forefront: that is, how do you make people care in the first place. As David Attenborough always says, you can't value what you don't know, and with knowing comes caring. So, we're getting people turned on to nature rather than banging them over the head, and we will never move into campaigning as in Greenpeace or Friends of the Earth. We present information. In ARKive, at the end we show what the threats are, whether it is deforestation, bushmeat or long-line fishing, and we will provide a link to where you can find out more. We don't make a judgement. We just present the information, but we will look for footage of the threat. (Harriet Nimmo, interview 9th March 2009)

Consequently, in seeking to understand conservation awareness and action, animals in human culture and their relation to natural history film and television, environmental documentaries, educational and campaign films and news photographs, we must seek to understand the media itself as an environment and the social, institutional and ecological environments as a media form (McLuhan, 1964). The media encompasses sound, image and a reality that can be either real or virtual, in two dimensions or three, large or small, in one colour or many. The media can convey intellectual argument or basic emotion, can offer visceral and intuitive messages or clearly reasoned and logical ones. The technologies and their contexts of use, production and consumption may offer complementary and contradictory messages of their own, perhaps contributing to a culture of denial and compartmentalisation. Exposure to natural history films, animal entertainment television, conservation campaign communications, zoos, YouTube, pervasive still and moving images of cuddly cuties and occasionally brutalised or slaughtered animals may resonate with one particular conceptual schema and not another, one particular interest and not another, one sense of political urgency or none. Television programmers are aware of this, as well as of the flows and cycles of public interest, sentimentality and concern. Asked what she felt the impact of wildlife and natural history programming was, the Chair of the 2008 Wildscreen Film Festival and a founder of the UK's Channel Four replied:

> Most of it I think is washing over, I have to say, in the sense that we have had films on television about the natural world as long as television has been going. You couldn't say that as a nation the general public were hugely aware of the dangers to biodiversity and the rest of it. I think there is a separation between the audience's enjoyment of seeing beautiful images of the natural world and that there is a threat to that beautiful world, let alone what they could actually do about it. Now there have been periods when the environmental aspects of programmes have been stronger. When I was at Channel Four I didn't want to do pure natural history films – the BBC, Survival, they're doing that. I wanted to do something different and we did do much more environmental programming than the other channels. Jonathon Porritt did a programme called *The Greening of Britain* and he attributed to Sir Richard Pusey and me more responsibility for the greening of British television than any other individuals which at that time, the 1980s, was probably true. Then in the 1990s nobody wanted to know. It was a dead area. Key gatekeepers in broadcasting institutions were not even remotely interested in the developing world. Since 2000 it is beginning to come up again. There is a much greater public awareness of climate change and other issues. It is partly the work of NGOs, partly programmes on television, partly good journalists. . . . It's a mixture. You'd be hard pressed to identify the key determinants of that change. (Carol Haslam, interview 20th October 2008)

Brian Leith, a senior producer at the BBC Natural History Unit and a trustee of Wildscreen, notes that the effects of natural history programming on audiences is something that has exercised the minds of film-makers and audiences at Wildscreen conferences for many years. He recalled:

There was a debate at Wildscreen Festivals years ago led by Derek Bouse. He came to various Wildscreen sessions and Jackson Hole in the US and to Missoula. He was always saying "We think we are making a difference; well, there is no evidence at all." I think it is very difficult to pin down because what I think is happening is a radical, social, upheaval of our values so that whatever we do as film-makers or as part of Wildscreen is just one tiny element in the unfolding changes. You can find specific examples where individual films have made differences to policies and have made governments tackle things, but it would be a momentous task to try and prove it. It's like looking at environmental stories on the news. They have probably gone from virtually zero twenty-five years ago to maybe 20% of stories described as vaguely environmental now. Now that's an effect of this great steamroller of change. If you talk to anyone of us here [BBC Natural History Unit], virtually everyone one of us would say that Attenborough for example inspired us to make films. This is important, for Attenborough has been, in the past, criticised for not doing enough in terms of environmental action and raising awareness, but I think the truth is he sees his world as trying to generate a passion for nature and wildlife which in turn leads to a desire and concern to protect it. In that sense he is one of the godfathers of the environment movement just as Ed Wilson is. Ed Wilson was never a campaigner, but he is such a guru on biology and nature that he inspired others to want to protect it and save places. (Brian Leith, interview 8th April 2009)

Whether the media is simply responding to or helping fashion this change is indeed difficult to know. Media analyst George Gerbner (2002) argues that the media has had, in certain circumstances, an important 'cultivation effect'. Others have argued that the media has an important agenda-setting function by the very fact they prioritise and communicate certain issues in certain ways and at certain times, and that certain types of programmes at some periods become the staple diet of many viewers. The films of English naturalist Peter Scott, French underwater explorer Jacques Cousteau, American zoologist Marlin Perkins and presenter Marty Stouffler, primatologist Jane Goodall, ethologist and presenter Desmond Morris and many others have been important and, to some extent, influential in changing the nature of wildlife television and its terms of public engagement. Greg Mitman (1999), Derek Bouse (2000), Jonathan Burt (2002) and Cynthia Chris (2006) have all written extensively, perceptively and sometimes quite personally on natural history film and wildlife television. Chris (2006: 199) acknowledges that "wildlife films and television programmes bring to our attention aspects of nature that might otherwise remain unknown". She also notes that the educative values underpinning films have changed over time. In the early days of wildlife film-making, up to the late 1930s, films tended to emphasise the difference between human and animal life. Expedition films saw animals being hunted and shot for sport or as a resource, with the white colonial order presented unquestionably as naturally superior to the cultures of indigenous peoples. The Disney Corporation's award winning *True Life Adventures* wildlife films of the 1940s and 1950s such as *Seal Island*, *The Living Desert* or *The Vanishing Prairie* emphasised the daily family life of animals including courtship, mating (though not copulation) and raising young. Since the 1980s and especially in the 1990s professional biologists have tended to influence the interpretative values framing many films with clear references to evolutionary theory, the genetic scripting of behaviour and social learning. She concludes (Chris, 2006: 209) that "what is projected onto nature reveals the most urgent struggles of human culture". Historian Greg Mitman recognises that screen-based media, particularly film and television, have an understated influence on how we see things, on what we recognise as true or as real and how we interact with the world beyond the image. He writes (Mitman, 1999: 2007):

> But the glamour of science and the drama of nature on screen match neither our experiences in the field or lab nor our everyday experiences with the nat-ural world. Nature is not all action. And science is filled with more method-ical and sustained labors than adventures. Conditioned by nature on screen, we may fail to develop the patience, perseverance, and passion required to participate in the natural world with all its mundanity as well as splendor. Trained as spectators, we make little effort to accommodate ourselves to nature. When presented to us through the hidden labor of others, nature is crafted to meet our demands, expectations, and values.

Chapter Two

Animals and visual culture:
on image–based communication

A number of cultural theorists have remarked that the Western world is saturated with images – that the Western citizen consumes more images in one day than a person in early modern or pre-modern times would have done in a lifetime. For some, we in the West have inhabited, and often revel in, a society dominated by media events, spectacles and images that basically refer to other images. This constitutes a simulacrum, an imitation of reality having little or no tangible connection to reality itself (Boorstein, 1961; Debord, 1995; Baudrillard, 1988; Eco, 1987). Whether this seems fanciful or not depends in large part on whether these ideas resonate with everyday life experience, but it is undoubtedly the case that screen-based media in all its manifestations from the iPhone to Imax, from 2-D to 3-D television, from low-resolution to high-definition digital film and photography, is an ever-present reality. Words and rational discussions are being replaced by pictures, and for pessimistic media ecologists like Neil Postman (1986) we are quietly and contentedly "amusing ourselves to death". Thomas de Zengotita (2005) has also captured the implications of this in his sharp commentary on our mediated relationship to nature and to animals. Zoos advertise themselves by producing posters of iconic species as if they were Hollywood film stars, and tourists often respond disappointedly when confronted with an animal in its natural environment rather than on the screen. De Zengotita (2005: 212-213):

> You go to Yellowstone, hoping to see wolves. . . . You time your ride through the park just right, you notice a cluster of cars and a battery of cameras and scopes arrayed at the edge of a particular turnout along the road, and you pull over and join the assembled wolf-watchers – and, by God, you see wolves.
>
> Except you won't see wolves, you'll see 'wolves'. You'll be murmuring to yourself, at some level, "Wow, look a real wolf, not in a cage, not on TV. I can't believe it."
>
> That's right, you can't. Natural things have become their own icons.
>
> Is that why you will get restless so quickly if the 'wolf' doesn't do anything? The kids will start squirming in, like, five minutes; you'll probably need to

pretend you're not getting bored for a while longer. But if that little smudge of canine out there in the distance continues to just loll around in the tall grass, and you don't have a powerful tripod-supported telelens gizmo to play with, you will get bored. You will begin to appreciate how much technology and editing goes into making those nature shows on the Discovery Channel.

However, this appreciation, should it occur, may not come automatically or naturally. It will depend on how we understand and experience our own consumption, production and use of images. This understanding will partly be influenced by our facility with image-based media and with visual culture generally – that is, our visual literacy and visual competence.

Advertisers and public relations specialists play with, and play on, our familiarity with images quite extensively. Conservation organisations eagerly endorse the rearticulation of familiar tropes from popular film culture if they can effectively communicate a preferred message. The *Rethink the Shark* promo co-produced by the Save Our Seas Foundation and Saatchi and Saatchi uses audience familiarity with the *Jaws* feature film franchise to communicate the rarity of actual shark attacks on humans. A sunny beach scene, people swimming and surfing, a dog fetching a stick, lifeguards on the lookout, a camera tracking down towards the sea, a cut to an underwater shot of a boy's legs. The POV (point of view) of a menacing creature. A woman, chest high in the water, stares directly at the camera and screams. A panic ensues as the lifeguard blows a whistle, initiating a mass rush to the safety of the beach. A montage of close-up shots of blurred legs running. A group of holidaymakers in their swimwear stand at the water's edge looking frightened as they stare out to sea. *Jaws* music plays as the promo cuts to a close-up of toaster bobbing on the ocean surface. A caption reads, "last year 791 people were killed by defective toasters. Four by sharks." Public understanding of the shark has been framed by the success of the Peter Benchley's novel, the spin-off feature films and are reinforced constantly by the fang and claw natural history programmes that can be regularly seen on Animal Planet and similar channels. The shark is generally assumed to be so very dangerous because of a feature film, an image, a story, and their popular cultural, inter-textual rearticulations over nearly forty years.

Visual literacy

In his sceptical introduction to the field of Visual Studies, Art Historian James Elkins (2003) asks, "What is visual literacy?" There can be numerous answers. Recognising an image as an image is one kind of literacy. Beyond this, there could be various interpretations as to what the image means, its significance and currency in the social world. Visual literacy could also refer to remembering or recognizing images as, in some way, culturally important or meaningful. Indeed, it is often stressed that visual literacy, and visual culture more generally, involves the ability to see what has been socially constructed and what has not, what gives images their ideological power or what constitutes their rhetorical impact. Visual literacy here suggests the spectator is able to see and make sense of the image in one way rather than another. In other words, visual literacy involves ways of seeing and ways of interpreting, contextualising and articulating meaning in other perhaps more discursive modes (Berger, 1972). Elkins also suggests that visual literacy encompasses a series of visual competences including being able to make, design and edit images so as to enhance awareness of the aesthetic and technical choices that inform the nature of media communication as an element of human social interaction, cultural tradition and perhaps acculturation. Michael Griffin (2008), in his discussion of visual competence, argues that a necessary distinction needs to be made between those images or 'sign-events' that are natural or transparent and those images that in some way have been intentionally created to convey a specific emotion or some meaning which we could or should infer. This issue becomes quite complicated when photographic images, digitally produced or otherwise, incorporate elements from what we would see naturally, leading us to see the image as a simple reflection of what exists rather than a product of an intentional and deliberate creative process. Griffin uses examples from the news media, but examples could be taken from science communication, natural history film-making and wildlife photography. The photographs of giant pandas by Chinese scientist Lu Zhi in *Giant Pandas in the Wild* (Lu Zhi, 2002) show the panda in what's left of its natural environment in a series of high-quality colour images. The large full-page image before the title page presents the profile of an adult panda cradled between two branches of a tree that make up a 'V'. The boughs are covered in green moss, and the thick black and white fur of the bear seems as inviting to the touch as the black rings around the eyes seem doleful and sad. Another full-page image has a one-month-old virtually hairless baby panda cradled in the cupped hands of a scientist. The cub is on her back, her stubby limbs outstretched, her round pink belly denoting health and the vulnerability of extreme youth. These images have an emotive pull. The animal seems almost unbearably cuddly, but the cub has been offered to the camera; the book has been produced to describe and promote panda conservation and the image of the animal itself has been used for nearly fifty years as the emblem of the World Wide Fund for Nature (WWF). The panda has become an image, a logo, an icon used and interpreted by many as an illustration of all that is wrong with the unthinking and uncaring impact of human beings on the natural world. The images have been created by a photographer, re-presented by a publisher and various conservation organisations to elicit a certain response and encourage a certain feeling and understanding from the reader. Visual literacy is about understanding how this process of image creation, reception and interpretation may work and how in other contexts the same or similar images might be enlisted to depict the futility of conservation policies and actions attempting to save a creature that to all intents and purposes is a genetic zero, an evolutionary mistake or evidence of God's creative design. Pandas, after all, eat a limited diet of bamboo rather than meat like real bears, seem to have little aptitude for sexual reproduction, are generally rather fat and defecate up to forty times a day. They have, however, survived for centuries . . . until now (Buchen, 2008). Jean Trumbo (1998) notes that computer graphics and other new media tools offer tremendous opportunities to communicate science effectively among scientists and the wider public. She argues that the image is a powerful tool in scientific learning, though when images and text appear together it is the image that tends to dominate. Written language must be processed cognitively, but images are processed in similar ways to direct experience. We react emotionally to images before they are cognitively understood. Nano-photography of nature offers marvelous images of a world that cannot be seen. Images are created by a scanning electron microscope directing a beam of electrons at a target which may be an organism consisting perhaps of just one cell. Its intricate structures and colours are brought out in fine detail. However, there is a problem. The original image is monochrome, though much of the nano-photography that finds its way into books, magazine articles and television documentaries has been colourised with little, if any, mention of the creative process – the drying and freezing of the target, spraying it with platinum or gold atoms to enhance its reflectivity, or choosing colours to bring out the object's visual dynamics and structural complexity. These images convey an understanding of science that is a product of an artistic intervention (Elkins, 2008; Jones, 2008). In other areas, the viewer may be engaged on a variety of perceptual levels that are further enriched when accompanied by a selection of sounds suggestive of other sensory experiences. Can you hear a caterpillar chomp a leaf?

Ann Marie Barry (1997:173), in her lengthy study of visual intelligence, also notes that images from film or television may enter our consciousness without any significant critical engagement. Such a state of affairs, she continues, is similar to daydreaming, making viewers potentially vulnerable to sug-

gestion and susceptible to emotional manipulation "at a critical point in attitude and idea formation". Thus, watching a succession of powerful images
may 'feel' as if they are logically or rationally connected when in fact they are
not. For Barry, if this is so, then 'television daydreams' may lead to an accept-
ance of a distorted image of reality, as the speed and rhythm of moving image
montage working at a subconscious level enable critical judgements to be
bypassed. This is perhaps the reason why so many prestigious natural history
productions, with their high definition colour images and stereo sound, are so
emotionally powerful and so popular with audiences. But, this is not to say that
it is impossible to know something because rational thought processes have
been eluded. It is surely possible to know some things intuitively or emotionally, and for Rick Williams and Juliet Newton, visual intelligence is closely
associated with intuitive intelligence and visual cognition. Williams and Newton (2007:7) define visual intelligence as "the ability to observe, understand,
and respond to images, light, symbols, shapes, patterns, colors, contrast, composition, and balance". Human beings have this visual and intuitive intelligence naturally, but rarely do Western educational institutions develop this
outside art, design and media departments. In his three-part discussion of
'omniphasism' Williams (1999, 2000) seeks to redress the imbalance. For
Williams, visual literacy must encompass a holistic approach to cognition, perception and aesthetic appreciation. Barry (2006) shows how this relates to the
neural processing undertaken in the left and right brain hemispheres, where
increased knowledge enables an appreciation of complexity through the dis-
cernment of patterns rather as a collection of discrete details. Consequently,
without a visual education encompassing both the rational and intuitive minds
and developing visual and linguistic intelligence combined with an understanding of aesthetic influences on the emotions, it is conceivable that the twenty-
first century visual media business will increase its capacity to shape public
awareness, publicly shared values, assumptions, perceptions and predispositions towards both the social and natural worlds. As Newton (2001) notes,
human visual communication is inseparable from culture, functioning beyond
mere representation in spheres of human social and symbolic interactions.
Thus visual literacy involves an ecological understanding of image-based media
and the contribution of the visual to concept formation.

Bergmann (1997) argues that photographs do not simply visualise the outer
surfaces of things but can be used to depict ideas, develop interpretations and
direct perceptions. They can at various levels enable people to think, to dwell
on issues and problems they would not possibly have done otherwise. W.J.T.
Mitchell (1987; 2002) writes that all media are, in effect, mixed media with

varying ratios of sense impressions and sign-types. We can see hot colours and can hear cool sounds. All cultures are, and have been, visual cultures, but not essentially so. We see the way we do because we are social beings and our social arrangements take the form they do because we are seeing beings. Images also invariably interact with words, thereby sustaining each others' existence and effectivity. For some ecologists, the beauty and holistic integrity of nature has to be seen to be appreciated, and this leads them to 'essentialise' the image, nature and (wild) animals (Ito, 2008).

However, the meaning of visual images, and by extension natural history, environmental/conservation or nature films and photography, develops as a result of the interaction between the viewer and the object. Meaning occurs through the activity of making sense of what is seen and heard. Meaning is created dialogically. It is influenced inevitably by style, context, culture, emotion and reason (Bal, 2003). Images are 'go-betweens' serving to structure our relationships with each other and with non-human others and the natural world. In discussing the contribution of the philosopher Susanne Langer, Christine Nystrom (2000) suggests that 'presentational forms of representation' such as film and photography structure symbols that call to mind feelings and ideas, but they do not themselves say anything about their subjects because their elements do not have fixed connotations or denotations. For Langer, presentational forms "articulate the life of feeling" (Nystrom, 2000: 30) and unlike language which enables analytical reasoning and linear thought, "presentational forms foster the instantaneity of recognition, of gestalt apprehension, for the meanings of pictures, music and dance must be grasped as wholes or they cannot be grasped at all" (Nystrom, 2000: 31). For Langer herself, a picture is only a symbol, not a duplicate of what it represents; and unlike a sign, which is basically something to act upon, a command to action, a symbol is an instrument of thought redolent with, or of, meanings, connotations and conceptualisations. Those symbols which we apprehend through our senses of sight and hearing are often non-discursive, non-verbal and non-rational, but they nonetheless outlive the momentary experience, perhaps triggering the imagination and memory. Visual forms therefore articulate meanings as do music and the calls of whales and songs of birds. For Langer (1942:145), "the first thing we do with images is do envisage a story; just as the first thing we do with words is to tell something, to make a statement." Music can reveal, represent and articulate emotions, moods, and sentient experience, a "morphology of feeling" rather than feeling itself. Music is, as Langer (1942: 240) puts it, "an unconsummated symbol" having articulation and expressiveness "as its life". Symbols make things conceivable rather than store up a set of verbal propositions. They help weave our sense of reality. Thus, although the viewer may be vaguely aware of the music and sound effects structured within a nature or wildlife film, he or she will rarely be conscious of the subtle effect the music has in shaping meaning or a disposition to make or consummate a particular array of significant connotations, moods or emotional states.

There is more. For Messaris (1998), visual images are intimately related to analogical thinking – an analogy being something that is comparable to something else in significant respects. Thus a colour photograph of a wolf, or a baboon or a hedgehog is like the real thing in many ways. The way it is filmed and photographed orientates the viewer towards it in a certain way to elicit a response that is equivalent to the viewer's own experience of interacting with other people, things, objects, actions or animals. A close-up may convey a sense of intimacy or empathy, just as being physically close to an actual person or object may do so. However, images on their own – even in juxtaposition with others, as in a film montage or graphic novel – may require the addition of words to anchor a preferred meaning or interpretation. This is clearly evident in the captions explaining magazine photographs or the voiceover in a television commercial, and is necessary because images can say many things, mean different things to different people, at different times and in different cultures. Images and the visual culture of our times, and other times, are visualisations of our social world and social relationships. As for wildlife, nature and environmental film and photographic imagery, it is important to remember that these are invariably creative productions rather than transparent windows on the world. As Bouse (2000: 11) notes in his important book *Wildlife Films*, "the question is whether, or to what extent, audience members recognise this". Another question could refer to the kind of reality these films and photographs are presenting.

Mainstream film and television usually purvey a realist aesthetic that seems, and is, plausible; and, because audiences may have little experience of wild creatures beyond those seen in the media or at zoos, it may be difficult for them to evaluate actually how realistic or true television programmes and films are. The use of presenters, authoritative voiceovers and 'making of' sequences showing camera people up trees, in caves or submerged in miniature submarines, are attempts by film-makers and programme producers to demystify the film-making process and to invite the audience to trust the veracity of what is seen. Bouse (2000: 8) writes that certainly we are shown what has been photographed, but:

> The problem is that although wildlife films may show us things we might really have been able to see, they typically do so in ways we could never see

them, and in which nobody ever has seen them directly, including the people who film them. Obviously, the natural world does not reveal itself to them in the highly contrived and cinematic way it appears on the screen.

Thus in discussing the influence of wildlife film, television and perhaps photography too, it may be impossible to differentiate them from the effects of film, television and photography in general, although different interpretative communities will certainly have their own takes on what they see and hear. There are also many different ways in which media producers, professional and amateur alike, can construct the realities they perceive (Gamson, Croteau, Hoynes, Sasson, 1992; Moores, 2000). Then again, a qualitative study by the Glasgow University Media Group (Philo & Henderson, 1998) for Wildscreen on why viewers relate positively to wildlife programming found that audiences watch natural history films because they differ significantly from their mundane everyday experience. Nature programmes often feature exotic and distant locations, conjuring up in the minds of viewers images of romance, peace, freedom, untouched nature and remoteness. Viewers may also identify with some animal behaviours such as nurturing, may like the human presenter and so consequently wish to learn more about the 'natural' world and the process of filming it. Some viewers may even change their own behaviour as a result. Holbert, Kwak and Shah (2003), in their analysis of lifestyle data from the advertising agency DDB Chicago, note that environmental concern is an important reciprocal influence on television viewing and pro-environmental behavour. TV news tends to concentrate on negative elements such as pollution and natural disasters, while nature documentaries tend to concentrate on more positive aspects of animal habitats and animal behavour. They write (Holbert, Kwak and Shah, 2003: 191):

> The use of television news, even with its episodic and overly dramatic coverage of the environment, has a positive influence in creating a greater desire within individuals to recycle, purchase products that are environmentally friendly, and be more energy-efficient in their daily routines. The same can be said for the influence of the viewing of nature documentaries, programs that often provide a discussion of our responsibilities as stewards of the environment. . . . Nature documentaries do present a very positive message about the environment that every effort put forward by responsible citizens aids in keeping our world a little cleaner.

Studies like these are important, but what they do not explore in any detail is the how and why. Meyrowitz (1998) notes that most media analysis concentrates on content, but to understand how the media operates it is important that media literacy and media analysis encompasses much more. Meyrowitz therefore writes of multiple media literacies which, although each one can be analysed separately, in practice interlink and interconnect. These literacies include:

Content literacy – being able to analyse messages in a variety of media taking the form of ideas, topics, values, ideologies, appeals, settings, actions, narratives, genres, etc;

Media grammar or language pertaining to each media – with print media e.g. size/shape of page, use of italics or bold, use of blank space; with still photography e.g. depth of focus, colour balance, angle, type of lens; with audio e.g. sound perspective, tone, echo, silence, volume; and, with TV/film e.g. visual fade, cuts, pans, focus, montage and so on.

Medium literacy – that is, the type of setting or environment, the fixed features or characteristics of a medium, influencing communication in one way or another e.g. the type of sensory information conveyed – visual, oral, olfactory; the form of information within each sense such as picture or written; degree of definition, resolution and fidelity (a radio voice is closer to a live voice than a TV close-up is to a live face), degree and type of human manipulation as in an oil painting or snapping a photo.

With media convergence, all of these elements may be combined in a single product and experienced on a single device, albeit at varying levels of image and sound quality. Ulmer (2004) has noted that with the growing impact of new media communications, these various literacies and skills are being combined and enhanced to form something new – 'electracy'. Our use of the internet and computer technologies means we can download or upload movies, twitter, blog, write, sing or dance in a space that is virtual rather than real. These actions and possibilities may be leading to new and distinct cultural forms, social ideas, communication relationships and perceptions of the natural and social worlds. Where mainstream television production is concerned, the effectiveness of media grammar tends to be equated with its invisibility. This is not necessarily the case with new media productions, where seeing the join is part of the fun. As well as content there is a need for medium analysis, for the most powerful messages may really lie here. Meyrowitz writes (1998: 106):

. . . medium analysis involves explicit or implicit comparison of one medium of communication with another medium of communication (or with unmediated interaction). Because it is impossible for a medium to have any influence without content, and because most media messages also involve the conscious or unconscious manipulation of grammar variables, each media environment (a surrounding, curved-line shape) contains content elements (letters) and grammar elements (polygons) as well.

This is why it is useful to consider the media as an environment in itself that may for some people lead to both increased awareness of ecological and conservation issues and also to action. However, research on the influences on individuals' environmental sensitivities has rarely explored the media in any significant detail. Palmer (1993) noted that 23% of her survey respondents referred to TV/media as influencing their practical concern for the environment, but Louise Chawla's (Chawla, 1998) respondents mentioned education, books and particularly the outdoors – but not film or television as being in any way important. Chawla (1998: 381) concludes:

> One conclusive finding of research on responsible environmental behaviour is that there is no single all-potent experience that produces environmentally informed and active citizens, but many together. This complexity may make the challenge of environmental education more difficult, but it also makes it more hopeful. Just as ecosystems are more resilient when they contain an abundance of species that can form diverse adaptations to change, so is the future more hopeful if diverse paths lead people into environmental commitments.

Times change, and you don't have to be an environmentalist or pond dipper to be concerned about wildlife and biodiversity loss.

Advertising animals

Animals frequently appear in commercial advertising, and not surprisingly in public relations campaigns promoting animal welfare, zoos, animal focussed theme/safari parks and 'edutainment' venues such as Sea World or Disney's Animal Kingdom. As Gamson, Croteau, Hoynes and Sasson (1992) have discussed, media texts may incorporate both manifest messages and assumptions which are clear and obvious to the viewer. Other messages may be relatively invisible because they articulate commonly held assumptions. Herzog and Galvin (1992) have identified nine categories of animal representation in tabloid articles, photos and cartoons. These include: animal as loved one, as saviour, as threat, as victim, as tool, as sex object, as person, as object of wonder and as figment of the imagination. In many children's films and TV programmes animals, particularly cats and dogs, appear as pets or surrogate humans. The popular Australian 1960s children's series Skippy featured a bush kangaroo who had the uncanny ability to communicate with people, use radio transmitters, dial telephone numbers, play the piano as well as capture criminals and other undesirable types. Advertisers have frequently used animal imagery to symbolise qualities such as loyalty, affection and strength, and in many cases animal advertisements are unashamedly and deliberately anthropomorphic. Lerner and Kalof (1999) analysed 72 American TV commercials and found that six primary themes or categories appeared, including animals as loved one, as symbol, as tool, as nature, as allegory and as nuisance. Ads that portrayed animals as a means of transport, as sport or as food do not anthropomorphise, and a distance is created between pets and farm animals lest audiences identify with a creature whose life is sacrificed to make a burger. Thus, the class a particular species is placed within determines the media treatment it can expect.

Anthropomorphised animals are humanised and usually gendered as a male. Spears, Mowen and Chakraborty (1996) discovered that anthropomorphic animals were most often associated with food and drink, services and pet foods. Wild animals were usually used to sell durable goods like cars. Consumers are therefore influenced by the symbolic meanings that animal images convey, and Lancendorfer, Atkin and Reece (2008) noted that an image of a dog, 'man's best friend', in an advert could elicit a quick response that seemed to bypass any desire to think too deeply about what was being sold or any other implications of the message communicated. In the 1970s a long-running series of TV commercials dressed chimps up as humans and placed them in various tea-drinking scenarios mirroring popular attractions in zoos known as 'chimps' tea parties', where the humour resided in the contrast between the civilised absurdity of primates dressed as middle-class ladies sipping tea from china cups and the relatively unrestrained slapstick behaviour preferred at the zoo. More recently, Budweiser ran a series of humorous ads featuring animals. A chimp dressed in a T-Shirt and shorts sits on a sofa next to a young man's girl friend. She praises his apartment and his pet who is "so well behaved". As the man turns away to get some Bud Lights, and as she observes "he's so cute" the chimp places his arm around her. The chimp, Frank, says "I think you're cute too . . . baby. I do a little bit more than talk." The young woman looks startled as the chimp rocks back and forward, looks swiftly in the direction of the woman's breasts and suggests "let's cut the chit chat and go upstairs, you know . . . .". The man returns to the sofa. "Wow, here he comes. Act natural." Frank withdraws his arm and scratches his head. The ad cuts to a close up of a can of Bud Light and then swiftly back to the sofa as the man, now sitting, gets up again and leaves the frame screen right. Frank turns to the woman, replaces his arm and asks "so how do you feel about back hair?" This theatre of the absurd plays on the incongruities of anthropomorphism and inter-species social interaction without totally undermining either.

Sometimes, however, a different gender designation can bring out a wide range of cultural assumptions, as the campaign to "de-sex your bitch" by New Zealand's Royal Society for the Prevention of Cruelty to Animals did when bill-boards in the late 1990s carried this message next to a photomontage of a dog in a ruff, wig, lipstick, skirt, ankle bracelet and high heels. The Auckland-based campaign to neuter dogs and so reduce the number of unwanted animals cre-ated a mini-furore, with accusations levelled against the NZRSPCA of sexism, bad taste, ill judgement and ugliness. The visual image certainly created unease for those who pointed to the inequality in gender relations, and pleasure for those who saw the campaign imagery as 'just a joke'. The basic message about neutering, however, was not lost on the New Zealand public, but the contro-versy also led to a reassessment of what constitutes boundaries between humans and animals, and the gendered nature of animal representation (van Stipriaan and Kearns, 2009). More controversial perhaps is the US-based organisation PETA's use of images of sexually attractive and often scantily clad young women, often fairly well known actresses or models, in their highly suc-cessful *Go Naked* campaign. Bart Welling (2009) argues that in these images the boundaries between ecoporn (highly idealised images of landscape and ani-mals) and standard pornography are blurred, reifying ways of seeing that authorise all manner of oppression. A sweaty and distressed-looking Celina Jailty has large rusty chains round her arms and thighs. Her ankles are shack-led and the caption reads "Shackled, Beaten, Abused. Stop Cruelty to Ele-phants." A pouting young woman in a short leather skirt, fishnet tights, boots, small top and a police officer's hat kneels with her legs parted over two young rabbits. The caption reads, "Touch the buns and you're busted. DON'T WEAR FUR." A naked Jamelia photographed by Mary McCartney lies on her stomach resting on her elbows. She looks at the camera. A white rabbit nestles in the small of her back. The caption reads, "Be comfortable in your own skin, and let animals keep theirs." A naked woman poses side on in a glass doorway – "I'd rather go naked than wear fur." Similar ads and videos support PETA's campaign to 'go vegetarian'. Poorva Joshipura, Director of PETA Europe, reflected on the success of *Go Naked* in grabbing media attention and contesting oppression, saying:

> It is attention-grabbing images and stunts that get people to our website, get people to see our undercover videos and that's what results in real change. . . . The *I'd Rather Do Naked Than Fur* campaign started in the early 1990s and it is just as successful today in getting media coverage and getting the public's attention to the issues. Celebrities are just as interested in being part of that campaign and no matter what anyone may think of public nudity it is one of those campaigns that has been one of the most memorable in raising awareness about cruelty to animals. And not only on fur farms, we've been using that tactic to highlight the cruelty of bullfights, animals used for meat and animals used by other industries. These campaigns have perhaps been covered by every major newspaper on the planet. Major magazines and television shows have been inspired by the campaign to do their own stories and other organisations have been inspired too. In the UK even pensioners went naked to campaign against being stripped of their pensions. (Poorva Joshipura, interview 7th April 2010)

PETA's media campaigns often subvert corporate influence on consumer and media culture. For PETA, their campaign which depicted feeding children meat as a form of child abuse successfully did just that.

A great deal of television broadcasting is dependent on corporate sponsorship and advertising, and this also influences the way animals are depicted. Lerner and Kalof (1999: 380) write:

> It certainly follows that the commercials produced by the corporations themselves would also present images that failed to challenge the relatively unconscious divisions that support showering affection and money on some animals while killing and consuming others.

Animals are seen by advertising agencies as having the capacity to sell a range of products. Pandas can sell credit cards (Mastercard), gorillas can sell chocolate, especially when playing the drums (Cadburys) or hair gel (Wella), meerkats can sell insurance (comparethemarket.com) and elephants can seemingly sell everything – credit cards again (Mastercard), mobile phones (Optus 3G), soft drinks (Coke), and in India a wide variety of products (Pepsi, Happydent). Some ads exploit the popularity of popular film and television, including animal behaviour programmes such the TV soap opera Meerkat Manor made by Oxford Scientific Films for Animal Planet. The puppet meerkat Aleksandr Orlov, created by the advertising agency VCCP, has a massive following including over 700,000 Facebook fans and 36,000 followers on Twitter. His own personal website has an array of downloads including jingles, wallpaper, movies and a series of 'bloopers'. A gentle humour has been used by General Electric to promote an environmentally friendly brand image with a strapline 'Ecoimagination'. One ad features a baby elephant in a dripping jungle setting dancing daintily to music of Gene Kelly's 'Singing in the Rain'. The surreal nature of the scene, the sharp computer-generated imaging and the obvious reference to a Hollywood classic is clearly designed to lighten the enviromental message, sell a service – green energy – and, to some extent, rebrand the power and utilities industry. It also plays on viewers' love of elephants, Hollywood fantasy and the innocence of childhood. Spears and Germain (2007) surveyed the appearance of animals in print advertisements between 1900 to 2000 and found that although dogs, horses and birds were used regularly throughout the century, the depiction of animals changed in relation to the climate of the times. In the 1950s themes including relationships, family and light-hearted fun dominated, with dogs being used to convey this experience. In the late 1960s themes including rebellion and war and equine images, conveying a sense of power and strength, were preferred. In the 1990s individualism, consumer identification with products, economic prosperity and a concern for nature predominated. Dogs were most frequently used again, and the human-animal distinction was often blurred. Images, and particularly images of animals, are repositories of social meaning that change over time, and advertising images form part of the cultural and ideological framework through which groups and individuals indirectly make sense of conservation campaigns, policies and actions, and the images used by NGOs to communicate, motivate, inspire or sell a different, perhaps more ecocentric, message.

Not surprisingly, zoos and animal parks use images of their own animals to promote the range of entertainments, activities, conservation and educational work they are engaged in. Often this involves little more that a photo-collage of an iconic animal, usually in close-up, surrounded by a kaleidoscope of images indicating what else the zoo has to offer. Sometimes though, budgets willing, zoos employ prestigious advertising agencies to develop ingenious, humorous and visually powerful promotional campaigns which are virtually indistinguishable from the interpolation of animals in the commercial promotion of other goods or services. Being conscientious and socially responsible organisations, zoos invariably include significant conservation messages in their communications. In 2008 Buenos Aires Zoo presented a series of eye-catching images to increase visitor numbers. Close-up photographic portraits of an orangutan and a male lion with a black eye served to announce the arrival of some kangaroos.

Images of hippos, lions and monkeys yawning indicated the zoo would open in the evenings. Others placed images of lions, polar bears and giraffes adjacent to images of stuffed toys of the same creature. The strapline was "get much more for less" contrasting the price of the toy with that of the zoo's entry fee. Using Bates Y&R agency, Copenhagen Zoo initiated a series of bus ads with actual city vehicles seemingly being wrapped and slowly crushed by a gigantic python. Madrid Zoo ran a campaign created by Sra. Rushmore United advertising agency using a portrait of an animal next to that of a human being. Messages inserted in the bottom left corner included small captions such as "elephants never abandon the elderly", "a lion never uses his strength to humiliate another" and "when a dolphin finds a hurt dolphin, he helps it stay afloat". And finally, when the last polar bears died in St Louis Zoo in April 2009 they were replaced not by other captured creatures but a few proxy electronic bears as elements of its Wild Lights winter holiday exhibit. This act, highly praised by PETA, which sees zoos as cruel and unnecessary, is a grim but prescient message about the effects of global warming on a key iconic species as well as a pertinent comment on the future of zoos themselves.

Linking art movie pretensions, conservation and jewellery advertising, Godfrey Reggio, director the 'Quits' trilogy of films visually exploring what could be termed 'the condition of man', released *Anima Mundi* ('Soul of the World') in 1992. First screened at the 48th Venice Film Festival, the film, financed by the jeweller Bulgari to celebrate WWF's Biological Diversity Campaign, is a formalist exercise in structural montage and brand management – Bulgari, WWF and Gaia. Stock footage from a range of film archives was complemented by newly shot film, and throughout *Anima Mundi*'s 28-minute duration the viewer is invited to marvel at the wonders of nature. Close-ups of eyes – lions, tigers, owls, frogs – are followed by a succession of other image sequences of cloud movement, molten larva flows, aerial shots of running bison partially obscured by dust, monkeys licking lips, and slow-motion chases involving a lioness and fleeing gazelles. The conservation message is conveyed somewhat pretentiously just before the final credits in a quotation from Plato's Timaeus which appears in a number of languages to symbolise its global significance – French, German, Arabic, Spanish, Chinese, Russian, Italian, Japanese and English:

> . . . this world is indeed a living being endowed with a soul and intelligence . . . a single living entity containing all other living entities, which by their nature are related.

The meaning of the images is not anchored by a commentary – or indeed any captions other than its opening title and final quotation. The sound track by American composer Philip Glass, whose hypnotic and repetitive music has been used in Reggio's other non-narrative films, offers a visceral experience of nature. It is the music, as much as the images, which provoke a largely emotional engagement, perhaps inviting meditation on and immersion in the profilmic lifeworld. It is a stylish film, mirroring the brand image of the stylish company that used the film to promote its new naturalia range of jewellery by borrowing the conservation credentials of the WWF. However, although *Anima Mundi* today is a historical curiosity it does have some affinity with other non-narrative, theatrically released, films such as Claude Nuridsany's *Microcosmos* (1996) but clearly does not have the same visual or political dynamic as Nikolaus Geyrhalter's *Our Daily Bread* (2005), which overtly addresses a range of interconnected issues relating to factory farming, animal welfare and modernity through a juxtaposition of images that challenge the viewer to consciously make a cognitive, political and ethical judgement.

Circuit of communication

Anima Mundi is still available as an iPod download on the internet, although watching it on a screen a few centimetres across produces a diminished viewing experience as compared to seeing it on the big screen. Other images also do the rounds in what is essentially a circuit of communication. Many images seen in magazines, newspaper and websites are purchased from image banks such as Getty Images (which licenses the National Geographic image collection), Corbis or more specialist picture libraries such as Animal Photography or Nature Picture Library. Of the photos available, a large percentage will have been commissioned from photographers with a commercial brief to capture images that provoke feelings or evoke ideas rather than being strictly representative of an event or issue. The important thing is that these images can be used in a variety of contexts and design layouts. In addition, the image manipulation software Photoshop enables photographs to be easily adapted to match the perceived demands of the market (Frosh, 2003). Visual researcher David Machin (2004: 317) writes:

> The more they are multi-purpose, generic and decorative, the better they will sell. There has been a shift, it is suggested, from an emphasis on photography as witness to photography as a symbolic system.

Stock images are frequently decontextualised, interchangeable and to a degree stylised representations of general categories such as work, industry, nature, wildlife, love, friendship, Africa and sometimes even conservation. An online search through the categories will reveal a series of generic and predictable images whose validity lies in their emotional resonance, mood or 'sensory' truth. Their 'meaning potential' is partly a product of the nature of the image itself and partly derived from the assumed context of consumption. Searching 'conservation' may reveal a selection images of elephants, rhinos, lions, bush rangers, tree planting and occasionally an individual conservationist posing with a member of an endangered species. They might appear with options to buy or simply store temporarily in an online 'light box'. Theodore Adorno (1991) wrote that the culture industry, like most others, needs to be able to predict the market, and it can develop this predictability by providing audiences with predigested conceptual images and spaces where recognition is direct and effortless. On 1st May 2009 the *Independent* newspaper published on its front page a large colour photograph of an orangutan mother sitting with its baby in the Borneo rainforest. To the left and wrapped around the image of mother and child and imposed upon the out-of-focus greenery of the forest backdrop was the bold headline "Victims of the oil rush". A pointer to the special investigation on the palm oil business and deforestation printed on pages four and five was also visible. The image is recognisably that of two orangutans, and the faces of the two apes are, thanks to the headline, connotive of fear and desperation. A search of the Corbis image bank from which the image was purchased reveals the photographer to be Theo Allofs, the date of the image as unknown and the location as Tanjung Puting National Park. Allofs, a professional wildlife photographer, has over 1,000 similar and related images available from Corbis and on his own website. All are promoted as being useful in advertising, editorial and design contexts. Photographers obviously need to make a living and the way many do this is by selling stock images to corporate image agencies and their corporate clients who over time have developed a recognisably, corporate, visual lexicon. A good image will sell many times.

Take two more sets of images that were circulated widely in the popular media in Britain in 2009. The first shows a small family car in Knowsley Safari Park beset by a large troop of baboons who, apart from liberating the car's windscreen wipers, have managed to bounce open the rooftop luggage box and have proceeded to distribute its contents to others around the vehicle. Some are on the car, two are sitting inside the luggage box, a group are looking up waiting for an item to come their way or just enjoying the show. Through the window on the passenger side a woman with mouth open can clearly be seen looking both aghast and amused by these antics. The online *Daily Mail* version of the story shows six pictures: the first an establishing shot and the others detailed close-ups, depicting the animals pulling a toy monkey from the luggage or closely inspecting shirts, bras and a straw hat. This piece of public relations for the Safari Park during a quiet news period offered opportunities for viewers to be, like the passenger, simultaneously amused and outraged. The accompanying written text refers to the baboons as "opportunistic primates" or "pesky primates", highlighting their intelligence and capacity to entertain even if it is to the detriment of the Park's paying visitors. Only if the text is read carefully will the reader become aware that the event has been staged, ostensibly for educational purposes. David Ross, general manager, of Knowsley Safari Park is quoted as saying:

> 'Their technique involves the largest baboons jumping up and down on the box, flexing it until the lock bursts open, then the rest of the baboons pile in to see what they can find.'

> 'Obviously, we're well used to them helping themselves to the odd wing mirror or wiper blade, but this has taken things to a whole new level.'

> 'Let's face it, nobody wants to see a baboon running up a tree with their underwear.'

But Mr Ross said some visitors continued to ignore the warnings and paid a high price, with staff forced to re-enact the scenario for park guests so they could see the effect for themselves.

> 'Unfortunately though, we still get drivers who don't think it will happen to them and they decide to take a chance,' he said.

A week earlier the *Daily Mail* had featured the plight and recovery of a rather sad-looking hedgehog called Spud who, having been found completely spineless in a domestic garden, had been taken to an animal sanctuary in hope of a cure. The staff applied lotions and regular massages with baby oil and the national newspaper appealed to its readers for advice. There are two photographs. The first is a close-up of Spud with scaly skin and a caption informing the reader that he is miserable and barely alive. The second, also in close-up, shows the whole of the animal's body, taken some months later. Spud is sprouting new, but fairly short bristles and a caption reads "sharp dresser". Both photos depict the animal against a white background suggestive of a veterinary clinic. Unlike the baboons, though, Spud is directly looking at the camera – clearly an attempt by the photographer to elicit sympathy from the reader, for although a hedgehog hardly resembles a human being the sight of soulful downcast eyes encourages both viewer empathy and identification. Anyone can have skin trouble, and undoubtedly many *Daily Mail* readers will have experienced the pain, discomfort and embarrassment that goes with it. The hedgehog is an animal like us. The short text ends:

> But to their [sanctuary staff] delight, Spud's spines, a crucial defense against predators, are making a dramatic comeback.
>
> 'He's looking good,' said a spokesman for the sanctuary in Buckinghamshire.
>
> 'He doesn't feel embarrassed about his state any more.'

Both Spud and the Knowlsey baboons also made it on to national television, and from there on to YouTube where similar story lines have been produced. TV presenter Michaela Strachan on UK Channel Five spoke with a veterinary nurse about Spud's condition as she brushed and applied cream to the animal. It was brought about by mites, the nurse informs us. Concluding the report, Michaela Strachan looks to camera and with a laugh explains, "So that's Spud's beauty treatment over – exfoliate and moisturise". A two-minute roughly shot and edited video of the baboons shot by park staff and released at the same time as the photographs is available on YouTube. There is live sound but no post-production and no contextualising commentary; within six months the video had been viewed over 230,000 times. Whether or not these photographs, YouTube videos and television items are culturally innocuous, they certainly demonstrate one aspect of the cultural representation of animals in the Western popular media. They are both wild and not wild, different and similar, abstracted from their own environment and firmly placed within ours so as to be returned to the wild or at least a simulation of it.

Similar stories often culled from home videos are the staple of many TV series. These are cheap to produce, formulaic, predictable and popular. Animal Planet's *The Planet's Funniest Animals* (1999-present), has run for seven series featuring regular spots such as 'Pet-centricities', 'Snout Takes', 'Animal Sports', 'Privacy Please', 'The Hard Way' and 'Animals Who Think They're Human.' Although the humour in many of these stories inevitably anthropomorphises the animals, there is a sense this is largely due to the amateur video-maker seeing his or her pet, invariably a dog, as an actual person. Indeed, for some philosophers certain higher animals are indeed non-human persons (Singer, 1993), but the *All New Planet's Funniest Animals* is pure entertainment, having American comic actor Keegan-Michael Key offering a high-octane banal commentary on various animal antics such as a raccoon falling down a toilet (needs potty training) and a calf licking a domestic dog inside someone's home ("Hey you two, go get a room"). A British spin-off, *Animals Do the Funniest Things*, has run from 1999 to the present. Presenters have included comedian Michael Barrymore, former DJ Tony Blackburn, glamourous celebrity socialite Tara Palmer-Tompkinson and former magician and TV host Stephen Mulhern. Shown on ITV1, the later series sees the presenter doing a brief introduction to camera, often holding a featured animal while giving snippets of factual information about the species, the animal's behaviour and/or its natural habitat. This nod to ITV's diluted public service remit to inform, educate and entertain frames the stories, home videos, reports and 'sign-events' filmed specially for the show. 'Funny' stories have included a kestrel flying into and bouncing off a glass window pane, a zoo bear licking another's urine as she pees, a singing dog competition, a dog wedding and a wedding of two giant rabbits officiated by "a genuine vicar". The human participants also offer short pieces to camera explaining the normalcy of such events in a manner comedians refer to as 'dead pan'. Perhaps they are genuinely serious. Who knows? Clips of these shows are unsurprisingly on YouTube together with footage that has not found its way on to national prime time television. But anthropomorphic humour has been taken to another creative level by Nick Park and Aardmann Animations in the *Wallace and Gromit* animations, and in the animated TV series *Creature Comforts* where the recorded, unscripted, regional 'vox pop' voices of the general public are matched with animated animal characters who quickly become regular and familiar personalities. *Creature Comforts*, together with a set of television commercials for the UK Electricity Board and a less successful Americanised version, originated in a five-minute film made in 1989 for UK's Channel Four which featured plasticine zoo animals being interviewed about their lives in captivity. The humour is situational and gently ironic, as much related to the viewer being invited to perceive the off-screen humans as animals as the opposite, with political and moral connotations very close to the surface. The five-minute short won the Academy Award in 1990 for Best Animated Short Film.

Battle at Kruger

Battle at Kruger is an eight-minute 23-second video shot by an American tourist, David Budzinski, at the Transport Dam watering hole in South Africa's Kruger National Park in September 2004. Still photographs were taken by fellow tourist Jason Schlosberg. Its unedited footage – complete with fast pans, shaky camera positions, abrupt zooms, occasional glimpses of a top of a safari vehicle and offscreen voices – exudes a verité aesthetic. The tourists are amazed at the sight of a herd of large buffalo confronting a pride of lions at the water hole. The buffalo approach the lions, seemingly unaware or unperturbed by their presence when suddenly a group of lionesses attack, making straight for a calf. The buffalo run and one of the lionesses jumps and pulls the calf into the water. "Geez, she's got him" exclaims an American female tourist in a hushed but excited voice. The camera tracks the action and zooms in a little closer as the animals struggle in the water. Very soon they are joined by the other lions. "God, did you see that . . . unbelievable." The lions sink their teeth in the calf who, still alive, stands helplessly in the water up to its stomach. "Are the other buffalos coming to help, Frank? Is it too late?" While the lions attempt to drag the calf on to the bank two crocodiles surface, accompanied by an excited exclamation from one of the South African tourists. There follows a brief tug of war between the two crocs and the lions, with the latter being victorious. Just over four minutes into the video, the buffalo herd reappears. The sound of electronic lens focus changing and whispers of "it's too late" and "look at their teeth" correspond with the camera operator zooming out for a long shot to show the large herd screen left and the small pride around their catch centre right. The water fills the bottom half of the frame. The camera zooms in again as the buffalos edge closer. One large bull makes a tentative charge at the lions who, sensibly, take avoiding action. A South African voice, belonging to the safari guide Frank Watts comments on the rarity and feverishness of this spectacle: "You guys cannot believe what going on here, you have crocodiles, lions and buffalo." The tourist, although watching the action and recording it as it happens, describes what is happening, confirming that they too can't believe their eyes. One lion is chased away and then the herd attacks. One lioness is tossed into the air and the herd, then surrounding the group, turn on another and chase her away too. The camera follows but then swiftly pans left to recapture the action with the youngster. Four lions stay with the calf, which is still alive and trying to stand up despite the fact that at least one lion still has her teeth sunk into its flesh. The buffalos come closer and attack again. Two lions make off and the two remaining give up the calf, who stands up and walks into the safety of the herd. The large bulls at the front charge again ensuring the lions definitely make off. "Go on buffalo, go on." "Did you get him?" "Yeah, I got him being thrown in the air." "I've never seen anything like this. I mean, I've seen it on video and on movies." "You can sell the video."

The video was posted on YouTube in 2007 and instantly became one of the most popular contributions, generating nearly 50 million viewings by 2010 and 58,000 comments. The video was discussed by *Time* magazine, featured on ABC News and became the subject of a National Geographic documentary in 2008. It won the Best Eyewitness Video in the second Annual YouTube Video Awards in 2008. Ironically, Budzinski had earlier tried to sell the footage to various television networks but they turned him down, curtly explaining that they do not buy film footage from amateurs. Writing in the *New York Times*, Brian Stelter (2008) shows how new media has quickly changed everyone's reality, including that of the major media networks:

> For almost three years the film essentially sat on the shelf. But a year ago, when Mr. Schlosberg used YouTube to share the video with a friend — it was easier than making a DVD copy and mailing it, he said — *Battle at Kruger* started spreading virally on the Internet. Before long, National Geographic contacted Mr. Schlosberg, who in turn called Mr. Budzinski. That tourist turned online star had never heard of YouTube.

> The two men struck a deal to share in the profits. Mr. Schlosberg, a photographer, now sells prints of the video clip and runs battleatkruger.com, listing merchandising and licensing opportunities.

> The National Geographic Channel producers took Mr. Budzinski back to Kruger National Park to film the scenes needed for the television version: the group riding in the S.U.V., the tour guide pointing toward the watering hole, the cameraman zooming in. But the documentary ends with the real action: the original YouTube video.

> Enhanced by professionals, the television video is clearly superior to the blurry and heavily compressed version viewed online. Then again, television viewers can't immediately comment on the video, share it with friends or produce a video response.

This short piece of amateur wildlife film-making does indeed have all the ingredients of a perfect wildlife feature. It has iconic predators chasing down prey – a defenceless baby. It has vicious crocodiles attempting to steal the prey by confronting the lions. Then there is the rescue and the return of the victim to the warmth and safety of the family. In addition, it is an unstaged actual event taking place in a game reserve managed for the benefits of the tourist as well as the wildlife. This video, lasting less that nine minutes, compresses what is often seen on TV wildlife documentaries as staple iconic fare. It also suggests how with the advent of a social networking site like YouTube anyone who happens to be in the right place at the right time can distribute what professionals produce over much lengthier periods of time at a cost of millions of dollars. The fact that the image quality is of fairly low resolution is unimportant. It adds to the aesthetic authenticity of the event, and the action is followed well enough by the camera operator who seems to adopt a similar visual grammar as that evident in professionally produced BBC or National Geographic specials. *Battle at Kruger* certainly resonated with viewers, who learnt of the adventure not via TV Guide but from each other on the YouTube channel, other social networking or other new media sites where the viral story appeared. The fact that National Geographic turned the episode into a 'making of' story four years later is testimony to the significance of a circuit of communication where amateurs are able to successfully produce, distribute and exhibit their own material to a global audience both free of charge by simply passing on links via email or even as a commercial product sold via their own personal websites. New media allows for a diversity of communication users and producers, even if the visual grammar was, in this instance, a relatively familiar one. In some ways, though, *Battle at Kruger* is reminiscent of early cinema where, as film historian Tom Gunning (1990) writes, a cinema of attractions privileging spectacle and visceral engagement was the norm. Rizzo (2008) notes that many video-sharing websites like YouTube demonstrate similar characteristics, exhibiting short videos that barely develop a narrative but show instead, tricks, stunts, jokes, curios, novelties and sensational spectacles of one description or another – a dog performing tricks or a buffalo calf being rescued from the jaws of hungry lions. Rizzo writes of the new medium:

> Social networking sites such as YouTube are populated by subscribers actively looking for novelty. Therefore, YouTube clips engage an audience that is highly attuned to attractions. This may have also been the case in relation to the cinema of attractions, but there is something more intense about the way this search can take place anywhere at anytime. Its immediacy means that exhibition, shock and sensationalism become everyday events. This should not be surprising as these qualities are found, and indeed have always been found, in the media — but today's proliferation of media makes it a very intense experience.

Wildlife film and photography more generally is packed with shock and awe, love and sympathy, and depending on the nature of the programme or storyline, a series of visual and auditory attractions that may span a whole of an animal's life in sixty or thirty minutes, with breeding seasons compressed temporally within the limitations of a single minutes-long sequence. A lot happens very quickly in wildlife films.

Zoo Time

The art critic John Berger suggests that the mediated presence of animals in contemporary culture is testimony to their absence in our working, productive lives. They are playthings and entertainments, less than human and no longer wild. In the essay 'Why Look at Animals?' Berger writes (1991: 26):

> Zoos, realistic animal toys and the widespread commercial diffusion of animal imagery, all began as animals started to be withdrawn from daily life. One could suppose that such innovations were compensatory. Yet in reality the innovations themselves belonged to the same remorseless movement as was dispersing the animals. The zoos, with their theatrical decor for display, were in fact demonstrations of how animals had been rendered absolutely marginal. The realistic toys increased the demand for the new animal puppet: the urban pet. The reproduction of animals in images – as their biological reproduction in birth becomes a rarer and rarer sight – was competitively forced to make animals ever more exotic and remote.
>
> . . . . In zoos they constitute their own disappearance.

With the proxy electronic polar bear at St Louis Zoo and the development of still and moving image archives such as Wildscreen's ARKive, E.O. Wilson's *Encyclopedia of Life* or the IUCN's list of endangered species, it is perhaps the electronic zoo rather than actual physical ones that are best able to show the many species that are about to disappear from our world. However, species extinction and habitat loss have given actual zoos a new lease of life and a new public purpose. From once being seen as animal prisons, symbols of colonial exploitation and extravagance and an echo from an era of nineteenth-century scientific curiosity and obsession with classification and categorisation, today's urban zoos, animal parks and 'safaris' – and even overtly commodified tourist traps such as Disney's Animal Kingdom or Florida's Sea World – have become symbols of, and for, planetary care and inter-species responsibility (Davis, 1997; Beardsworth and Bryman, 2001). Designers of zoo exhibits and themes draw on a great deal of social knowledge and shared images which visitors will have seen on television, film and advertising. These images of conservation, of killing, of habitat destruction, of animal behavour, of animal capture and quasi-wildlife representation are sometimes transplanted to the zoo. While for some animals the zoo may be a last stop before extinction, and while the evolutionary process raises questions about the concept of species preservation and to an extent conservation too, animal stories and wildlife narratives frequently articulated in blue chip and other documentaries may frame and organise visitor expectations within these attractions.

Acampora (2005) states that the goal of naturalistic zoos, first pioneered at Berlin Zoo over 100 years ago, is to create a captive environment that acculturates the animals sufficiently to ignore their human spectators while they act 'naturally', as if they were in the wild. Usually, this does not happen, so what spectators see is at best a simulacrum – an unsatisfactory imitation. Zoos lack adventure, for like a museum they present and display representatives of species rather than take their visitors on imaginary excursions. As Eugene Hargrove writes (1995: 18):

> ... the triumph of narrative thinking could encourage the development of partially zooless zoos in which the animals live in remote locations, roaming under nearly natural conditions, away from the direct observation of zoo visitors, who would observe them indirectly through narrative documentaries ....

Acampora suggests that conservation areas that allow restricted and regulated spectatorship may be a model for the future, and Edinburgh Zoo announced in late 2009 that the UK's last living (and ageing) polar bear, Mercedes, would be moved not to another zoo but to four acres of land, complete with pond and a tundra-like environment, in the Highland Wildlife Park in Scotland. There she would be protected, enclosed by an electric fence, but otherwise able to live out her remaining years 'naturally'. Visitors can observe her from a distance on a raised viewing platform (*BBC News*, 2009). In the winter of 2009-10 she made her first ever snow den. As Finlay, James and Maple (1988) found, the context in which an animal is viewed influences what and how a person thinks of that animal. Mercedes' biography, Edinburgh zoo's action and the public appeal that led to raising the necessary £75,000 for her transfer together with the ensuing media reports suggests that Norton (1995: 108) is possibly wrong when he writes that "our moral decision to value wild animals as wild isolates us from moral obligations to wild animals as individuals". Zoos may, as David Hancocks (2001), Director of the Open Range Zoo at Weribee in Australia, argues, be able to cultivate environmental sensitivity, gentleness towards all other creatures and compassion for the well-being of wild places.

Bristol Zoo in the UK has a number of local animal conservation field projects and is increasingly using television screens to convey the nature and extent of their conservation and scientific work and ways in which visitors can participate. Simon Garrett, the Zoo's Education Officer, said:

I have literally come from the Director's office talking about how we can put more screens up – each one talking about a field project, getting a screen by the gorillas, by the fruit bats, by the doves. We have a lot of footage by our people working out on the field projects. By putting together a little two-minute video clip and placing either a collection box next to it and/or a list of things the public can do – such as looking out for FSC labels, buying certain products or not buying certain products – we can encourage visitors to support the project. It's turning a social day out into something where we are trickling a little bit of information so that although people aren't going to go away as committed conservationists but if the next time they are shopping in B&Q they see an FSC conservation label they will link it with something good they've seen at the zoo. (Simon Garrett, interview 4th June 2009)

Before television screens entered the zoo, actual zoos and animal capture expeditions appeared on television and film. Louis Lumière filmed pelicans, caged lions and tigers at London Zoo in 1895. In one film a keeper can be seen taunting the big cats with a stick, piercing some meat and poking it through the bars to create some action and silent growling. Mitman (1999), Bouse (2000) Chris (2006) and Palmer (2010) have offered interesting and detailed accounts of zoos on the television screen attempting to offer entertainment that is also educative. In 1950 NBC transmitted the first episode of the long-running series *Zoo Parade* based at Lincoln Zoo in Chicago and presented by Jim Hurlbut and the Zoo's director Marlin Perkins. Perkins was an excellent communicator, intuitively understanding the homespun nature of the new medium. He was relaxed, well informed and conversational. He used his co-presenter as an audience surrogate, almost a stooge, and seemed to be completely unflappable. The 190th episode saw Perkins opening cages in the bird house, talking and singing to the birds to evoke a response, allowing them to perch on his and Hurlbut's hands. Interspersed in his running commentary were bits of information designed to correct popular misconceptions. The owls, for example, shouldn't be hunted because owls are useful predators of mice and other vermin. The camera, constantly tracking both Perkins' and the birds' movements, offered audiences a guided personalised tour that was very informal and very accessible. American viewers were encouraged to identify with the zoo animals as if they were pets, and in order to minimise the effects of the iron bars, so were the keepers. As Mitman (1999: 140) writes:

The thematic focus on animal personalities, the pet-keeping practices of zoo caretakers, and the promotional advertisements for pet products all helped create a more intimate relationship between the audience and animals of *Zoo*

Parade. The names of animal celebrities and the Ken-L-Ration [dog food] ad starring Rover and his family also point to the intentional blurring of the distinction between animals and humans on the show.

One programme broadcast on an Easter Sunday conveyed the faintly radical idea that both animals and humans were loved by God, but this wholesome entertainment was genuinely loved by many American children and their parents. The show ran from 1950 to 1957 but intermittently, and often from different zoos in its final two years. Commercial sponsorship was sometimes a problem, and for its final nine months it had none.

In 1954, the BBC broadcast the first series of *Zoo Quest*, which combined film footage of animal collecting expeditions in Africa, South America and elsewhere with live shots of animals being handled and talked about in the studio. British audiences got their first sight of a young David Attenborough, and reviews and ratings were good (Attenborough, 2003). Naturalist Peter Scott and author, animal collector and conservationist Gerald Durrell also appeared regularly on the public service BBC. However, it was with the advent of commercial television that a loosening of the animal and zoo programme format came about. Desmond Morris, a former Oxford academic and then curator of mammals at London Zoo, presented *Zoo Time* on Granada Television. The series ran for twelve years from 1956 to 1968. Morris had originally intended and wanted to produce serious animal behaviour films, but the filming process was too slow for the television executives: it took too long a time to document the reproductive cycle of an animal, so Morris was persuaded to present one weekly live half-hour programme broadcast from London Zoo itself. Morris refused to take zoo animals to the studio as they become stressed and behave unnaturally. Instead, he had a studio built in the zoo thanks to the hijacking of an outside broadcast unit designed for the Wimbledon tennis tournaments. Morris (2000: 4) remembered:

> So I won my point, my zoological point, which is, let's take the cameras to the animals, don't let's take the animals to the studios. And this was new, and this had never been done before. All previous animal things, I'm not talking about films now, but live television with animals, had been done in a studio where animals had been brought along in a bag or a box, and then taken out, and looking around and blinking looking at the lights and wondering where they where. So, we actually got a lot of behaviour out of the animals . . .

In his autobiography, *Animal Days* (Morris, 1979), he writes of learning a great deal about media communication from the programme's first director

William Gaskill, who told him to stop lecturing to a piece of machinery. Gradually he learnt to treat the TV camera as a single person and to create an imaginary family in his mind. *Animal Days* is consequently full of funny anecdotes, but for Desmond Morris *Zoo Time* was little more than television fluff, with later episodes featuring chimps' tea parties and elephant baths. However, particularly in the late 1950s when the shows were broadcast live he challenged the somewhat puritan morality that pervaded public broadcasting and avoided some of the criticisms which later dogged many animal and natural history programmes as being misleading by exhibiting a disrespectful anthropomorphism. The latter criticism eventually led to the closure of the long running UK children's TV show *Animal Magic* as producers were accused of encouraging animals to behave for the camera in ways that were considered unethical or unnatural. Morris, on the other hand, wanted audiences to see animals behave and respond to the presenters and keepers more or less in a normal manner. Consequently, they would sometimes escape, urinate, bite and even demonstrate signs of sexual arousal. In an interview conducted for Wildscreen's *WildFilmHistory* project by Christopher Parsons, Morris (2000: 8) recalls:

> We had a young chimpanzee called Congo who appeared on many of these programmes and who became a sort of television personality. And Congo again, one of the things I refused to do was to dress him up. I was asked to put nappies on him because he was a male with a conspicuous penis. And I refused. I said, "If this chimpanzee is dressed up I'm leaving." I used to get very stroppy in those days because I was a scientist and I wasn't going to appear with dressed-up animals. And I remember there was a long debate about this. Could they risk viewers seeing a chimpanzee's penis? And I said, "It's not very impressive, I don't think you need worry, it's not like a human penis, it's a tiny spike, even." I suppose Congo must be the first being ever to have an erect penis on British television. But even when it was erect, it wasn't very impressive. And in the end they accepted this and nobody complained. We didn't have a single complaint about that.

Zoo programmes continue to be popular. In Australia, *The Zoo* airs on Channel 7 and is based around the animal inhabitants and keepers at Taronga and Western Plains Zoos in New South Wales. Following a familiar format, the programme relates stories about the animals, their keepers and the vets and the accompanying website offers information about the careers of the human participants and individual biographies of the featured animals. The conservation message is clearly and directly presented as an integral part of the zoos' work and at least one of the reasons why viewers should be watching. Short clips from the programmes and media releases are also available on the website. One shows a young female keeper, Renae Zammit, feeding and bathing Monifa, a baby Pigmy Hippopotamus, while simultaneously explaining to an offscreen interviewer the dangers hippos face in the wild from poaching, war, pollution and habitat loss in their native Sierra Leone and Liberia. Showing an animal's young automatically engages viewers emotionally, perhaps making them more sympathetic to the problems faced by wild hippos trying to raise their young in their native homelands. London Zoo also offers web users access to an extensive range of downloadable moving image material. ZSL TV features a fair selection of cute animal babies which again act as hooks for viewers to attend to the more serious conservation messages communicated in the keepers' commentaries. There are additionally a few extended and unedited video clips of animals in the wild just yawning, looking around and doing very little else.

BBC's *Animal Park*, first shown in 2000, has presenters Kate Humble and Ben Fogle introducing viewers to wardens and their charges at Longleat Estate and Safari Park in Wiltshire in the UK. Each episode explores a particular theme, such as animal enrichment, which is about making the lives of captive animals more interesting and natural. A keeper explains to viewers, via the presenters, how this is done – puzzles, scattering food round their island to encourage a type of foraging and also, occasionally, watching TV. A sequence in one episode involved a large silverback gorilla, Nico, being presented with a mirror and then a television monitor in which video footage of various animals in the park could be viewed. This replicated an experiment the keeper had recently learnt of in an animal behaviour course she had attended. The keeper comments that images of sea lions and other creatures get little response, but when an image of a rhesus monkey appears and later shots of other gorillas including Nico himself, the ape becomes totally transfixed. A close-up of the gorilla's eyes illustrates how attentive he is of the images as the viewer is told of the intelligence of great apes. "They can recognise their own reflection." Nico is then seen abruptly turning away and hitting the side of his cage. "He is basically getting a little bit agitated, a little unnerved. He just wanted it to end I think", explained the warden. Ben Fogle's soothes any potential viewer concerns about the experiment stressing the animal by stating "it was time for the animal to go out anyway", and the next image is a long shot of the gorillas moving around outside in their enclosure. A final shot is a close-up of the gorilla's face, with the sound commentary stating that the activity "may have given him something to think about for the rest of the day".

Monkey Life, made by Primate Planet Productions and shown on Channel Five and Animal Planet, is based on the work of Monkey World Ape Rescue Centre, a sanctuary for primates located in Dorset, UK. Its format resembles that of a soap opera, with continuing storylines and cliff-hanging endings. Both the animals and wardens play the heroes and victims. One storyline told the tale of 80 small primates being transported from a research lab in Chile to the UK sanctuary. The complicated logistics were explained by the sanctuary's director, Dr Alison Cronin, who is filmed supervising the transfer. Like other dramas, the main story alternates with a series of sub-plots, scenes and locations shifting from one to another, from Chile back to Dorset and back again. The viewer's interest is maintained by a breathless commentary, quick editing and a series of questions which amount to: will the animals be saved?, will a sick animal recover?, can all the animals be transported safely to England?, will the existing inhabitants at Monkey World accept the new arrivals? The programme deliberately and effectively dramatises, in a serial form, conservation and animal welfare issues such as the effects of habitat loss and poaching. When first shown in 2007 Channel Five's early evening ratings tripled, but in late 2009 the Channel announced it was cutting the series. This provoked a group of viewers using the social networking site Facebook campaigning for Five to reverse its decision. Two comments illustrate a general reaction:

> . . . no way can you axe the best reality TV show that's ever been on the box! There's drama (Alice – who turned out to be Mary Chipperfield's tortured chimp Trudy!),Whodunnit (When Paddy flipped and Jimmy got blamed), Romance Twan and Gordon with their lady friends, action (amazing rescues from around the world), compassion (all the gentle moments from staff and surrogate mums like Sally), friendships, new beginnings (babies being born) and sad goodbyes (the sadness news a great man like Jim passing on and of course the adorable Charlie.[1] Everything is in this show, please channel 5 don't take it away!!!

> . . . if either 5, or another channel, don't show programmes like Monkey Life the barbaric treatment that these animals endure from humans won't be brought to the public's attention and we won't be educated on the inhumane things that are done to them and it will continue. Some people who keep some of these animals as pets really aren't aware that they are being cruel to them until they see programmes like this and it may stop other people buying them as pets.

Channel Five's decision made the national press, with *The Guardian* quoting the managing director of of Primate Planet Productions, Louise McCance-

---

1. Jim Cronin, Monkey World's founder and husband of Alison, died suddenly in 2007.

Price, saying the programme had been a genuine educational force motivating some owners of primate pets to re-home their animals with Monkey World and other viewers 'adopting' monkeys living at the park. "This is not just a TV series to us and to our viewers, but an important tool in creating awareness of primate conservation." (Tryhorn, 2009)

Zoo Days, made by Granada Wild for Channel Five, was first screened in 2007. Shot at Chester Zoo in the UK, the educational, zoo promotion and justification themes dominate the storylines. This time the enrichment theme shows keepers preparing a feast of meat sown into an animal's hide. They have never done this before and one of the keepers remark that when the "lion goes for the kill" it will give him "a good workout". The unseen narrator states that the visitors, filmed holding their own DV cameras, will have the privilege of seeing a beast devouring his prey. Sabu, the lion, is then shown slowing leaving his den and moving towards what is essentially a furry bag of meat. He starts to take the fur off the hide, baring his teeth and allowing scent particles to enter his system. The viewer is assured that the animal is behaving totally naturally as he would in the wild. A brief shot follows of the lion picking up the bag and moving off screen to finish his meal. There is a cut to the visitors showing each other what they have just witnessed in the viewing screens of their digital cameras and the programme then moves gently on to another item.

This sequence may be compared with a report by Peter Sharp first shown on Sky News TV, 'China's Killer Zoos', and winner of a Panda Award at the 2008 Wildscreen Festival. It is feeding time at Harbin Wildlife Park in northern China. Tourist buses full of Chinese visitors are entertained by various live animals including a cow, a chicken and duck being fed to a group of overweight Siberian tigers who proceed to tear the creatures apart. The action is accompanied by cheers and shouts from the spectators safely located in their tourist bus. In China, the correspondent says, this is considered to be "good family entertainment". A chicken costs £2.60 and a cow £100. The kills are long and drawn out. The cries of the dying cow are clearly audible on the report's soundtrack. Sharp also shows footage of a three-year-old bear dressed in an orange dress roped to a car and attempting to pull it. This entertainment goes on twice a day at another Chinese zoo. Other scenes in the report show a caged tiger pacing up and down, a chimp hitting himself and other monkeys performing tricks to entertain the human visitors. Animal Rights campaigner Dr John Wederburn, founder of the Asian Animal Rights Network, is seen in one sequence making on-the-spot inspections, but conditions in Chinese zoos, he says, have not improved in ten years (Sharp, 2008). To reinforce the point perhaps, in 2010 the international Chinese news agency CCTV reported the death of 26 animals in Shenyang Forest Wild Animal Zoo in the north east Liaoning Province. Four of the animals were Siberian tigers and the others were also on the list of protected species in China. The tigers were reported to have died of malnutrition as the largely privately owned zoo could only afford to feed them with cheap chicken bones (Bristow, 2010). David Hancocks (2001) and other zoo professionals in the West have criticised the animal mistreatment in China, but animal welfare and enrichment issues generally are not always so straightforward. Putting lumps of meat in a tightly sewn-up animal skin is enrichment and a spectacle for visitors to Chester Zoo, while Chinese visitors are treated to a feeding time when the meat to be consumed is still living, breathing and most certainly scared. Financial, cultural, ethical and political issues inform both practices and both media representations. What isn't really addressed in either the Sky News report or in *Animal Park* is whether it is legitimate to have wild animals confined and captive at all – anywhere.

Within days of the news breaking internationally, the Chinese government agreed to fund Shenyang Forest Wild Animal Zoo.

Conserving Images

Images of animals in the wild or in captivity pervade Western culture, but one issue that needs to be addressed is perhaps whether the prevalence of animal imagery and animal stories in the media enables or hinders the communication of serious conservation messages. It is possible that if a cultivation effect is at work, then what is being cultivated is a rather warm comforting reassurance that some people somewhere are doing some things to help some creatures. In her brilliant study of photography, the critic Susan Sontag perceptively suggests that we should be more careful in our use and understanding of images, recognising that "images of real things are inter-layered with images of images" (Sontag 1979: 175). She concludes her essay 'The Image World' (1979: 180) by writing:

> Images are more real than anyone could have supposed. And just because they are an unlimited resource, one that cannot be exhausted by consumerist waste, there is all the more reason to apply the conservationist remedy. If there can be a better way for the real world to include the one of images, it will require an ecology not only of real things but of images as well.

Chapter Three

Blue chip and beyond:
gender and nature in natural history film–making

Possibly all cultures – but certainly Western cultures – demonstrate contradictory attitudes to animals. On the one hand we love our pets and other non-human companions, watch fascinating natural history documentaries and support animal welfare initiatives; but on the other hand there is a disquieting record of cruelty and disavowal of animal suffering in much food production and biomedical research (Arluke, 2006). A Gaumont Graphic newsreel from 1922 shows what is heralded in the inter-title as a 500-year-old giant turtle, an 'old man of the sea', turned into the plaything of bathers on a Miami beach. Two men push and then lift the turtle from the ocean's waves carrying him to the water's edge. There they are shown in close-up roughly pulling the turtle's head back for the camera. The film cuts to a young woman in bathing costume standing and dancing on the turtle's back, a rope in its mouth in mock simulation of a donkey/turtle beach ride. Although clearly fun for the human participants, the film conveys to contemporary viewers a sense of disrespect, shame and embarrassment. Other films from the early part of the last century depict a similar casual disregard, or perhaps ignorance, of the sentience of other creatures. Often today's viewers, particularly in many Western countries, recoil at the casual brutishness of the circus, the mock heroics of the great white hunter shooting an elephant or the matter of factness inherent in early film actualities depicting the bloody heroics of traditional whaling fleets. In the early twentieth century only George Orwell (1957: 97) in his essay 'Shooting an Elephant' seems to have captured the terrible senseless horror of killing another creature:

> In that instant, in too short a time, one would have thought, even for the bullet to get there, a mysterious, terrible change had come over the elephant. He neither stirred nor fell, but every line of his body had altered. He looked suddenly stricken, shrunken, immensely old, as though the frightful impact of the bullet had paralysed him without knocking him down. At last, after what seemed a long time – it might have been five seconds, I dare say – he sagged flabbily to his knees. His mouth slobbered. An enormous senility seemed to have settled upon him. One could have imagined him thousands of years old.

Times change, and with them the cultural mentalities that people inhabit and reproduce in their actions, thoughts and sensibilities. Natural history film-making since the Second World War has contributed to a shift in cultural attitudes and dispositions towards animals and the natural world (Baker, 2001). From the early Oscar-winning wildlife documentaries, the *True Life Adventures* made by the Disney Corporation from 1948 to 1960, to long-running television series about animal behaviour and habitats presented by both naturalists and academics such as Peter Scott, Jacques Cousteau, Desmond Morris, Marlin Perkins and David Attenborough, the media has offered viewers a combination of entertainment, education, wonder and spectacle.

The BBC's Natural History Unit (NHU) was formed in 1957 in Bristol which has since become a centre for environmental, wildlife and natural history media productions. Geographer Gail Davies (2000) has argued that there have been three discernible phases in the NHU's development. The first phase saw the emergence of the amateur naturalist film-maker whose work was characterised by an educational ethos and fieldcraft skills that concentrated on capturing images of animals in the wild, collaboration with scientists and communicating an enthusiasm for the natural world to the viewing public. Direct experience with animals was highly valued and was perceived as guaranteeing the authenticity of the television programme, which was often reflected by the lack of telegenic attraction in much of their work. This was partly due to the film-makers' priority in learning more about the animals in the wild and partly by the constraints the cumbersome film-making equipment imposed on the creative process. The real creativity of the amateur film-making/naturalist was in scouting locations, understanding species behaviour and building up knowledge. Material was often unscripted, with very basic editing and minimal use of post-production effects.

The second phase centred around the production of keynote, often collaborative, mega-productions most clearly associated with David Attenborough. The 13-part *Life on Earth* series first broadcast in 1979 took years to make and involved film-makers for the BBC, National Geographic and Granada travelling the world. The series exemplifies the type of programme which has since become synonymous with BBC quality and brand image, where the skills of the presenter/facilitator are extremely important as the mode of address is to audience members directly and personally. The science, although still important, is more accessible, as the major drive behind these productions was, and remains, audience maximisation and international sales.

The third phase, which came to the fore in the 1990s, exhibits a more cost-consciously managerialist approach, with major blue chip blockbusters often made as co-productions with Discovery or National Geographic. These programmes are themselves media events – large televisual beasts surrounded by a variety of far cheaper, smaller and sometimes trivial programmes whose stars are frequently presented on a quest to find an elusive wild animal. In these productions library footage is very important, as relatively little time is spent in the field and, as Davies notes, the NHU's specialised archive of still and moving images has been commercially exploited by the BBC with sales to advertisers, feature film and music video-makers and to cable channels in the USA and Europe for use in TV dramas and multi-media CD-ROM products. For many years there has been a close association between the BBC and the Discovery Channel, with Discovery winning preferential access to NHU resources. Davies writes, 1999:55):

> This extension and control of the television networks around the NHU [Natural History Unit] has enabled a trade in animal images of a magnitude comparable to the huge trade in animals previously associated with zoos.

From the late 1990s, long-running series or 'soap operas' focussing on zoos, sanctuaries, animals parks and animal hospitals have also become a scheduling staple. Some series have focussed on the killer content – Maneaters: *Sharks, Blue Water Predators, Predators, Ultimate Killers, Shark Summers, Rogue Predators, Anatomy of a Shark Bite, Predator X, Up Close and Dangerous*, and more. For Cottle (2004: 93) the 'money shot' in these films is the kill. He writes:

> Such scenes, like the 'money shot' in pornography, are widely thought to be what the audience wants, and this helps account for their increased prevalence within recent programmes as well as the increased numbers of programmes devoted to the big predators, often sharks, and even more specifically the Great White. To put it another way, the political economy of natural history programmes disenfranchises invertebrates.

Even programmes such as *Hero Animals* made by Big Wave TV, whose storylines tell of humans being rescued by altruistic animals from the jaws of dangerous predators have all the blood, excitement, claws, thrill, teeth and chill one could wish for – often in slow motion. In 2010 *Hero Animals* was nominated for a Royal Television Society award for best factual series. Generally, though, audiences and film-makers expect a variety and mix of approaches that frequently extend from the serious and worthy to the carnivalesque, but even the trivial can have a serious side, and despite changes in format, approach and image quality many natural history programmes have an exceedingly long shelf life. Programmes first broadcast over thirty years ago are still repeated somewhere in the multi-channel environment, and many of the cheaper series are re-run many times.

Full-length documentaries often feature trophy species such as lions and tigers and culturally significant researchers, with sympathetic and complementary articles regularly appearing in *National Geographic* magazine and large-format coffee table books published by the Sierra Club or other respected organisations. But Barbara Crowther (1997) has noted that natural history film-making has also been dominated by male presenters, producers, and technical staff, and unsurprisingly the programme aesthetic has essentially been male-orientated, serving to reinforce the appeal of science to male audiences and reproduce the values and perspectives of a sociobiology that has tended to marginalise the interests of women. However, in the last ten years women have become increasingly prominent as television national history presenters, scientific experts and important and influential conservationists, although Jane Goodall, Birute Galdikas and Dian Fossey are relatively early examples of pioneering female conservationists – all initially employed by Louis Leakey – whose media profiles developed as their work gained international academic and public attention. Occasionally the personal lives of these media-friendly conservationists adds a mediagenic human interest dimension to an otherwise well-known straight scientific story. Photographer and cameraman Bob Campbell shot over 70,000 feet of footage of Dian Fossey and her gorillas in the early 1970s. Many of his still photographs were also published in *National Geographic* magazine. His influence on her research and indeed her life was profound, but not acknowledged in Fossey's own book *Gorillas in the Mist* (Fossey, 1985) or elsewhere. Wildlife film-making or scientific observation can be not only a very solitary activity but also intensely emotional. Campbell and Fossey had a brief romantic attachment but Fossey, like Galdikas and Goodall, developed deeper and perhaps more profound attachments to their research subjects as the National Geographic Special *Mountain Gorillas: the lost film of Dian Fossey* (2003) poignantly demonstrated. In the cases of Dian Fossey, and to a lesser extent and film-maker Joan Root, their violent deaths have become subjects of Hollywood biopics (*Gorillas in the Mist*, 1988) or documentary features (*Murder at the Lake*, BBC 2009) and so have extended their media lives beyond their actual ones. For Charlotte Uhlenbroek, it is her attractive looks and PhD in Zoology that have made her both a respected and popular television presenter as well as being described as "an eco-friendly Lara Croft" in some newspapers (Williams, 2009). Her informed contributions as presenter of the BBC's *Chimpanzee Diary* (1998-1999), *Cousins* (2000), *Congo's Secret Chimps*

(2001), *Talking with Animals* (2002), *Jungle* (2003), *Secret Gorillas of Mondika* (2005) and Channel Five's *Among the Apes* (2009) have been critically well received. In the 1990s she had undertaken research for her doctorate with Jane Goodall and acted as scientific advisor for PBS on the programme featuring the work of Jane Goodall in the long-running Nature series *Jane Goodall's Wild Chimpanzees* (1996). She seems to offer everything TV producers want.

Jane Goodall is, perhaps, in a league of her own. Now one of the most revered, respected and publicly recognisable conservation figures in the world, she has also become one of the most celebrated although she is not exactly a complete media celebrity. Once married to wildlife film-maker Baron Hugo von Lawick, her ground-breaking research on chimpanzee behavour in Gombe, Tanzania, has become widely known to the general public through a number of wildlife feature documentaries, television programmes, books, photographs and journal articles. Many of the moving images of her in the 1960s and 1970s were shot by her husband. Born in 1934 she has the title of 'Explorer-in-Residence Emeritus' with the National Geographic Society, and images of her going back nearly fifty years can be found on the Society's website. She has frequently appeared on the front cover of the Society's journal, and has been credited with a number of field-based discoveries such as chimps using tools, contracting human diseases like polio, acting as social beings, waging war and expressing awe and other emotions when in front of a spectacular waterfall. Goodall's autobiography (Goodall and Berman, 2000) and the PBS documentary based upon it, *Reason for Hope*, emphasise the spiritual and philosophical motivation informing much of her research, conservation and public education work. She values chimps because they are genetically very close to human beings and because they are important sentient life forms in their own right with their own perspectives and experiences of the world. She gave the chimps she studied names at a time when doing so was vigorously condemned by many scientists as being damagingly anthropomorphic and basically unscientific. However, as she explains, her science is framed by a deep wish to see the world as chimps do, to enter their minds and to empathise with the life experiences of these nearly human others. We are imprisoned within our own confining human lifeworlds. We only see the human view of the world, and as even as cultured, educated and intellectually superior beings we still find it hard, often impossible, to see the world from other perspectives, even of another human culture or from the opposite sex. She writes of one chimp, David Greybeard, whom she had once observed using twigs to dislodge termites from their mound (2000: 81) as offering her insights that objective scientific methods would have undoubtedly missed:

As David and I sat there, I noticed a ripe red fruit from an oil nut palm lying on the ground. I held it toward him on the palm of my hand. David glanced at me and reached to take the nut. He dropped it, but gently held my hand. I needed no words to understand his message of reassurance: he didn't want the nut, but he understood my motivation, he knew I meant well. To this day I remember the soft pressure of his fingers. we had communicated in a language far more ancient than words, a language that we shared with out pre-historic ancestor, a language bridging two worlds. And I was deeply moved. When David got up and walked away I let him go and stayed there quietly by the murmuring stream, holding on to the experience so that I could know it in my heart forever.

There are many images of Goodall touching or hugging chimps and chimps touching or hugging her. Some are intentional re-enactments or echoes of the important moment mentioned above, symbolic of Goodall's under-standing of life and an attempt to stimulate a tactile or haptic experience through a visual communication (Paterson, 2007). The images taken through-out her career with different primates mean the same thing whether the chimp or Goodall herself is young or old. In fact the composition and form of this iconic image is more than faintly reminiscent of Michelangelo's fresco *The Creation of Adam*, painted on the ceiling of the Sistine Chapel in around 1511. God reaches out to touch the finger of Adam, to give him the gift of life and to remind him that man is made in the image of God, just as perhaps Goodall reminds us we are made in the image of the ape. It is therefore all the more telling that much of this world, including the small isolated patch of for-est that is today the Gombe National Park, has been denuded or destroyed by economic development.

Miss Goodall and the Wild Chimpanzees, the first film National Geo-graphic ever produced, was directed by Marshall Flaum, photographed by Hugo von Lawick, funded by Gulf Oil (as were eight other Specials) and nar-rated by Orson Welles. It was first broadcast on CBS in the United States in December 1965 and has been described by Donna Haraway (1989: 179) as a "first contact narrative" celebrating the grace of touch across cultural and species divides. For Goodall, this chimp language of touch, of hugs and grooming communicates for them, and for us humans, love and friendship. In fact, the film is a synoptic reconstruction of Goodall's first five years in Gombe, with the film's narrative journey tracing the major landmarks of Goodall's early career including the slow process of getting close and gaining trust, the discoveries that chimps use tools, have an image of self, make beds or nests in trees and eat meat. The film is as much about Jane Goodall, "the

26-year-old girl from England", as it is about the chimps, the footage of whom visually confirm Goodall's discoveries. The shots of Goodall herself vary between self-conscious posing with note book or binoculars, occasional romanticised shots of her in silhouette against the light or, as in the final shot, walking off into the sunset. The National Geographic film aesthetic is thus similar to the magazine's still photography, perhaps hiding as much as it reveals and rendering *Miss Goodall and the Wild Chimpanzees* as the first media exercise in building Jane Goodall's conservation media status – aided no doubt by her relative youth, blond hair, slender figure, middle-class English accent and social poise. Haraway employs biblical terms in her discussion of this first film. Goodall is "a second Eve" naming the animals "in the garden". She is a "virgin-priestess". In a later 1971 film, *Monkeys, Apes and Man*, also a National Geographic Special, Jane Goodall's ability to touch animals is re-emphasised as she looks to her apes' mothering behaviours almost as a model for her own which is presented not so much as a scientific exercise but rather as "a feminine gender-coded practice of identification and compassion" (Haraway, 1989: 184). In 1984, when National Geographic's third Goodall film was released, *Among the Wild Chimpanzees*, the sponsor published an advertisement titled "Understanding is Everything". The top half of the image has a chimp's hand gently curled round that of woman's with a lengthy text underneath starting, "In a spontaneous gesture of trust, a chimpanzee in the wilds of Tanzania folds his leathery hand around that of Jane Goodall – sufficient reward for Dr Goodall's years of patience." Four paragraphs later the text reads, "Association with the National Geographic Society and the television specials is only one aspect of Gulf's lively concern for the environment. But it is an especially proud one." To the left of this, the Gulf Oil Corporation logo is discreetly printed, enabling its brand to borrow some of Goodall's and National Geographic's benignancy.

All three of these pioneer scientist-conservationists can be said to have developed a feminine-coded approach to primatology and to science more generally. Whereas a masculine approach to science is based on mastery, Goodall's, Fossey's and Galdikas's was based on a trust with the animals, the terms of which were those of the chimps, gorillas and orangutans themselves; this led Sy Montgomery (1992) to speculate that these women developed a spiritual bond with their animals similar to that of a shaman. Dian Fossey began to see herself as a gorilla and Jane Goodall frequently uses chimp calls in her public talks, media appearances and lectures. All three women's approach to their scientific activity was by the standards of the time, and probably in many circles remains, unconventional. Montgomery writes (1992: 274):

Western scientists do not like to talk about these things, for to do so is to voice what for so long has been considered unspeakable. The bonds between human and animal and the psychic tools of empathy and intuition have been 'coded dark' by Western Science – labelled as hidden, implicit, unspoken. The truths through which we once explained our world, the truths spoken by the ancient myths, have been hushed by the louder voice of passionless scientific objectivity.

Film can convey this passion and other worldliness through a carefully crafted symbolic aural and visual aesthetic, a particular technical format and controlled context for reception. In 2002 the Bank of America and the National Science Foundation financed the 40-minute IMAX film *Jane Goodall's Wild Chimpanzees*. This large-format production, later digitally remastered and released on DVD, is a celebration of Goodall's work and of Goodall herself. Many images are of her standing meditatively or looking contemplatively or once again holding, kissing and caressing her chimps. She is now not so much the virgin priestess but a saint whose media image is akin to Mother Teresa, only kindlier and gentler. The lingering images of the chimps, often in close-up and themselves looking contemplative, are contrasted with the cruel and deadly experiences Goodall's project has saved them from. Many are orphans rescued from meat markets and others have been rescued from disappearing forests, which is matter-of-factly presented as yet another problem motivating Goodall's conservation work. Unfortunately and significantly, the economic and political reasons for these disappearing forests are not explained, although there are magnificent aerial shots of what's left, but again not of the surrounding deforestation. The deeply romantic orchestral music accompanying these scenes is described by the composer, Amin Bhatia, on the DVD extra as "a homage to mother Africa . . . the way Jane is paying homage to her children, her chimps". The music, the strong male voice offering a linking commentary and the wistful utterances of Goodall herself create an aural harmony complementing that of the image track. Over a montage of restful chimps looking directly into the camera lens, Goodall asks rhetorically and perhaps sentimentally, "If these chimps could speak, what would they say?" The pathos is clearly and obviously encoded, and overwhelms the audience particularly if they experience the film in an IMAX cinema. But significantly, many of Goodall's talks and speeches to international organisations, conservation bodies and conferences are now widely available and accessed on the web. The aesthetic impact is less but the message is the same, invariably of the need for communication, compassion, education, action and understanding. She remains constant and her reputation is unblemished although she does have, like photographer and journalist Karl Ammann, a few critics.

Conservation, science and edutainment

Telegenic presenters, who if not attractive are invariably enthusiastic and usually both, are able to add entertainment value to what might otherwise be considered a worthy but dull educational endeavour. *Springwatch*, both in its UK (BBC) and US (Animal Planet) variants, succeeds in engaging viewers directly with the natural world as it unfolds around them. Kate Humble for the BBC and Vanessa Garnick for Animal Planet, together with their more numerous male co-presenters, encourage viewer participation in wildlife surveys, competitions and educational activities that are reinforced by well designed, interactive and informative websites. In the UK, *Springwatch* has had higher ratings than the reality show *Big Brother* and labelled 'edutainment'; such programmes combine a number of approaches to education, social learning theories, diffusion and communication strategies that have been fashioned by organisations including Disney, National Geographic, the BBC and most expertly by NGOs working on social and gender issues in developing countries (Singhal and Rogers, 1999; Singhal, Cody, Rogers and Sabido, 2004). The term was first used by Robert Heyman in 1973 when making documentaries for National Geographic, and is now used widely by those working in interactive digital television, serious gaming and computer-based education (Rey-Lopez, et al 2007). Recently there have been conservationists-cum-entertainers like the late Steve Irwin, whose widely seen TV series *Crocodile Hunters* and *Crocodile Diaries* have mixed showmanship, adventure, business acumen, masculine bravado with a genuine commitment to animal well-being and environmental sustainability. Some critics have questioned the overall desirability of celebrity-led conservation and the para-social relations with animals that these presenters encourage (Brockington, 2008; 2009), but Irwin and others like him have certainly stressed the educative significance of their work. Celebrity is important in edutainment just as it is in campaigning, for the symbolic vibrancy of images of wilderness, iconic animals and 'the power of nature' can be lent additional impact when a well-known and respected celebrity emotes and endorses the requisite awe, wonder or despair. The viewer interacts with nature and perhaps conservation through the presenter's seeing and experiencing of what is presented on the screen. It is thus a form of parallel or para-interaction which is, or at least can become, extremely important in its own right as a means of audience self-organisation, mobilisation, creativity and direct action, as Jenkins (2006) and others have noted. This para-social interaction with nature though is sometimes eased, as Cottle (2004) suggests, when the presenters are young and female (Charlotte Uhlenbroek) or physically energetic (Steve Irwin) and so, like the animals or land-scapes depicted, essentially telegenic. For Vivanco (2004) this adventurism, including the inevitable wrestling with snakes and crocs is key to *Croc Hunter*'s success with television audiences and with visitors to Irwin's zoological park in Queensland, Australia.

Irwin's conservation message is simple and clear: certain animals are dangerous but humans are more dangerous to them than they are to us. The format of these programmes are hybrid documentary/realityTV/soap where representation morphs into simulation, where the boundaries between fact and fiction are intentionally blurred. Vivanco suggests that audiences are more drawn to Irwin's actions and his 'madness' than his ecopolitical messages, which are perhaps incidental to the action of tying up and moving an angry animal from his natural habitat to a safer one fit for human entertainment such as a zoo or animal park. The historical and political context of some of his programmes are consequently marginalised. In one programme, Irwin goes to East Timor under the protection of the Australian-dominated UN peacekeeping forces to rescue Timorese crocodiles which he states are greatly respected by the local people. There is no mention of the Indonesia's violent repression of the attempts of East Timor's people to gain political autonomy, but the interests of international conservation, Western modernity and Australian zoos are assumed, and presented, as being one and the same. The views of local people are not heard, and as Christophers (2006) argues in his discussion of natural history production in New Zealand and the UK, much of it is still subject to a lingering colonialist heritage. This can be seen by the fact that New Zealand's natural history programming is dominated by the BBC and many of the locations used by the NHU, such as those for *Big Cat Diary* filmed in Kenya in 1996, are luxury safari destinations which were once the former residences of colonial officials.

Anthropomorphism is not eschewed completely by scientific researchers or serious educational programme-makers. Oxford Scientific Films, whose highly accessible *Meerkat Manor* (2005-2008), screened on BBC television and Animal Planet, communicates many findings of a long term academic study of meerkats' social behavour by researchers from Cambridge University led by Professor Tim Clutton-Brock in docusoap TV format. Although Clutton-Brock does not anthropomorphise in his scientific papers for *Nature*, both the TV series (at the time of writing in its fourth series) and his publications for a more general audience do (Clutton-Brock, 2007). As Guthrie (1997) argues, a critical anthropomorphism can be a useful heuristic device for developing scientific understanding. Pollo, Graziano and Giacoma (2009) are also undoubtedly correct when they argue that a reflective use of visual and verbal metaphor in natural history programming improves the public understanding of scientific research and conservation awareness. However, audiences are themselves interpretative communities, framing what they see and hear according to a value and conceptual framework not necessarily shared by either the programme-makers or their scientific advisors. For instance, the highly popular US version of Luc Jacquet's *March of the Penguins* (2005) has been read by fundamentalist Christian groups in the USA as supporting the claims of 'intelligent design'. The reasons are various. Cultural observers have suggested that religious audiences who believe the intelligent design theory are very receptive to stories about isolation, family values, community perseverance and self-sacrifice. Many religious communities perceive themselves as battling with mainstream America's corporate media culture and are struggling, like the penguins, as the chosen people they are (Wexler, 2008). Jacquet himself has stated that he wanted the film to be open to any reading, although the film's aesthetic invites an anthropomorphic reading by encouraging viewers to identify and empathise with the penguins' life experiences. Camera work and editing include penguin point-of-view shots, visual depictions of fictionalised penguin memories, and sensitively filmed and edited scenes of penguins caressing chicks with their beaks, 'kissing' or mourning, which are well established classical devices used in Hollywood narrative cinema. For Wexler, these common filmic techniques in narrative documentary, clearly seen in *March of the Penguins*, are sufficient reason to be critically mindful of the status of film in general as a medium for the representation of science; although Luc Jacquet's earlier films such as *The Leopard Seal's Share, Springtime for the Weddell Seals, The Tick of the Birds* and *Penguin Baywatch* do not support this position. They are ingenious and artistically creative, but far less open to readings that undermine the scientific worldview.

However, even some highly respected documentary series such as those written and produced by David Attenborough, himself an avowed Darwinist, may offer support for intelligent design to those audiences predisposed to accept its logic (Dingwall and Aldridge, 2006). Some programmes though are produced clearly and distinctly to contest culturally alternative interpretations. With the four-part series *Inside Nature's Giants* (2009), independently produced by Windfall Films for Channel Four and National Geographic, and made in association with the Royal Veterinary College in London, autopsies are carried out on a giraffe, a whale, an elephant and a crocodile. Promoted as natural history "as you have never seen it before" and presented by veterinary scientist Mark Evans, its explicit purpose is, as Professor Richard Dawkins says in the pre-credit sequence, to reveal the 'illusion of design' in the evolutionary process. David Glover, Channel Four's commissioning editor for Science, has been quoted as saying that the series offered viewers "a unique chance to see for themselves how evolution has shaped the anatomy of some of nature's most magnificent animals" (Evans, 2009). Professor Alun Williams, Professor of Pathology and Infectious Diseases at the Royal Veterinary College, was also quoted in the same media release as saying that televised post-mortems are of great educational value as they extend knowledge of anatomy, animal handling and pathology for people studying veterinary science and for the general public. Despite the series' potential for sensational and macabre voyeurism, the programmes are relentlessly rational, reserving the spectator's wonderment for the unfolding process of scientific discovery and the fact of evolutionary adaptation. This is reinforced by *Inside Nature's Giants* webpage, hosted by Channel Four, where online learning materials include two autopsy games whose design was funded by the global health charity, the Wellcome Trust. One explores elephant anatomy and the other the whale's. The game, played against time, starts with the web user cutting open the computer-drawn animal and placing images of internal organs in their appropriate places. A number of other exercises follow, each demonstrating various aspects of the animal's behaviour. The whole game is graded and operates at three different levels of complexity. The comments on the programme message board are varied, expressing a mixture of appreciation with frustration at the rather challenging timing built into the game's design. The comments on the individual programmes themselves are generally highly favourable and only occasionally critical. Some of these explore issues the series does not address, indicating yet again how the ethical and conceptual frameworks audiences have influence the way a film or media text is understood. For instance:

SUE BERRY on 1st July 2009 at 05:16

Your programme on dissecting the elephant was interesting though probably for science students – otherwise it was just voyeuristic and titillating. The best bit was at the end, then left without discussion: why did the elephant die? I can tell you why she died; she died of captivity, her arthritis having developed through standing on hard ground at Blackpool Zoo, eating a crap diet and getting hardly any exercise (apart from performing tricks for customers). I suppose the programme's comparisons of the dead animal with the wild ones on film would lead us to make the links for ourselves, but then there was insufficient information about the zoo. So what can we say about this particular elephant?

Well, she spent her life entertaining zoo visitors, and after she died she continued entertaining television viewers. By the way, her name was Crumple.

Science and visual spectactle is also the dual attraction in the series *Animals in the Womb* and *Extraordinary Animals in the Womb* which has been produced by Pioneer Productions, Fox Television Studies, National Geographic television and Channel Four. They combine spectacular HD photography of elephants, kangaroos, dogs, emperor penguins and sharks developing in the womb with a concern to enhance the popular understanding of science. However, the film-makers' marketing emphasis is on the visual spectacle. The director Peter Chinn told Andrew Pettie when the first season aired on UK television in October 2008 (Pettie, 2008):

> There are plenty of amazing animals still to be done. Such as the Surinam toad, whose young hatch out of its own back. And sea horses are pretty funky, in that they develop inside the father. So I'm sure there'll be another *Animals in the Womb* film next year.

Blue chip

'Blue chip' is the term given to natural history and wildlife film and television that have high production values, privileging spectacle and wonder as part of an educational excursion designed to demonstrate the beauty of the environment and the technological sophistication, distinction and cultural importance of the media production. The film historian Derek Bouse (2000: 14-15) suggests the ahistorical and decontextualised blue chip documentary exhibits the following tendencies:

The depiction of mega-fauna – iconic species such lions, tigers, elephants, bears, whales, sharks, etc.

Visual splendour – unspoiled and uninhabited wilderness often enhanced by a heavily romanticised soundtrack, close-up sounds of animal and even insect behavour which would otherwise be inaudible, and high definition or 3-D images.

Dramatic story line – a compelling narrative, often an animal biography or quest with obviously melodramatic moments and climaxes.

Absence of science – or at least scientific controversies or detailed explanation of scientific methods.

absence of politics – little or no overt mention of conservation issues, politics or depressing themes.

absence of historical reference points – timelessness in story and image (sometimes belied by image and sound quality).

absence of people – or at least white people, to preserve the illusion and allusion to a nature unspoiled by development.

The globally successful *Planet Earth* (2006), for example, is a BBC Discovery and NHK co-production depicting a wide range of animals inhabiting pristine spaces and presented in glorious HD colour and stereo sound. Picturesque scenes of animals running, often shown in slow motion from the air, are accompanied by an appropriately romanticised musical soundtrack aiming to marry admiration with respect and conflating spectacle with an intuitive knowingness. One visual feast is quickly followed by another, and as communication and art theorists remind us, it is frequently through the affective engagements with images that things are remembered (Barry A.M., 1997; Williams, 2003). Guy Debord (1995) suggests we inhabit a society of spectacle, a culture of vision, where we can only understand nature and environment by understanding the images we create, construct and consume. And as Ulmer (2005) argues, images have ramifications that words do not. They bypass critical reason and directly influence how people relate to each other and to the natural world. The environmental educator David Orr once noted that all education is environmental education, and it could equally be said that all images are also environmental images. What is seen or not seen helps to socially construct our world, our reality. Animal images can either be archetypal or 'econic', representative of actual species or an idea of them (Morey, 2009). An image of a panda may be a cuddly and cute symbol of one endangered species (itself) or of all endangered species. Artists, film-makers, television producers and photographers often say their work is designed to help people to see, learn and understand, which means that "the question of visual nature is therefore a central and unavoidable issue, along with the role of animals as images and spectators" (Mitchell, 2002: 170).

Much natural history film-making, from its very beginning and certainly long before the arrival of CGI (computer-generated imaging techniques) (Bouse, 2000; Scott, 2003; Bagust, 2008), has traded on the wonder engendered by visual spectacle. Like other narrative genres, the close-up is frequently employed to conjure up a false intimacy or identification between the viewer and animal subject (Bouse, 2003). Many elements within blue chip films directly solicit spectator attention by inciting a visual curiosity and supplying visual pleasure through a succession of exciting and dynamic spectacles. *Winged Migration* by Jacques Perrin, winner of the 2002 Oscar for Best Documentary, follows various bird species on the wing during their migratory travels across the Earth's six continents. The aerial photography enables the spectator to see birds in close-up and in flight. This was only possible because the film-makers themselves nurtured the birds from the moment they hatched, applying ethologist Konrad Lorenz's theory of 'imprinting'. The birds were from the beginning made familiar with human artifacts, machines, noise and other demands, which makes the film neither a documentary or a fiction, but as the voice over dubiously says in the 'making of' featurette, "just a tale of nature". In these 'extras', the film-making process and the film-maker become central to the story, revealing perhaps a susceptibility for media practitioners to focus on themselves as an important story. Film and filming no longer becomes a medium of communication, but the message itself. There is in this tendency towards self-referentiality a genuine professional pride and an educative attempt to demystify the creative process, even addressing perhaps the ideological implications of the aesthetic naturalism of the wildlife and nature film.

Computer-generated imaging techniques have enabled other attractions to be developed. The BBC's *Walking with Dinosaurs* and other series in the franchise have challenged some of the complacencies surrounding mainstream natural history television. Dinosaurs and other extinct beasts like mammoths may be seen walking, swimming or eating, requiring the audience to suspend its disbelief in order to accept what cannot actually have been filmed or photographed – a moving image of a prehistorical animal (Scott 2003). *Walking with Dinosaurs* and *Walking with Beasts* offers audiences a genuine spectacle in the digital reconstruction of a prehistoric landscape through which the presenter/scientist walks as he explains the lives and behaviours of what he supposedly sees and occasionally runs into. Although some critics worried about audiences believing what they saw on the screen, being unable to distinguish between an imaginative CGI fabrication and the documentary authenticity of a photographed image, Michael Jeffries (2003: 540) suggests there is much value in the format. Comparing the message boards of various series he writes:

> Contrast the contents of the *Walking with ...* boards to that of *The Blue Planet* and *Wild Africa*, both broadcast during the same late 2001 period as *Walking with Beasts*. During the transmission dates for these series the mes-

sage boards for both were dominated by praise for the technical and aesthetic quality of the footage, viewers' own experiences of marine life or Africa and career advice. (. . .)

Audiences appear to be responding to the *Walking with* ... series differently from other natural history programmes. Perhaps it is simply the topics, with dinosaurs and extinct mammals seen as science. However it may be the broad editorial style, with the *Walking with* ... ecosystems provoking questions whilst the conveyor belt of wonders in *The Blue Planet* or *Wild Africa* do little more than evoke a passive wonder, perhaps even complacency. The *Walking with* ... series are a challenge to the dominant portrayal of natural history, and their message boards have provided a forum for questioning, debate and exchange in contrast to the passive delivery of science evident in most other natural history television.

On the other hand, it could be argued that blue chip documentaries, replete with their graphic images of reality, are themselves fictionalised and creative fabrications located outside recognisable times and spaces. For Bouse, blue chip documentaries are political by default. They are political in that they leave so much unsaid and unseen.

BBC's *Blue Planet* series, first broadcast in 2001, consisted of eight episodes which seemed to give the impression that the oceans were brimming with fish, were unpolluted and problem-free. Sean Cubitt (2005) suggests that *Blue Planet* is a work of art, in which case it is aesthetics rather than ethics that dominates its mode of presentation. The series foregrounds the beauty and wonder of the marine eco-system rather than the beauty of any individual marine species. Aural and visual pleasure are key to understanding the nature of this and other blue chip series. It is a "structured respect for that subjectless creativity" (Cubitt, 2005: 51) that values nature intrinsically in the same way a plant values sunlight. As we learn more about the role of nature, of ecosystem services in providing human beings with food or digesting our waste, nature becomes humanised, exploited and diminished. Cubitt seems to suggest that the necessity of conservation and sustainable development is there in the re-presentation of nature as something mediated in the actual process of imaging. He writes (2005: 58):

> Montage, including composite cinematographic and CGI images, can only produce a virtual image of the unimaginably complex and vast processes of the oceans. Yet this virtual nature is a remarkable solution to the question of natural virtue. Imaging technologies capable of transcending their human origins allow the natural to remake what it is to be human. Human, natural

and technological are three moments of a single process, for if we cannot know, we cannot care, and if we cannot recognise nature as at once ecologically bound to our own survival as a species and as an utterly distinct and to a great extent unknown category of existence, there can be no way of mediating the needs of these two torn halves of an integral world.

Blue Planet was heralded as a fine example of quality public service television, "albeit according to a specific set of upper middle-class taste codes" (Wheatley, 2004: 337). Fierce criticism by conservation groups of the series, however, focussed not so much on the aesthetics but the ethics of what was overtly and intentionally ignored. This led to the BBC hastily producing an eighth episode titled *Deep Trouble* which explored the more difficult issues of overfishing and marine conservation. This episode was screened separately from the rest of the series, on the more cerebral BBC2, late in the evening, and was not sold to Discovery nor did it later became part of the DVD boxed set sold in the US. Film, photography and television may not tell us what to think but informs us about what we might think about, and the public service broadcaster has a clear mission to entertain and to inform and educate.

The 2006 broadcasting White Paper, *A Public Service for All: the BBC in the Digital Age*, suggests that "the BBC's output will achieve its maximum impact only by entertaining its viewers and listeners" (DCMS, 2006: 10). It is this insistence to "make clear the importance of entertainment to the BBC's mission, whilst ensuring that its content should offer something distinct from other broadcasters" as well as being "high quality; challenging; original; innovative; and engaging" that has led some broadcast analysts to suspect that the BBC will remain quite conservative in its programming policies. Debates on public service broadcasting frequently attempt to reconcile market with public interest imperatives, that is, giving the public what it wants (to buy) with giving the public what it really needs (even if it is ignorant of those needs). Market-led arguments have been accused of putting profit before quality, and public interest arguments have been accused of being paternalistic. Natural history film-making seems to square many circles – it is, or at least can be, entertaining, informative, educative, of high quality, technologically innovative, highly marketable overseas and a prime almost unending opportunity for co-productions. So long as nothing too difficult or emotionally bleak is conveyed apart from the odd (thrilling) high-speed chase by a lion of its prey, suitably repeated in slow motion, then audiences seem to continually return for more of the same. When first broadcast by the BBC in the UK in 2006 *Planet Earth*, narrated by David Attenborough, secured nearly eight million viewers.

Ratings and DVD sales were very high in the US, and within two years the series had been sold to 130 countries. In America the series was narrated by Sigourney Weaver, who had played Dian Fossey in *Gorillas in the Mist*.

The world changes – even if wildlife and nature documentaries have been rather slow in representing some of these – but by 2007 even mainstream television producers and media executives recognised the need to do something a little different. In that year, the BBC commissioned *Saving Planet Earth*, its first natural history series overtly promoting conservation. Unsurprisingly perhaps, viewing figures were less than impressive and the series sold poorly. Only the first three of the eleven-part series gained over three million viewers, although £1.8 million was raised for conservation projects in the two years following. Interestingly, a feature film version of *Saving Planet Earth* was produced for theatrical release in UK and Europe, where its box office takings were greater than that for *March of the Penguins*. Called *Earth*, the feature-length version was released in the USA on Earth Day (22nd April) in 2009, and exhibited theatrically and on television through the Disney Corporation's new venture Disney Nature. As the trailer states, the film follows one day in the life of three families – whales, elephants and polar bears – and at the beginning of the film the narrator (Patrick Stewart in the British version and James Earl Jones in the American one), contextualises their stories within an ideological framework emphasising the precariousness of the planet's natural ecology and the dangers of extinction that many animals, including those featured, currently face. Author and wildlife film-maker Chris Palmer (2010) was impressed with the film's scientific accuracy, its entertaining and engrossing nature, its use of recycled footage (that helped reduce stress on animals) and a storyline that incorporated global warming. Most of the 62 comments on the film posted on the IMDB website entry for Earth are also highly favourable, although some people commented they would have preferred something a little more politically and aesthetically challenging.

> But the biggest crime of all is that while *Planet Earth* uses the tragic story of the polar bear as evidence that we are killing this planet and as a catalyst for ecological change, Disney took that story and turned it into family-friendly tripe. After the male polar bear's demise, they show his cubs grown significantly a year later, and spew some garbage about how they are ready to carry on his memory, and that the earth really is a beautiful place after all. No mention of the grown cubs' impending deaths due to the same plight their father endured, no warning of trouble for future generations if we don't get our act together, nothing. Just a montage of stuff we have already seen throughout

the movie (and many times more, if you are one of the billion people who have already seen Planet Earth). (Chicago, 22nd April 2009).

Aside from incredible cinematography, it was a typical Disney disappoint-ment for me. Preceded by a half-dozen Disney movie trailers, rife with Disney cliché ("circle of life", "falling with style"), over-dramatic music, recycled footage (Disney claims "40% new footage"). . . . And what is Disney's obses-sion with showing predators chasing and killing baby animals? There were a half-dozen such scenes, complete with bleating youngsters on the verge of getting their throats ripped out. I think Disney needs to recognize that ani-mals have a rich and interesting life outside of life and death struggles that appeal to the action-movie oriented teenagers that got dragged to this film by their parents. I was also cognizant of how Disney stopped well short of implying that man had anything to do with the climate change. Are they so afraid of the tiny minority of deniers that they think it's still a controversial subject? (Denver, 23rd April 2009)

The ten-part nature series *Life*, a BBC production made in association with the Discovery Channel, Skai TV (a Greek TV station, part of the large media conglomerate known as the Skai Group and co-funder of the *Life* series) and the Open University, is another blue chip effort shot entirely in HD with a clear educative purpose. It focusses on the lives, behaviours and struggles of the planet's flora and fauna. The genre format is familiar, the photography is as usual impressive, and each sequence typically short enabling each pro-gramme's editing rhythm to carry the audience's attention along with the var-ious shapes, sounds, colours and movements. This series, for all its magnificent qualities and 'television firsts' – including film of komodo drag-ons hunting a water buffalo on the Indonesian island of Rinca – is 'nature porn' pure and simple. The voice of David Attenborough gives the series an air of public service worthiness, but in many ways the programmes are little different from many other similar documentary series screened in the preced-ing thirty years. Premiered on BBC One and BBC HD in October 2009, the first episode, 'Challenges of Life', attracted according to BARB figures, 6.84 million viewers, that is, over 26% total audience share. The final one, 'Pri-mates', shown in December 2009, secured 5.14 million viewers, nearly 22% audience share. Audiences remain comfortable with the familiar, the spectac-ular, the comforting and the reassuring. Nothing is said in *Life* about the the problems that wildlife confront because of human economic development.

Natural history's emphasis on spectacle and story has often compromised its capacity to claim the status of documentary, whose aesthetics are often claimed to equate with truth and realism. Film theorists and historians, though, have debated and argued over the idea of cinema truth for nearly one hundred years, and interestingly they have rarely included discussions of wildlife or nature films in their work. The status of the natural history film has always been somewhat ambivalent, and its subject matter not perceived as being as important as war or politics; that is, at least until comparatively recently. For some theorists and practitioners these debates are rather academic for all film is a fiction to some extent or, as BBC NHU producer Brian Leith put it, "a lie":

> A story isn't truth. A story is a story, and I think you have to trust film-makers. None of the things that happen in a novel are real, but if they have a resonance with the readers' world then they can incorporate a very valuable lesson about life. Every time you put a cut in a shot say of an elephant . . . . you cut to something else – a sunset. Well that didn't happen at that moment. The whole business of film-making is inherently a lie and we shouldn't be so stupid, naive or pedantic to blame the film-maker for telling a lie. You add sound effects, you add music, you add narration. If we get really pedantic we will ruin our films and you will end up with some very sterile documentaries that are entirely factual and incredibly boring. The best films are the most imaginative – more lies – because imaginative means romance, wonderful images, lyricism . . . . These are not reality, and this is what is exciting about the [film] business. On the one hand you have objective truth, and on the other hand you've got magic. Magic is what will move somebody to change their life or to save a place. Objective truth is the raw material you have to work with and somehow you have to bring these two things together without destroying either. (Brian Leith, interview 1st May 2009)

Re-enactments, studio-based shots capturing 'natural' behaviour, retiming of and repetition of key sequences or 'money shots' and the post-production creation of appropriate sound effects and music for mood and texture abound in blue chip wildlife/nature/environmental productions. These are part of Leith's 'lie', the way film and television tells 'the story' which, as film pioneer John Grierson once noted of the documentary form, is in effect "the creative treatment of actuality", that is, a film form in search of a greater truth (Grierson, 1930/1979). Many natural history film-makers are comfortable with this definition not least because they are well aware of pressures from funders, distributors and audiences for a product that will be watched and is watchable. Many stress the need for a good story with images and sounds selected to serve this fundamental purpose. The idea is to carry the audience along with the narrative's trajectory, and even if the story is emotionally difficult viewers must not be allowed to disconnect, withdraw, deny or even worse – switch over. In her detailed study of the phenomenology of the film experience, Vivian Sobchack (1992) writes that the spectator has an intentional consciousness and film an intentional project. If both are transparent, the relationship between the two is compatible and easy. In other circumstances, the spectator may need to adjust and will need to choose a time during the viewing experience to align his or her thoughts/consciousness with the intended direction of the film. If the film's meaning is clear and comprehensible this may happen without any conscious translating, deciphering or making of meaning. The trouble comes when the meaning is comprehensible but disruptive or challenging to an audience's established worldview, assumptions, aesthetic or ethical values. Then there is more work to be done by both the film-maker and the spectator if any alignment is to (re)occur and for it to have a real significance.

Many documentaries produced for, or by, the major media corporations insert, sometimes egregiously, conservation messages within their story lines, as with National Geographic's *Whales in Crisis* or *The Last Stand of the Great Bear* (2005) or documentary series such as *Orangutan Diary* or *The Secret Life of Elephants*. Some like Dereck and Beverly Joubert's *Eye of the Leopard* (2006), a conventional blue chip documentary for National Geographic and winner of a Panda Award for best film on animal behavour in 2008, says little about the wider ecological issues – just as similar films have done in the past like Hugo von Lawick's *The Leopard Son* (1996). However, unlike the earlier film, which wallowed in a sentimental anthropomorphic discourse on motherhood, attachment and loss, the Jouberts' *Eye of the Leopard* is web-linked by the National Geographic Society's Big Cats Initiative. If you want to see cats like this in habitats like this, donate now! is the message on the website, though not in the film, for the producers wished to avoid depressing audience figures with a depressing animal story. For this husband and wife team, making blue chip films enables them to undertake other more overtly conservationist work. For Dereck Joubert, conservation films on their own do very little, but when clips from them are used as he does in lectures and seminars he is able to open up discussion about a range of issues (interview, 22nd October 2008).

At the 2008 Wildscreen Festival there were numerous formal and informal debates and discussions about sustainability, conservation and the media industry's ethical responsibility to informing, entertaining and educating the public in a more pro-sustainability direction. Asked his view on whether the industry is doing 'too little, too late', the actual title of the main discussion, David Attenborough replied:

I speak as someone who has worked for a public service institution for a long time, and I think this particular public service institution [the BBC] is not doing too badly. The fact of the matter is other organisations throughout the world have reduced their output of serious natural history, and other organisations have felt that natural history is not as important as everyone in this room thinks thinks it is. We have to demonstrate that it is not only important but that people want to know about it, and so we can't just use it as a boring or academic exercise – we have to make sure people want to watch it. It is very important we do that.

Human interest and animal interest

For Virginia Mckenna, star of the 1966 feature film *Born Free* and long-term conservationist, telling the story of an individual human or non-human animal is a good way of communicating conservation messages. Such stories can touch peoples' hearts, and if the story of the animal and its habitat are brought together the audience will then be able to form a more sophisticated and holistic understanding of the world. At Wildscreen Festivals there are practical workshops, master classes and opportunities for existing and prospective film-makers to pitch their story to programme commissioners. The most important question is always "what is the story?", closely followed by how is it set up, why would anyone continue to watch and how will the viewer be carried along by the narrative. Winner of a Panda award in the Children's category at the 2008 Wildscreen Festival, *Bama's Journey*, made by Nicola Lankester and commissioned by Al Jazeera International to be part of its Witness series, is the story of one man. Alfred Bama works in Limbe Wildlife Centre in Cameroon caring for eleven gorillas orphaned as result of the bushmeat trade. The story follows Bama on a journey to Chester Zoo where he will learn more about how animals are cared for in the UK, but the film goes far beyond this. After a short sequence exposing the connection between the bushmeat trade, logging and habitat destruction, including shots of a tree being felled and joints of ape meat being fished out of a cooking pot, the film focusses on Bama himself. The viewer is invited to see Cameroon, the gorillas and the developed world, England, through his eyes. There is some rough play between Bama and the gorillas. They know him, and he refers to himself as their father. They are so like us, he remarks, and unlike many people who live near him he refuses to eat ape meat. The viewer then sees his small home and garden, which has no electricity or running water and by

Western standards is extremely poor. Nevertheless, there is richness to his life and his community that is clearly evident when contrasted with the lack of society and the superficialities of material wealth in the commercialised entertainments available in London or even at the zoo. In Cameroon there are still natural forests, so there is no need for zoos. After work people congregate in public spaces to socialise, whereas in England they retreat to their private homes. By the end of his four-week keeper exchange, in which he had seen some African animals for the first time, he is glad to return. Throughout the film's 25-minute duration the audience can see and hear Bama's spontaneous reactions and more reflective considerations on his experiences in England. Many of these are delivered directly to camera, although Nicola Lankester's off screen voice is occasionally heard asking a question or prompting a comment. The director's presence is felt more prominently through the contextualising 'voice of god' narration that once or twice becomes a little intrusive.

Bama's Journey intentionally directs the viewer's attention to the difference between Cameroonian and Western culture and the challenges and discrepancy in resources of the two animal-centred organisations. However, the film is also a human interest story, and Bama's reflections are also a vehicle for an exploration of animal welfare issues, ecological values and the purpose of conservation. The emotional import of the film is through its open invitation to empathise with Bama's personal commitment, dedication, frank honesty and expertise. It does not rely on high production values or a celebrity presenter, but in many ways is far stronger for it, as the authenticity of the subject, the image and message are, in their raw aesthetic, a witness to what is being lost and what must be recovered.

Sometimes such a contextualised holistic view occurs accidentally during the film-making process, but at other times it may be the very purpose of the film's script and screenplay. Canadian Rob Stewart raised money to make a non-narrative film full of beautiful images which would be "an underwater Baraka". He had trained as wildlife photographer but soon discovered the actual process of making his film, eventually released as *Sharkwater* in 2006, led to a very different product. It is a feature-length adventure movie starring the film-maker himself, who teams up with Sea Shepherd conservationist Paul Watson to do battle with the shark poachers of Guatemala. Fourteen days into filming he had collided with a fishing boat, had been charged with attempted murder, had been exposed to the corruption of the Chinese mafia, had filmed himself and his crew "to stay out of prison" and escaped from Costa Rica with the coast guard firing their machines guns at his craft. Stewart told the 2008 Wildscreen Festival audience:

We marketed the movie in a completely different way which really got people
into it. It had a cool story – textbook story structure. It had an exciting incident, set-ups and pay-offs, concentrically mounting obstacles and people
jumped on the journey with this twenty-two-year-old kid who wanted to make
a shark movie while everything went catastrophically wrong. I wanted to make
the coolest, adventure-led action-filled, sexy documentary I could. We put the
coolest music in it. We wanted to make it hip and edgy so we'd get kids.

For Stewart, story and event, excitement and thrill, is what will engage
young people in conservation. As evidence he noted that *Sharkwater* has
spawned numerous websites, has led to other productions and sharply con-
trasts with the blood-and-gore-nature-porn-predator movies that too often
have sharks as their major character. The film certainly mixes generic conventions and expectations that are already fairly loose, fluid and without strictly
delimited boundaries. These boundaries are blurring further as film-makers
seek new ways to convey conservation messages and values. Animal Planet's
Whale Wars, a six-part made-for-television series first shown on the US cable
channel in November 2008, is based on the exploits of Paul Watson on his flagship vessel *The Steve Irwin*. Its documentary, or possibly reality TV qualities
merge with those of melodrama and the adventure of a real-life thriller. First-
person testimony is intercut with shaky action footage, climactic music and
regular cliff-hanging moments designed to keep the viewer hooked between
commercial breaks and each episode. Some individual episodes attracted over
one million viewers on the series' first screening in the USA. Average viewing
figures suggested that 529,000 adults between the ages 25 and 54, of whom
309,000 were men, watched the series. According to Nielsen Media Research
Data, *Whale Wars* delivered a 0.7 percent household rating in the Friday 9pm
slot which was 75% higher than the time slot average the year previously
(Reynolds, 2008). The combination of adventure and the growing public oppo-
sition to Japanese whaling among many sectors of the US public enabled Animal Planet to have a success and a way of tackling anticipated criticisms that
'terrorists' like Watson should not be made into media heroes.

Human interest stories engage audiences but the weaving together of an
individual's story, the impact of human culture and economic development on
the environment and the future life chances of many animals requires a complex formal structure to a film that may place it outside the major commissioning categories that determine what gets funded, what gets distributed and what
gets seen. Too often it is an either/or: natural history or conservation, documentary or wildlife storytelling, the sorrow or the wonder. Randall Wood's

Rare Chicken Rescue, co-produced by Film Australia and Freshwater Productions and commissioned by the Australian Broadcasting Commission interweaves the story of Mark Tully, a former community development worker who experienced burnout in 2000 and retreated to his family home in Queensland, with that of the need to conserve rare-breed chickens, 'chooks', which are rapidly disappearing because of the standardisation within the global poultry-rearing and food industries. Mark suffers from depression and anxiety, and his chickens have in effect saved his life and his sanity. At one point he says:

> In all honesty, I would owe my sanity, my living and breathing existence, to the birds. Without you they don't get fed, without you they don't get watered, and without them I wouldn't be coming out of the house.

They have understanding and compassion, he says. They give him purpose and a connection to a world greater and in many ways more meaningful than the transitory one that humans create in their towns and cities. The story follows Mark on a 10,000 kilometre round trip to Tasmania in search of some rare-breed poultry, particularly the endangered Sumatran and Azeel, that he wishes to add to his collection. On the way he meets a range of poultry fanciers and rare-breed enthusiasts who exude a similar passion and empathy for the animals and a deep sadness at their disappearance from our world. The film is shot throughout with a humour expressed via the music, graphic inserts and the comments of Mark Tully and other enthusiasts, often made direct to camera in medium close-up and often against a vibrant yellow or green background, bringing out the vivid colours of birds' feathers and plumes that the speakers invariably hold. These non-naturalistic shots were taken while on the road, sometimes in rotting chicken sheds full of turkey manure, with the subject sitting in front of a screen with a phosphorescent reflective background covered with coloured gels before being illuminated by a strong light.

Tully is a big fragile man with dark rings under his eyes and usually seen wearing a bright blue polo shirt. Maintaining his trust and confidence in the film's making was key to Randall Wood's success, and it is Wood's own sensitivity that enables Mark Tully to unselfconsciously display his love and gentleness before the camera. What the chooks give Mark is what a more sensitive approach to the natural world would undoubtedly give to others. "Peace and tranquility . . . or as some would say, tranquility", he says. As Randall Wood remarked:

> The greatest success of the film is that it has actually helped Mark. Ultimately my goal as a film-maker is to give the person who has actually devoted their time to the film something back. All good films are a transaction. I was

happy that Mark was happy with the film. He actually had input into the edit to make sure he could feel [he was] represented fairly. He came to the edit with some good suggestions. He wanted to up the final section where we talk about the UN and their evaluation of the status of rare breeds internationally. (Randall Wood, interview 24th October 2008)

In one sequence, shot against a yellow background, Mark can be seen with an egg in the palm of his hand. He watches a small chick struggling to break out. With his thumb he gently lifts part of the shell and the chick finally emerges, almost falling from Mark's hand to the ground. The connection to the wonder of life extends perhaps beyond the notion of biophilia or the practical therapeutic uses animals may have in human health care to something deeper and more complex. Human animals can only thrive so long as other creatures thrive, and rare breeds can only survive in our world if they are bred for a food market and therefore eaten. At the Devonport Poultry Show in Tasmania, Mark and other birders line up at the canteen for a chicken lunch.

In Australia the film is used as an education resource in schools for classes in Biology, Media, English, Health Sciences and Personal Development. It is a film that works on a number of levels and has been well received at many different types of film festival, but for Wood the film is primarily about mental illness which emerged from the story of a man obsessed with chickens.

In some ways Mark Tully is the grizzly man of the chicken world. He is really quite obsessed beyond passionate. [Werner Herzog's] *Grizzly Man* is a great film to watch because it is about that threshold between 'normal' and stepping into that other world. (Randall Wood, interview 24th October 2008)

A number of other films have explored human-animal relationships and although some of these can be amusing using the bizarre and eccentric to convey the sense of love and affection many humans feel for animals others can be extremely distressing. Errol Morris' *Fast, Cheap and Out of Control* (1997) can in no way be categorised as a natural history or environmental film, but by interweaving interviews with an animal trainer, a topiary gardener who fashions bushes into animal shapes, an expert on the naked mole rat and a robot designer, Morris is able to show that what at first glance appears decidedly odd is in fact decidedly human and social. Similarly Mark Lewis's first film, *Cane Toads: an unnatural history* (1988), approached the unwise introduction of this large and almost indestructible amphibian into Australia in 1935 in the hope it would control the cane beetle that was decimating the country's crops. Lewis shows the surprising affection this animal has gained among many sections of the population despite the uncontrollable and devastating effect it has had on

Australia's natural ecology. Like Mark Lewis's later films, *Cane Toads* is laced with a visual and verbal humour that he uses to reveal ignorant prejudices, deep cultural assumptions, social conflicts and the inherent dignity and sensitivity of animals that croak, have beaks or regularly appear on the menu. *The Natural History of the Chicken* (2000), screened on PBS in the United States and the BBC in the United Kingdom, is a subtler and in some ways a politically more sophisticated film than *Cane Toads*. In it Lewis demonstrates the extremes inherent in social attitudes and practices by sympathetically juxtaposing the bizarre with the normally invisible horrors of industrial factory farming. Some more affluent interviewees complain about their 'redneck' neighbours keeping noisy roosters, while their redneck counterparts remind the film-maker that they are living in an agricultural area and noise is to be expected. One woman takes her prize bird swimming or shopping or out for a drive, and while inside the house clothes her in a red nappy to match the cover of her sofa. Another woman tells the story of having to give her chicken, Valerie, Cardiopulmonary resuscitation (CPR). The press got hold of the story, and it travelled across America and over to Australia and Russia. It was a newspaper report of this CPR story that first prompted Lewis to make his *Chicken* film but, like Randall Wood, Lewis is not sentimental and does not trivialise. Chickens are respected for their use and intrinsic value. Images of chickens abstracted against a black background display their beauty in isolation from any social and environmental context, and these are soon followed by rural workers in a diner waiting for their fried chicken. For Lewis, it is important to celebrate creatures that are not the A-list animals who star in blue chip natural history documentaries. His aesthetic and stylistic choices provoke questions in the audience's mind about what is normally consumed and accepted under the banner of television natural history. His *Wonderful World of Dogs* (1990), for instance, is a sly comment on the Disneyfication of the natural world by certain film-makers, and *Cane Toads* has been described by one critic as *Monty Python* meeting National Geographic. In an interview for the BBC, Mark Lewis (2005) explained:

> The style I developed for *Cane Toads* came absolutely naturally. I wrote a treatment, sequences and a lot of storyboards. I made it a very structured film because I wanted to visualise certain elements. I guess the greatest influence on natural history film-making at the same time had been the BBC and David Attenborough's programmes. There was always one person leading you through all of the stories. In this case the layperson was so much more interesting and had such a good connection to the animal that I found them much more appropriate to use than the so-called experts. So it evolved through a combination of things: finding great characters and deciding that they were the

best people to tell the story. At the same I decided to do all of the interviews directly to camera because I felt the interviewee engaged with the audience in a much more direct fashion – the audience became a receiver of information rather than being a witness to a conversation. The other element that I really thought a lot about was filming the cane toads themselves. I never tried to look down on the cane toad with the camera; instead I always tried to shoot it from its own eye level. That was instinctive too: that if you're telling an animal's point of view you want to be looking across at it as if you're another cane toad.

Using the 'C' word

For many TV executives, conservation has to be woven within the schedules, has to be implicit rather than explicit, and this view correlates very closely with those natural history producers who believe that nurturing a love of nature is a sound way of developing conservation awareness among the viewing public. Public service channels like the BBC must deliver audiences, for otherwise licence payers will not be getting value for money; and commercial digital channels, of which there are now very many, still have to deliver audiences to advertisers. Audience fragmentation and the new media ecology has not really changed the structure of the media industry (Chris, 2002). Discovery, launched in the USA as a cable channel in 1985, now offers up audiences to advertisers in distinct segments – those whose taste in non-fiction television relates to science, to animals, to nature, to history, to home and health, to crime, to adventure, to mystery and so on. It has been argued that Western media culture tends to infantilise our relationship to nature and wildness by making it safe and palatable while ignoring the more difficult and depressing issues, but new media offers new opportunities for messages to be disseminated. Some Channels like Five in the UK 'do not do conservation with a big C', or as one TV executive put it, "blatant" or "upfront" conservation, although some programmes Five screens – like *Nature Shock: Alien Ice Bear* about the shooting of a bear in the Canadian arctic that turned out to be a cross between a grizzly and polar – do include a discrete conservation message. The main story is about an American hunter, Jim Martell, who recalls at length being fined $65,000 by the Canadian government for killing a polar bear. His words are over laid with dramatic reconstructions to provide visual interest to a storyline that largely fits round a simple question: will he/won't he have to pay up? Brian Leith, a senior producer at the BBC Natural History Unit, suggests that these films should not be too readily dismissed:

It's a bit like the argument that used to fill every Wildscreen Festival like "OK, we make the occasional conservation documentary but are we making any difference to actually saving animals around the world?" It's kind of a sterile argument because it is almost impossible to prove, but I think the question being framed has moved on. We would no longer say "are we having any impact?"; I think we would say "it doesn't really matter if a programme doesn't have an impact. It is part of a wider dissemination of information which stimulates an interest in nature and an interest in nature *per se* will create an interest in conservation." So even an *Animal Planet* frivolous blooper show, if it means people love pets . . . well, loving a pet is a good step towards loving animals, it's a good step towards saving animals. (Brian Leith, interview 1st May 2009)

Perhaps. The consequence of this could equally be that this love allows us to deny, disavow, ignore, compartmentalise, tune out from what is too uncomfortable or too challenging to acknowledge (Jeffries, 2000; Cohen, 2001; Monbiot, 2002). Viewers looking for relaxation, entertainment and a little education are not encouraged to take responsibility for their actions, although they are always invited to 'learn more' about the true stars of Disney Nature, National Geographic/Discovery/Animal Planet/BBC blue chip television co-productions, who are diminishing in numbers year by year as the IUCN's *Red List* makes painfully clear (IUCN, 2009). The fear that the 'c' word will cause viewers to switch over or switch off always seem to win out, but the problem may also have something to do with the way industry ratings, audience demographics and programme impact are gathered and evaluated too.

Kelly Anderson (2008), in a short article for Realscreen, noted that Planet Green, a multi-platform green initiative with a 24-hour eco-lifestyle television network and part of the Discovery network, does not use conventional demographic criteria to evaluate audience impact. Rather, it employs a marketing technique known as psychographics, which purports to measure what people think. Very recently some green psychographic metrics have been developed, and a number of scales have emerged:

- the 'LOHAS' (lifestyle of health and sustainability) are considered to be truly green;
- the 'Naturalites' are more concerned with health matters;
- the 'Conventionalites' are practical people who although interested in green issues are not won over by end of the world scenarios;
- the 'Drifters' are not really concerned by green issues but want to be seen

as fashionable and will watch green programmes when fronted by important celebrities;

- the 'Unconcerned' may watch a green programme but take no notice or not even recognise its conservation or sustainable message.

With audiences fragmenting according to platform and subject preference, highly specialised and highly targeted films are likely to be the future. The size of these specialised audiences will still likely determine whether a media product is considered niche or mainstream, but this will in turn be influenced by the way broader social values and eco-consciousness in different parts of the world co-evolve with the experience and increasing knowledge of climate change, environmental degradation and species extinction. Prospects are grim, and are unlikely to disappear in the short term. Cottle (2004) argues that the failure to produce more environmentally informed documentaries is related to the need for expensive productions to have a market longevity and broad audience appeal. Films that deal with current issues and problems soon date and become unsaleable, and some media scholars such as Gerbner, Gross and Signorelli (1986) have noted that the more TV you watch the less you tend to know; but for Martin Atkin, head of media at WWF International, the key point is that:

> ... a lot of audiences are turned off by too much doom and gloom, too much reality when it comes to talking about the environment. We've all seen those hundreds of films of glaciers falling into the sea, smoke belching out of chimneys, people dying of drought, and all the studies show people just turn off from that type of thing. The question is then, what do you do? How do you convey an essentially depressing message in a way that's not depressing? And, that's really a tough one and I don't think anyone has really got the answer to that. (Martin Atkin, interview 22nd June 2009)

Some films do make a difference and do not avoid difficult issues and disturbing images. Victor Schonfeld's and Myriam Alaux's *Animals Film*, (1981) initially made for cinema release but bought by UK's Channel Four, to be broadcast in the Channel's first week, is a powerful indictment of animal welfare practices in the food production and medical experimentation industries. Its filmic techniques, in large part derived from the 1960s political film-making of Jean Luc Godard and Chris Marker, effectively communicate its central message, and despite (perhaps because of) several vested interests attempting to get the film banned, led to both significant public discussion and legislative changes in some countries. It then disappeared but resurfaced in 2008 as a DVD. Few wildlife, environmental and nature documentarists have followed such an uncompromising path. Some, however, have. Perhaps more should.

Chapter Four

Films for conservation:
trying to get it right

Richard Brock, a veteran film-maker with the BBC, believes there is room for a whole spectrum of nature and wildlife films. After many years with the NHU and after working on prestigious projects such as *Life on Earth* (1979), Brock came to the conclusion that audiences were not getting the full picture. The desire of programme controllers to avoid doom and gloom meant there was too great an emphasis on the cute and cuddly. He recalled one incident while filming David Attenborough attempting to do a piece to camera about orang-utans on the edge of a forest in Borneo, when the soundman kept asking the take to be delayed because of the noise of a chainsaw. Brock (2007) recalled:

> . . . even David just didn't want to know about the problem. He just wanted – alright he had to do a programme and he had to do a sequence. But people know this was happening but it wasn't being seen by the audience. No-one knew and that was really frustrating.

As a result, he set up the Brock Initiative to, amongst other things, make locally orientated films in less developed countries offering screenings mainly to local people. In 2005, in collaboration with the international environmental charity Earthwatch and with a communications grant from the Vodafone Group Foundation, the Brock Initiative made 15 short films with local schools, communities, charities, businesses and government bodies in the East African Rift Valley about the serious environmental degradation and changes to the local ecology and wildlife brought on by the rapid economic development and population increase around Lake Naivasha in Kenya. In six weeks the films were shown to over 2,500 people, gathering enthusiastic and positive responses. Today they are a permanent educational resource in the area. For Richard Brock it is important that good stories are told using the language, environmental and cultural references that audiences recognise, enabling them to see the causes of environmental destruction or species extinction and to identify with the experiences of non-human animals who are also effected by the changes.

In the past I have taken the point of view of the animal. So if you then become the animal you can use technology to be a bird or a mole. The other thing it can do without preaching is to show you what the problems are for that animal because of us. (interview 22nd October 2008)

South African independent film-maker Willie Steenkampf believes that multimedia approaches that adopt a positive rather than a negative issues-driven approach engage audiences more directly. They tend to lead to higher audience loyalty and can make a significant contribution to environmental management. Steenkampf (2008) has studied the three public service television channels in the South Africa, two of which regularly screen natural history programmes – Channel 3 tends to focus on international blue chip co-productions like *Planet Earth*, and Channel Two broadcasts *50/50*, which combines environmental and human interest stories within a public service ethos articulating conservation as being in the interest – and for the good – of everyone. Additionally, DSTV M-NET's pay channels have around 14% national audience share, and broadcast an investigative journalism series *Carte Blanche*, regularly featuring environmental topics. The Afrikaans series *GROEN*, first shown on the Afrikaans channel kykNET in 2004, focusses on the wonders of the natural world as an escape from 21st-century urban life. There is also a related children's series, *GROENtjie*. Subscribers to DSTV will also receive Animal Planet, National Geographic, National Geographic Wild and Discovery Channels in their subscription package. Overall, Steenkampf concludes that if film-makers and conservationists target a niche market, they can maximise their influence through communicating information and fostering understanding that has a capacity to lead to positive practical action. Steenkampf suggests well known and telegenic presenters may be an effective way of engaging and retaining audience interest, and possibly a key to *GROEN*'s success. The programme is also well informed. *GROEN*'s producers work closely with conservation bodies, universities and even government departments. Willie Steenkampf recalls (interview 9th May 2009) a particularly sensitive issue during his time working on *GROEN*:

A good example is when our Minister of Environmental Affairs had to make a decision about the culling of elephants. We were approached by them because we were basically friends with the department and they said to us, 'how can we get involved without making a fuss over the actual shooting of elephants?' Being conservationists and zoologists we understand why you might you might need to cull animals, especially in a country like this where you've got booming economic development and natural areas are becoming more and more threatened. The country is now focussing more on an ecosystem approach to conservation rather than species conservation. We decided we could help him. Yes, let's show that an elephant is a destructive beast and a social animal, so you can't just take one animal out. We didn't talk about culling. We said how amazing this animal is and we have so many different places that can accommodate elephants and yes their habitats are threatened. Then two weeks later the Minister announced Plan Four, the new elephant management programme and we believe we helped people accept that decision much more easily where it could have been a very big controversial problem. The management of elephants includes these things and the last resort will be culling.

As newspaper reports continually demonstrate, any suggestion of elephant culling is likely to generate a rapid and critical public response – bad for conservation, bad for the elephants, bad for the tourist industry and just ethically wrong (Lekotjolo, 2010). Programme makers and conservationists are well aware of this, and have conducted research on alternatives including the use of chili peppers and the strategic siting of hives of honey bees in villages. Both seem to deter marauding elephants from raiding villagers' crops. Bees and chilies also provide the villagers with an additional source of income. Episode Two of *The Secret Life of Elephants*, broadcast in January 2009 on the BBC, featured Saba Douglas-Hamilton exploring the possibilities of the Elephants and Bees Research Project, which is one of her father's (Iain Douglas-Hamilton) Save the Elephants' conservation programmes undertaken in partnership with the University of Oxford. Even the pre-recorded sound of angry honey bees acts as a deterrent, but being intelligent creatures it is the sound combined with the actual threat of being stung that is really the deciding factor. Bees are attracted to the elephants' watery eyes and can go up their trunks, although their stings cannot actually penetrate their tough hides. Such schemes, however, have been by no means commonplace. BBC NHU producer Brian Leith recalled that he once made a film, part of the 1995 series called *Africa's Big Game*, in which the necessity and cost-effectiveness of elephant culling in some circumstances was discussed. "It would never get a big audience on BBC One". He continued with a telling anecdote:

I was staying in a lodge near Mount Kenya, and we came back from having filmed all night because elephants do a lot of their crop-raiding at night. We sat down for breakfast, and there were people who just got up and were about to go off to do their wildlife tours in the morning and I got into a conversation with a family from England. There was a daughter, about 15 years old, and they were asking what we were doing and I said 'We're filming a series about the interactions between people and wildlife here, and we've just been out filming the Kenya Wildlife Service having to shoot elephants because they are raiding crops.' This daughter blanched and she said, 'You've just been filming . . .' I knew I'd made a terrible mistake. It was a complete culture clash. The truth in Africa is very different from the truth for a 15-year-old girl from England with a romanticised view who doesn't realise . . . (Brian Leith, interview 1st May 2009)

The film won the Best of Festival award at Missoula International Wildlife Film Festival in 1996.

Programme-makers are usually aware that certain issues will likely play well or badly to their anticipated audiences. Producers at *GROEN* have sought hard audience data on how different approaches to conservation are received. They decided that after a four-week period the series would shift its emphasis away from the wonders of nature to a more difficult issue-driven approach. Data was gathered on audience reactions from viewer feedback posted on the series website and from the usual information on the programme's ratings. The first week elicited a genuinely angry response to the issues raised, but audience ratings dropped steadily as the experiment continued over the following three weeks. Steenkampf and his colleagues concluded that people who watch natural history programmes care for nature but they largely watch it for pleasure and relaxation. It took six weeks for audience ratings to recover after the series switched back to the normal 'wonders of' format.

Now and then give them all the facts. But also given them the answers. What can we do? (Steenkampf, interview 9th May 2009)

South Africa, like many other countries, is culturally and socially diverse, and although conservation organisations want to reach the widest possible audience, for Steenkampf effective conservation communication has to be targeted according to the attributes, values and predispositions of the particular audience segment watching the programmes. *GROEN*'s audience profile is largely white, middle class, well educated, propertied, and they tend to go on safaris. Thus, unlike other poorer urban dwellers, these audience members can conceive of and understand the problems of the lion and the elephant because in some ways they have seen and have associated with them. In South Africa, as in other democracies, the old and new media are an important element of the public sphere, where debate, discussion and increasingly political and conservation campaigns are organised or actually take place. Steenkampf sees this public debate as an important aspect of conservation film-makers' work:

You must also remember your decision-makers are just normal people at home watching TV. The more people who respond to your film . . . that's what they look at. It's politics. They look at the reaction of the public and then they react on that. We had the laws changed on elephant management because of a programme on *50/50* about poaching and how the government is not reacting to it. Your government is the public.

Supporters of public service broadcasting frequently argue that the public ought to be given what it really needs (even if it is ignorant of those needs) rather than simply what it wants to buy. On the other hand, critics of public service broadcasting tend to offer more market-orientated arguments, laying themselves open to accusations that their main interest is in maximising profits rather than ensuring decent programme quality or enabling broadcasting to effectively operate in the general public interest. Media theorist Nicholas Garnham (1996; 2003) believes that if the market is allowed to dominate broadcasting, a loss of diversity, quality, public debate, knowledge and understanding will inevitably occur, although with a multi-channel and multi-platform new media ecology the role of public service broadcasting (or indeed narrowcasting – that is, more targeted dissemination) is less clear than before. Public service broadcasters themselves tend towards the quality arguments and will often cite nature and wildlife programmes such as the *Natural World* series on the BBC or the *Nature* series on PBS as examples of excellent popular educative programmes serving the public and now planet's interest. By contrast, for Hartley (1999), Papacharissi (2002) and Jacka (2003) public service broadcasting is class-based and anti-democratic, pathologising everyday life and popular culture, whereas the new media technologies – the digital multi-channel environment combined with the growing significance of the internet – are inherently liberating, enabling new forms of cultural politics, programming, 'DIY citizenship' and public conversations to emerge.

Film presenting human ecology and conservation

The Wildscreen Film Festival debates frequently focus on conservation as well as the more technical and commercial matters relating to commissioning and programme formats. The assumption that blue chip documentaries, by conveying a love of nature are sufficient to stimulate action, is often challenged. However, there are examples of mainstream natural history programmes integrating a clear conservation perspective with not so much a feel-good sense of wonderment or inserting a brief conservation message but presenting a serious and complex analysis of human ecology, ecosystem processes, cultural politics and cultural values. Neil Goodwin's *Rachel Carson's Silent Spring* (1993) or Doug Shultz's *Silence of the Bees* (2006) for the American Experience and Nature series on PBS are good examples. *People of the Sea* (1997), made by Hugh Miles and Patrick Morris, started life as a conventional wildlife film but the more Miles investigated the issues, the more a very different story emerged. National Geographic had part-funded the production with the BBC, and when they first viewed the film, now about the diminution of cod stocks and the over-exploitation of capelin in the Newfoundland waters, the programme commissioners stated that it was not the film they originally expected or wanted. However, because *People of the Sea* presented such an important message as part of an intricate and integrated study of life in Newfoundland's once rich and diverse marine ecosystem, they accepted the version as made. The film offers a subtle and complex narrative, interweaving natural history concerns with issues relating to (un)sustainable fishing, regional politics and human economic development. The aesthetic facilitates both a cognitive and an affective understanding of the issues by using iconic archive footage, vibrant images of the threatened marine species, local music and sounds, and a narration by Shane Mahoney, then Chief of Wildlife Research with the Government of Newfoundland and Labrador, whose Newfoundland/Irish accent, deep scientific and local ecological knowledge and profound commitment to place lent a special integrity and authenticity to the film which it may have otherwise lacked if the film-makers had decided instead on an anonymous commentary or celebrity presenter. Mahoney, who appears on screen only once, is a middle-aged man with thick dark hair and a greying beard. He is a symbol of 500 years of European settlement, a rootedness in a particular place and the hard efforts entailed in making a living and a life from the marine environment. Mahoney is in effect as near to an indigenous person as a European can be in north America. Pocius (2001) in his anthropological study of Calvert in Newfoundland describes the culture, consciousness and commitment of the people in considerable detail and with deep understanding of the local people's commercial and spiritual dependence on the ocean.

Although the destruction of northern codfish stocks has now become an international symbol of unsustainable development, short-sighted political decision-making and a clear example of market failure, *People of the Sea* is concerned to demonstrate how a small change in one element can have multiple effects throughout the ecosystem. The cooling of Newfoundland waters has placed additional strains on the capelin, which as food resource for cod, gulls, seals, ospreys, whales and virtually everything else is also threatened by a human harvesting which looks to sell the pregnant females to Japan as a bar snacks. The rest are simply dumped. Thus, the capelin are denied the opportunity to reproduce, and a spiral of decline is likely to be reinforced even though more eco-friendly alternatives to making a living are available – examples of which act as the positive coda to the film. *People of the Sea* won awards at the Jackson Hole Wildlife Film Festival in 1997 and at Wildscreen in 1998 but, as Miles (2006: 18) later said:

> . . . the best result of all is that the Premier of Newfoundland saw it, who used to be the fisheries manager, and he was so impressed by it he said he wanted the BBC to supply us with 300 copies, so every school in Newfoundland can have a copy. So the children were brought up understanding about their environment and the dangers of over-exploitation of a wildlife resource, and that was just wonderful. Best I've ever had from a wildlife film actually.

Some years earlier a film by Jacques Gagne, *Cries from the Deep* (1981) financed by the Nation Film Board of Canada (NFB) and featuring Jacques Cousteau and his crew from the Calypso, hesitantly explored the human ecology of the region, having Cousteau delicately asking fishermen at one point whether the real problem for Newfoundland wasn't whales taking too many fish but human beings themselves.

Human culture is rendering the natural environment unsustainable, and in an elliptical way this theme is pursued almost unconsciously by some filmmakers working through the NFB, such as in the films made between 1963 and 1968 by the Quebecois film-maker Pierre Perrault. His trilogy of films about the disappearing traditional lifestyles of the peoples of L'Ile-aux-Coudres in the St Lawrence River presents the cultural dominance of modernity as a subject for deep reflection and contemplation. In *Pour la Suite du Monde* (1963) Perrault persuaded some local people to capture a beluga whale using the same methods they had last used in the 1920s when whale hunting was a major part of their culture and income. Local ecological knowledge lies exclusively with the elder generation, as in the previous three or four decades there has been no reason to pass it on. Additionally, the captured beluga will now go to an aquarium in the United States rather than go to slaughter. The film is consequently a retrieval and a homage to the past, a comment on economic development and cultural change with significant scenes of local discussions, home-making, social music-making and dancing symbolising both communal solidarity and dependence on the external environment. Shot in black and white, *Pour la Suite du Monde* is reminiscent of the folk reconstructions of Robert Flaherty and stylistically of the poetic realism of Humphrey Jennings, where the visual composition is often sufficient to encapsulate the felt meaning of the narrative. There is a long shot of the St Lawrence River with a big ship passing in the distance. Something extremely close to the camera, indistinct and blurred, is discernible in the foreground. The focus changes slowly although the camera position remains static. The blur turns into the leaves of a tree and the passing ship fades into the mists of time and space. The depth of field has altered before changing again to slowly reveal the weight and dominance of modern commerce and economic development. Both *People of the Sea* and *Pour La Suite du Monde* address the importance of place and the cultural loss that accompanies the global dominance of the market economy.

The use of a local person with local knowledge and a profound commitment to place is a device used in many environmental and some wildlife films. *Hawaii: a Message in the Waves* (2007) directed by Rebecca Hoskins, co-produced by BBC Worldwide and Animal Planet and shown in the UK as part of the long running *Natural World* series, is another complex film that conveys a very strong conservation message about human responsibility and culpability for environmental destruction, harming wildlife and the cultural degradation of the social world. Hawaii is presented as a sun-drenched paradise. There are iconic shots of breaking waves, beautiful bodies swimming and surfing, golden beaches and clear blue skies. The audience's guide is a local teacher of Polynesian descent, Iokepa Neale, who likens living on an island to living on a canoe, like his ancestors did when travelling the thousands of miles on their voyage of discovery to the archipelago a thousand years previously. Hoskins structures her film around four key principles that have informed the way Polynesian settlers learnt to live within their ecological limitations. They controlled their harvesting of the ocean, respected the environment, took responsibility for their use of natural resources and saw themselves as accountable to both other people and to the environment as a whole. Living these principles, being immersed in them just as a free diver is immersed in the ocean environment, is the path to ecological harmony, whereas economic development through tourism is a path to the destruction of fragile coral reefs and the aesthetic pollution of shorelines and oceans with tourist boats and high rise tourist hotels. Hoskins makes the point in a montage sequence that presents the argument in both a literal and metaphorical form. To call any place a paradise is a kiss of death, one person says, and Hoskins graphically shows this in scenes in the third part of the film where tonnes of marine debris – largely plastic artifacts discarded from the the throwaway culture of countries on the Pacific Rim – have been washed up on the beaches of Hawaiian archipelago by the ocean currents. Seals are caught by discarded ropes. There is a close-up of a monk seal with a ring from parcel tape around its snout that prevents it from feeding. An albatross chick attempts to free itself from a plastic coat-hanger. Adult albatrosses feed their chicks on floating plastic trash rather than fish. Dolphins play with and choke on plastic grocery bags. Fed on plastic, young birds are so malnourished they do not have the energy to fly or live to adulthood. One final scene shows the free diver, a young woman, on Midway island collecting plastic artifacts from the stomachs and boluses of dead albatrosses slowly decomposing on the otherwise idyllic beach. Within an hour she has collected a museum-load of plastic combs, hairbrushes, fishing equipment, golf balls, computer cartridges, toothbrushes, plastic forks and spoons, cigarette lighters, roller balls from deodorants, gluesticks and more. They are laid out neatly in rows, classified and categorised exactly as an index of the everyday, of Western civilisation's obsessions with accumulation, consumption and the status of material wealth. Hawaii is changing, has changed and as the music of eco-singer/songwriter Jack Johnson plays, the viewer is told directly that Hawaii is both a model of sustainable and unsustainable living, of conservation and material devastation – "We just have to decide where the real wealth lies". Hoskins' film has been seen widely on digital channels and on the internet. It is a favourite at environmental film festivals, and has been used as a mobilising tool for green groups. Hoskins herself was instrumental in initiating a ban of plastic grocery bags in her own village of Modbury in the the south-west of England, where her film was shown at a local arts centre. At the end of the screening the audience agreed to ban the bags (Vidal, 2007). The film's website provides information and tips on how individuals can clean up the world by changing their own everyday lifestyles, as well as showing a range of stills and clips. *Hawaii: a Message in the Waves* is not just a film with a conservation message but has itself become an effective campaigning and educational tool for a more sustainable world because its aesthetic offers the viewer beautiful pictures, ethical choices and a clear understanding that small actions do count, and that without them the beauty we value will soon turn into the ugliness we despise.

Ape Hunters (2002), another BBC film, this time made by Jeremy Bristow, is an award-winning film on the bushmeat trade. Bristow is unusual for a natural history film-maker in having a background in current affairs, and this is evident in many of the films he has produced. *Kings of the Jungle* (1998), *Warnings from the Wild* (2000), *Whale Hunters* (2002), *The Price of Prawns* (2004), *Can We Save Planet Earth?* (2006), *Wilderness Explored* (2008) and

Hope in a Changing Climate (2009) all have a political, economic and social dimension that shape the approach to environmental and conservation issues. For Bristow, the world is not only ecologically complex but socially, culturally and politically complex too. There are no easy answers and certainly no easy moral choices, even if the issue at first glance seems as clear-cut as did the poaching of gorillas for the illegal bushmeat trade. Gorillas are food, sources of income and like elephants destructive to crops and people's livelihoods. They may be genetic cousins to human beings but in Africa they are rarely perceived as such. Bristow's investigative techniques often mean that the story emerges during the process of filming with unexpected actions or comments becoming highly relevant structuring elements. Bristow therefore needs to be alert and open to what is happening around him. He recalled (interview 8th April 2009):

> With a film like *Ape Hunters*, I try to take the audience through the learning experience I went through in the three months making the film in an hour. . . . You have to tailor the film, to some extent, to the audience. I don't know how the film would be seen in Africa, or whether it would need to be re-versioned for Africa. I went there with the idea that it's us whites – we're really at fault, these people don't have the food so they have to hunt, to get their protein from the great apes and the elephants. And it is our fault because we build all these roads to get the logging vehicles in to chop down their forests. That is part of the story, but just as big a part is that they have a different attitude to animals. At the end the hero-guy just says 'Well actually, I do it [conserve the gorillas] not because you tell me but because you pay me and to me they are still beasts of the forest that must be eaten.' That was my discovery in the film. There is a huge cultural difference, but to address that for a different audience you make a different film.

Ape Hunters was voted Best Documentary at the FICA environmental international film and video festival in Brazil in June 2002, and in October the same year won the One Planet Panda Award at the Wildscreen Festival and the British Environmental Media Awards' Richard Keefe Memorial Award for best documentary on sustainable development. What is of real interest is how the film is seen by its various audiences, so although a film may garner many awards and great acclaim within 'the business' it is not always certain other audiences will react with similar enthusiasm. For example, Conservation International's nine-minute *Say No to Bushmeat* (2002) documentary, selected as a finalist in the 2003 Jackson Hole Wildlife Film Festival, highlights both the environmental destruction associated with the bushmeat trade and the health issues associated with the spread of the Ebola virus. Conservation International's campaign articulated the traditional belief that the survival of each local clan is inextricably linked to the survival of the clan's symbolic animal or totem, even though as the film notes nearly 98% of Ghana's 110 ruling clans are no longer found in their traditional territory. The overall impact of the film, together with the related TV spots shown on six stations to local populations, is unclear. A Conservation International project evaluation concluded in January 2004 (CI, 2004: 6):

> Outputs relating to cultural change take much longer period to be realized than the project's life period. This therefore falls out of the project implementation schedule. Support for monitoring evaluation after project implementation is very important, especially a project which is targeted to cultural and behavioral change.

Ape Hunters was shown to groups of villagers in rural Cameroon as part of a conservation education project undertaken by The Great Apes Film Initiative (GAFI), which aims to reach local communities, urban television viewers and decision makers. GAFI estimates that nearly 50 million people in 14 countries in both south-east Asia and Africa have seen films donated to the organisation. These have included productions by the BBC and Granada International: *Cousins: the Apes*; *Ape Hunters*; *Congo: Spirits of the Forest*; *Congo: Footprints in the Forest* and *Cousins: The Monkeys*. As Juliet Wright (2007; 2009) notes, raising awareness through showing films and achieving conservation objectives are by no means synonymous. As a GAFI project worker she organised a number of screenings to Cameroonian audiences, many of whom had never seen gorillas or chimps in the wild and were quite unaware of their behaviour. The films were originally produced in the English language, and although some of the audience had a sufficient grasp of the language to understand the commentary some screenings also involved an improvised commentary by a native speaker who explained various elements and references that were unfamiliar to the local audience. After each screening there was often a discussion and audience questionnaire. The research revealed that over half of the audience had eaten one or more primate species. Wright (2009: 3) writes:

> *Ape Hunters* may be effective when viewed by a Western audience who are shocked by the concept of eating monkeys and apes, but this shock tactic is ineffective in Cameroon. Where eating primates is an accepted norm, *Ape Hunters* could serve as a recipe guide or reinforce the notion that Americans

and Europeans like keeping primates as pets unless such films are properly interpreted by local conservation educators.

In one sequence towards the end of the episode *Cousins: the Apes*, Charlotte Uhlenbroek speaks about the sexual habits of bonobos. They resolve disputes by having sex, and footage is shown of the animals doing exactly this. "If a male gets aggressive, 'a quickie' soon calms him down." She then states that bonobos walk upright to gather food, explicitly stating that this is the clear link between them and us. Images of the animals walking are accompanied by soft soothing string music, emotionally preparing the viewer to empathise with the activities depicted in the close-up images of bonobos caring for and caressing their young. A hand is seen slowly and gently stroking the head of the baby. Uhlenbroek, using the obligatory hushed tones of a BBC wildlife presenter, then speaks of chimps and bonobos being able to think, and over a montage of medium close-ups of chimps in poses denoting thoughtfulness, asks what do they think about, how do they see the world, what sense do they make of it? The programme *Cousins: The Monkeys* continued this theme and seemed to have the most noticeable audience effect many of whom expressed surprised at the way adult primates cared so affectionately for their young. Some remarked on the obvious behavioural similarities between the great apes, chimps and monkeys and human beings.

A little later some audience members declared they would no longer eat pepper soup if it contained monkey meat, and other impressions and suggestions recorded by Wright (2007: 27-33) reveal significant learning experiences about the social and cultural similarities between chimps and humans, which clearly emanate directly from the film-viewing experience. A 42-year-old female pharmacy student speaks appreciatively of the similarity .of gorillas, chimps and humans. "They carry babies in the same way as people do", she says, but also feels that films should be made about the forest habitat as a whole. A 45-year-old female farmer says something very similar – she is amazed at how close apes are to human beings. A 54-year-old male trapper remarks that chimps hunt, play, wash food and have sex in similar ways to people. He is able to directly relate and compare his own experiences and his own activities to theirs. A 30-year-old female farmer is impressed with chimp courtship displays and food preparation techniques, and as a result feels that the forests should not only be protected but enlarged. A 20-year-old male student is taken by the fact that chimps breast-feed their young and teach them how to live socially.

In an interview Juliet Wright reviewed her thoughts about the influence of local culture on the interpretation of films used explicitly to promote a pro-conservation message. As perhaps to be expected, local audience interpretations did not necessarily correspond with the conservation messages local NGOs themselves wished to communicate.

> People do take in more of what they see than what they hear. One of the films shows mandrills congregating in big groups of 250, which is explained as an exceptional circumstance, a response to the level of predation. In some areas there is a safety in numbers, but the audience just sees hundreds of mandrills, and these images contradict what you are trying to say about the species being endangered. There are certain aspects of films that take an evolutionary perspective on their [monkey/ape] behaviour and human behaviour and in communities that have never been taught about evolution the message is lost. . . . I still show the Charlotte Uhlenbroek film but it is sometimes distracting. They [the audience] often focus on, and are completely amazed by what she does such as being hoist up a tree with cables. Audiences tend to focus on this spectacle rather than the animals. (Juliet Wright interview, 17th February 2010)

The images of Uhlenbroek in close vicinity with the animals suggested the apes were friendly, although there was also a hint that her own skin colour was perhaps a reminder of former colonial times when the white person knew best. There were other issues in the cultural translation of films made for one context to another, and the GAFI research indicated that, as many audience members themselves believed, if films are to be used successfully for purposes of conservation education in local areas within Africa or elsewhere, they ought to be made specially for that purpose by someone with local knowledge and preferably with a high level of technical expertise. This is currently being undertaken by the International Conservation and Education Fund (INCEF), founded in 2004 by film-maker Cynthia Moses whose films for National Geographic and Discovery have won many awards and wide professional and public acclaim. In 2000 her film *Odzala: Islands in the Forest* (1995) was instrumental in achieving a four-fold expansion of Odzala National Park in the Congo. In *Living with Gorillas* (2000) she developed a story around the work of Spanish primatologist Magdalena Bermejo who, influenced by the work of Jane Goodall and specifically the earlier National Geographic Special *Miss Goodall and the Wild Chimpanzees*, studied the lowland gorillas of the Lower Congo Basin. The film follows the same format as *Miss Goodall* – a narrative documentary reconstruction based on the work of a young female scientist using first-person testimony and Hollywood-style cutaways of both both humans and gorillas peering into the jungle. It is, however, a more complex and subtle work, for it carefully integrates three themes: a respect for gorillas as an important species, each member of whom has a distinct personality; an acknowledgement of the importance of the cultural traditions and ecological knowledge of the local people who had been displaced from their jungle homes fifty years earlier by French colonialists; and an understanding that conservation means human beings living with rather than dominating the environment which is able to sustain both them and other creatures. For Moses, conservation can only work if the local people are at the forefront as stewards and cohabitants of the forest. The final scene recognises the potential of film as a conservation tool. It shows local villagers sitting around a television screen watching film footage of the gorillas. Magdalena Bermejo provides the villagers with a commentary in French, who again remark on the similarities between the great apes and themselves, virtually admitting the apes, particularly the big silverback, as *de facto* members of their village.

The use of film as a means of giving voice to local people is developed in Moses' later work. Nowadays she focuses on enabling Africans to make their own films on conservation issues that directly impact upon their lives. The eleven-minute *Great Apes are Just Like Us / Ils son Comme Nous Les Grand Singes* (2006) starts with Catherine Missilou, an eco-guide with the Gorilla Protection Project, explaining in the local language and framed in a medium close-up head shot, that gorillas and chimpanzees live in the forest but poachers and hunters have killed many mothers and fathers. The film cuts to animals in the forest and then to a short montage of young apes being fed by their carers. A man, Florent Ikoli, Gorilla Sanctuary Conservator, invites viewers to look at the apes, to see how similar they are to human beings. They are presented in close-up – eyes, nose, lips – and then in a medium-long shot walking away from the camera. Another man, Dr Dieudonne Ankara, leader of the GRASP Project, reinforces this view, commenting in French on the similarity between ape and human behaviours. The film then cuts alternately between the three guides who explain menstrual and birth cycles, that apes make beds/nests to sleep on, hunt in groups and share the proceeds between themselves. The question is asked: why would we want to kill an animal like that? African drums play on the soundtrack, and the film cuts to images of human hunters with rifles. Dead apes are cut up on the forest floor, ready to be taken away. The audience is then informed that apes mourn the loss of one another just as we humans do. Shots of gorillas are followed by shots of Bonobos playing who, as the commentary relates, often resolve conflict through sexual contact: 'Make peace, not war; make love not war.' With a smile, Dr Ankara suggests this is a process humans should adopt. An ape is seen washing in a river. There is then a cut to a close-up of an animal looking straight at the camera lens and the viewer is told that today only a few genes separates us from the these primates. The apes also are good for the ecosystem, helping to maintain and regenerate the forest by spreading seeds through their faeces and thus ensuring that biodiversity is replenished and reproduced; a rich forest is an important resource for many traditional herbal medicines. The issue of species extinction is then relayed by Florent Ikoli, and shots of men using chainsaws to fell mature trees illustrates the point vividly and simply. A tree falls with a dissolve to a shot of a cleared area and then a cut back to Florent, who concludes by warning viewers that the loss of habitat, combined with the spread of the deadly ebola virus and illegal hunting, is threatening the great apes with extinction which would be a great loss to everyone. A short education and training video by Nicola Lankester, *The Takamanda National Park* (2007) follows a similar format, and one later adapted in *Bama's Journey*. The animals are a national treasure and the park is like a bank which if emptied will make Cameroon poor. There must be no fishing with chemicals that poison the river. A short scene dramatises the common practices of fishing with poison, food preparation and consuming a fish meal. The message is basic and obvious, told in both words and pictures, discursively and affectively. If you poison the river to kill the fish you will poison yourself. The film is also shown in rural communities as part of the Wildlife Conservation Society's (Cameroon) outreach programme and is one of a growing number of media-related conservation education campaigns.

Conservation and natural history films from the global South

A number of Indian film-makers have concentrated on the connectedness of all life, tracing the broad ecological and cultural contours of competition, co-operation and coexistence. At the root of these ecologically informed films, there is often a deep historical sense that conservation and human ecology has been a thread running throughout India's long history, diverse geography, social arrangements, religious rituals, values and beliefs (Gadgil and Guha, 1992). Mike Pandey's award-winning film *The Last Migration* (1994) follows the capture of a herd of wild elephants who, in losing their natural foraging areas to development, then encroached upon land used by local people for their own subsistence food production. The elephants destroyed many homes and killed a number of people. The villagers responded by taking pot shots at them or attempting to drive them away. This made the elephants increasingly angry as in effect they had nowhere to go. They had already lost their home-lands to development. Pandey's film carefully invites the viewer to identify with the plight of both the local people and the elephants, revealing a solution that will enable both to survive. The elephants are to be captured by a tribal group who for centuries have been adept at animal capture. They are super-vised by professional conservationists and veterinary staff who ensure the ani-mals are not harmed and are adequately cared for when transported away from the area. The elephants will then be trained elsewhere so that they can 'earn their keep' in the forest. Throughout the film Mike Pandey demonstrates visually the usefulness, intelligence, power and vulnerability of this iconic species. They are revered and worshipped by Indians, but also hated when they compete for the same resources humans need for survival. The film is necessarily dominated by images of the elephants, and Pandey is at pains to show how their behaviour is evidence of feelings and emotions that human beings themselves can recognise and empathise with. They comfort one another when distressed, look after one another when feeling threatened, and respond to the kindness of strangers with a trust and gentleness that is both rare and precious. The film's tempo is necessarily slow as Pandey must inform his audiences of urban dwellers of many things they will be unfamiliar with, including the natural world itself. Mike Pandey's cultural and eco-sensitivity defines his approach to film-making, which has been developed over time. He has acquired a respect and credibility well beyond the environmental and nature film-making business. He is trusted, believed and respected by many different audiences. His films are seen in schools, translated into a number of local languages including Urdu, and are now shown as far north as the dis-puted territory of Kashmir on the Pakistan border.

Vanishing Giants (2004) is a short television report graphically depicting the brutal and cruel treatment of India's elephants. The viewer sees shots of elephants being beaten, roped and pulled to the ground, stabbed, cut and killed. There are close-up shots of elephant tears, and frequently heard sounds of elephant cries. It is a very powerful and uncomfortable film, which instantly affected and probably shamed Indian audiences, for it led to a mas-sive public outcry and immediate changes to the law on elephant welfare. However, the film itself is apparently quite restrained, being suggestive rather than revealing the full horror of the beatings. It is perhaps this restraint that enabled Pandey to simultaneously raise awareness, provoke a sense of respon-sibility and inspire action among so many different people throughout such a large and diverse country.

Vanishing Giants was very tough to make. It was heart-rending really to see an elephant dying in front of you and nobody listening. I had to reach out to people. I had no doors open to me at a higher level. I culled out the most horrific images – when the elephant was falling in a pit and being cut into. I tried to minimise that by 90%. I was not witch-hunting. I did not want to over-dramatise. I wanted to explore the issue of how we as civilised human beings, who revere the elephant, can allow the animal to end up in that pit just because he wandered into a field. He cannot know that a man owns the field and that it is not for foraging in. We should have shot the elephant rather than torture it. . . . Visuals can make a difference, and if they are simply put they can touch the hearts and minds of people, whether a policy-maker or common man. That is what is needed – a little thinking. (Mike Pandey, interview 13th November 2009)

Similarly, his documentary *Shores of Silence* (1999) explores how the whale shark (*Rhincodon typus*), initially hunted for its liver oil used by fishermen to waterproof their boats, is now killed more profitably for its meat, fat and fins which are exported abroad. The fish, the largest in the world, is shown being hooked by fishermen, dragged to the surface where it struggles for breath and to shallow waters where, sometimes still alive, the animal is mutilated. The result of this profitable slaughter is the near extinction of the whale shark and a serious imbalance to the ecology of the Gujarat coastal region. To communicate with his audience Pandey employs religious references, cultural values and spiritual analogies. The whale shark comes to the coastal waters for food and comfort just as a young woman may return to the safety of her parents' home to have her first child. After two or three months the young woman returns to her husband, just as the shark returns to the open waters.

This [message] worked tremendously with local communities and we used a religious leader who said these things – Morari Bapu. He has a following of four or five million people along the coastline. That made a lot of difference. We showed the film to all 250 hamlets and villages along the coast and spoke to the women and the children. I showed them gory shots of fisherman thrashing around and dying in the water. I said to them, 'Do you want your husband to die like this – for ten pounds. Will you let your husband go out onto the high seas when the waves are cresting at thirty feet and fishing is banned? Do you need that ten pounds or do you need your husband?' Families then forced the fisherman, 'No, we don't want you to go.' That brought pressure from another area. (Mike Pandey, interview 13th November 2009)

Shores of Silence has been shown widely on Indian television as well as to local fishing communities, where it successfully changed attitudes through raising awareness and developing a new understanding of the animal and its shared ecology. The film has also inspired a successful campaign to have the whale shark added to the list of India's protected species, and in November 2002 it was screened at the international CITES (Convention on International Trade in Endangered Species) conference in Santiago, Chile), and was instrumental in changing the minds and votes of many delegates which ultimately led to the global protection of the Whale Shark.

Pandey's films frequently show the connectedness of the natural and human worlds, and how economic progress and development can have devastating effects on India's wildlife and traditional cultures. The Indian tiger is nearing extinction due to habitat destruction, poaching and ineffective protection measures. Ironically, it is also the country's national symbol. The vulture, of which India once had more than any other country in the world, has been decimated by the drug Diclofenac. This is used by farmers as a pain reliever for cattle, but leads to liver failure when the meat is eaten by the birds. Within ten years 99% of India's vulture population of 87 million had been killed. Rotting carcasses produced unwanted and dangerous viruses and harmful bacteria. *Vanishing Vultures* (2006) is a 17-minute advocacy film using existing and urgently shot new footage and made with the support of the RSPCA, Bombay Natural History and the British Council. It has stimulated awareness and action just as *Vanishing Giants* did a few years before. Within three weeks of the film being finished it was screened ten times on television, shown by volunteers in local farming communities and was instrumental in banning the drug's production and distribution in India. *The Fragile Web*, written, directed and produced by Pandey in 2005, offers a Darwinist interpretation of natural history and species interconnectedness that informs the commentary and the largely illustrative montage of sound and image. Only in the final five minutes is the intelligence and voraciousness of *homo sapiens* stressed as the main reason for ecological destruction and biodiversity loss. Interestingly, Pandey occasionally refers to "nature's design" or the "design" of a particular animal in relation to its own ecological niche, for as Gosling (2001) has noted, there is an inherent compatibility between Darwinism and Hinduism. Both systems of thought articulate the close connection between human life, conduct and history and that of the non-human world. Reincarnation and the recognition that many gods assume an animal form undermine the capacity of science to be spiritually subversive within a great deal of Indian culture. In India, 'design' is a word and a feeling that is not loaded with Christian fundamentalist connotations.

Pandey has also been responsible for the long-running environmental series *Earth Matters*, which is shown through India on the public service network, Doordarshan. The programmes are dubbed into local languages and are frequently used by schools and other groups, for the series covers a wide variety of highly significant issues ranging from HIV/AIDS and human ecology to tiger conservation. Many programmes are commissioned by the Public Service Broadcasting Trust of India from independent film-makers. The thirty-minute programmes have relatively low production values, for their average cost is around US $10,500. Many films have been made by women, some by completely new film-makers, some are financed personally by the film-makers but all aim to reach marginalised audiences to promote respect for cultural diversity and sustainable development practices. When screened by the state broadcaster these films have a potential audience of 600 million people or more.

Kalpavriksha (2000) written and directed by Nina Subramani and produced by Mike Pandey for UNESCO, emphasises the importance of traditional ecological knowledge by focussing on the medicinal use of plants by the Irula tribe of Tamilnadu, the Kani tribe of Karela, and other tribal peoples across India. These traditional remedies have been used for over three thousand years, but the destruction of both these plants and the attendant local wisdom is now imminent because of economic modernisation, habitat loss and the patenting of commercially significant plant products by international drugs companies. Using a gently pedagogic aesthetic and an authoritative female voice-over, *Kalpavriksha* demonstrates the dependence of human culture on natural ecosystems by comparing of the lifeworlds of indigenous, 'ecosystem peoples', with those of contemporary urban 'omnivores' who devour the produce of the whole biosphere (Gadgil and Guha, 1995). *Kurumbas – Children of the Blue Mountains* (2000) explores the need for ecological balance by examining the precarious existence of the the Kurumba tribals in the Blue Mountains of southern India, who annually harvest the honey of the Himalayan honebee from the sheer 300-foot cliffs within Nilgiri Biosphere reserve. Much of the surrounding forest land has been felled to make way for tea plantations where many Kurumba people, as Pandey's script states, exchange their freedom for the 'security' of waged labour. In doing so, understandably perhaps, these children of the Blue Mountains are surrendering to the vagaries of economic development and the anonymity of the global market place their unique ecological and cultural niche, their music (which mimics the sound of the bees and is heard periodically on the soundtrack), and their skills of making ladders from vines. In this context, cutaways to close-ups of plants, trees and the bees express neither a lament nor a sentimental nostalgia but rather a reverence for a way of life that was once in harmony with the ecosystem services that support it. In many ways these people exhibit a sustainable wisdom that others are trying to recapture and reproduce. Not all hives are destroyed in the harvesting, for at the root of the Kurumba's continued existence has been a conservation ethic enabling future generations to inherit a world that, although by no means wealthy in any material sense, was neither diminished nor degraded.

Social change, progress and economic development has been the hallmark of post-colonial India, but with it there has been a cost which the formal education system has only been able to partially address. Literacy levels in some areas are still extremely low and Mike Pandey, who has won many awards and was named by *Time* magazine as an Environmental Hero of 2009, has shown how film and television can be an important and powerful medium for environmental education, communication and change. This is particularly the case when the messages resonate with local cultures, beliefs, traditions and are linked to practical conservation campaigns and development projects, such as those initiated by his own not-for-profit foundation also called Earth Matters. Although many of the blue chip documentaries produced by the Discovery Channel, the BBC or National Geographic are shown in India, none have led to the practical conservation action, legislative changes or understanding as Pandey's own, sometimes self-financed, films. The relationship between loving nature or loving pets and saving animals is neither direct nor apparent, but that between education (through film) and conservation is. Pandey says:

> In India people revere and worship animals. The elephant, Ganesha, is the god of wealth and the tiger is called the chariot of Dhurga. Millions of people go out and pray on the special days, but the tigers are still dying. And monkeys are being killed, even though Tuesdays is the day of the monkey god, because they are called a menace. Man does what suits him, and what suits him makes him bend things. We are a very crafty species . . . but the sharing of information can lead to conservation. When the farmers saw the film [*Vanishing Vultures*] they realised what [they were doing]. You have to light lamps where there is darkness. (interview 13th November 2009)

Another Indian film-maker, Sheka Dattatri, suggests that a false distinction has occurred between development and conservation, and much natural history film-making has helped to reproduce and reinforce it. In most major eco-disasters it is the poor who suffer, but conservation is seen by many as a middle-class concern rather than a way of life as it was once in ancient India. *Mindless Mining* (2001) was made by Wildlife First in association with a number of other local NGOs campaigning against pollution and biodiversity loss caused by open cast mining in the rainforest areas of Kudremukh National Park in the Western Ghats area of southern India. The argument that economic development primarily benefits the local people and the local economy is methodically challenged and undermined. The film presents a range of scientific evidence with purely visual illustrations of polluted rivers and of habitat destruction. The film became part of a well organised and targeted campaign that exploited the power of social networks and professional contacts rather than attempting to raise general public awareness. In 2005 the mining company's licence to operate in the area was rescinded. Success was due to this focus, which in some ways mirrors the activities of Mike Pandey's efforts, but Dattatri tends to discount the value of making films to raise general public awareness as little more than 'a shot in the dark':

> This NGO also had people who had their own network of contacts who knew the private secretary of a minister and somebody else knew a very popular and powerful religious leader, and sometimes they just made cold calls. They sometimes would have a television screen and video player in their car, and they would go somewhere hoping to meet somebody or badger them. Sometimes they would say, 'Look, if you don't have time to discuss this in detail could you not at least see a ten-minute video we have done'. And sometimes they would say, 'What the hell, show it' – and once they saw it they were engaged by it and ended up speaking to the people for an hour or two. The film was a very important ice-breaker and a lot of the religious leaders are very important in India. They have enormous amounts of political clout. They often have a hotline to the chief minister of the state. They could call him on his mobile phone and say, "Eh, this is what is happening to our sacred river; how can you allow this to happen?' (Shekar Dattatri, interview 26th April 2009)

Dattatri's self-financed *The Ridley's Last Stand* (2002) starts with a personal recollection of the turtle-rich beaches of the Orissa coastline and then traces the reasons why so many turtles are today found dead and mutilated on the beaches. *The Killing Fields* (2003), a *pro bono* project distributed by the Wildlife Protection Society of India and freely available on the internet, is a shorter analysis of the same topic, this time with an anonymous narrator and an instructional aesthetic presenting a scientific objectivity designed to persuade policymakers and decision-makers who might otherwise be dismissive of emotive, personalised appeals or subjective-style journalism. The giant turtle, particularly the Olive Ridley, is a protected species but is in danger of extinction. If the turtle disappears, so do the livelihoods of the many local people who depend on the sea's resources to make ends meet. Ironically, the turtle, like the elephant and tiger, is also a Hindu deity, an avatar of the Hindu god Vishnu the Preserver, and this cultural reference features in one sequence in *The Ridley's Last Stand* where a campaign group, Operation Kachhapa, employs two folk singers to inform local village fisherfolk of their exclusive legal right to fish using their traditionally sustainable methods within five kilometres from the coast. By knowing and applying their legal rights, local fisherfolk can protect the turtle from the greed and cruelty of others. A series of painted pictures illustrate the song that speaks of the turtle's best interest being also the best interest of villagers. Unfortunately, big trawlers go close to the shore and catch the giant turtles in their drag nets which, despite a legal requirement to do so, are not fitted with a TED (a turtle excluder device) because the boat owners believe the subsequent loss of around 5% of the fish catch is too high a price to pay. In the five years prior to the making of *The Ridley's Last Stand* 75,000 dead giant turtles were washed up on the Orrissa coast. There has been no official attempt to enforce the law because of the economic and political clout of the trawler owners. The problems of indiscriminate mechanised fishing, local government indifference and other more ecological issues such as the Forestry departments' planting of casuarina on nesting beaches are presented as interlinked ones, capable of resolution only if there is political will to confront the issues and the various interest groups. The overriding factor is economic, and although national policymakers were sympathetic and everyone publicly professed reverence for the Olive Ridley, the film offers practical solutions but little hope. Dattarti explains:

> The film was taken up by the Wildlife Protection Society of India in Dehli and the Wildlife Protection society of Orissa, and although the solutions are quite simple the situation is quite complex – there are a lot of stakeholders involved, a lot of livelihoods involved and a lot of money is being made from the seafood export trade and a lot of powerful people including politicians and ministers own a lot of the boats. They are basically refusing to do anything. They are refusing to use turtle excluder devices in their boats, they don't want to stay away from certain no fishing zones and because there is no enforcement, even though there are some extremely good laws, nothing is happening with the Ridleys. (interview 26th April 2009)

The Last Dance (2006), a short emotive film made by Ashima Narain with funds secured from the British High Commission and British Council's Environmental Film Fellowship scheme, explores the illegal practice of bear dancing. The theme of the film fellowships was wildlife crimes, and an arrangement had already been made for the winning films to be shown on the Discovery Channel. The push to emphasise the conservation angle came largely from the British Council, although Narain argues that conservation cannot be addressed in isolation from the economics of development. The sloth bear has been a protected species in India since the Wildlife Protection Act of 1972, but these and other animals have been used by Kalandars for centuries to eke out a living by providing entertainment to village people and occasionally now to tourists. The story is a simple one. A sloth bear cub is captured by poachers, the mother is killed and the cub is sold to a Kalandar who then removes its canine teeth, drives an iron needle through its muzzle in order to pull a rope through so the animal can be led, tethered and restrained while beaten into submission. All this is conveyed graphically in dramatic reconstructions that make the viewer wince by facilitating his/her identification with the pain of the young animal. The film then cuts to actualité shots of dancing bears in action, villagers watching and their owners continuously prodding the animals to jump and perform.

However, Ashima Narain makes it clear that the Kalandars are not totally to blame, for it is partly their culture but more importantly their economic circumstances that have enabled this practice to continue. Kalandars are a poor nomadic Muslim group likened frequently to Europe's gypsy community, and officially categorised as a 'backward tribe' by the Indian government; without aid and education they have little opportunity to make a living in any other way. The work of a local NGO, Wildlife SOS, is featured in the film working closely with one Kalandar who decides to give his bear to a local sanctuary in return for 70,000 rupees compensation supplied by the government that will help him to buy an auto-rickshaw and make his family more economically secure. The message is positive, and the relationship between the socioeconomic circumstances of poor communities and wildlife conservation is addressed clearly and distinctly. As the narrator says in the English language version, "By rehabilitating both the Kalandar community and their animals, the wildlife crime is being tackled holistically." The problems are multi-dimensional and the solution matches this, as the bears, the Kalandars and indeed the poachers have all to be rehabilitated. The film is therefore a mix of factual presentation and emotive imagery but, as Ashima Narain recognises, there are other issues.

We have so many different dimensions to the audience in India which are demarcated by language, economics and geography. In India we are Eastern but within the Eastern there are also the English-speaking and the tribal peoples. I say the bears are treated very cruelly, so the immediate reaction is: "So you'd rather save a bear and make a man starve," but then you say there is also rehabilitation of the Kalandar and then they are willing to listen. You have to educate the educated. In India there is this very patronising feeling that people who aren't speaking English, or who are in the forests, are not us. But they are us and I will try to reach out to these people first as they are within my range of accessibility, my mental and cultural framework. This film is really meant for the urban audience. (interview 21st October 2008)

Religion is not referred to at all in the film. For Narain, religion is irrelevant to the economic and environmental issues being addressed, and its mention would divert audience attention from them. It would also be irresponsible for someone in the media to mention it – "There is too much communal disrespect." However, for animal rights campaigner and politician Maneka Gandhi, daughter-in-law of the former Prime Minister Indira Gandhi, religious affiliation is a factor in the continuing mistreatment of sloth bears. She told an Australian interviewer, "Because they are poached by a minority community, the Muslims, everyone was reluctant to create a situation where they would respond not as the criminals they are but as 'Muslims' being hard done by. In fact all the illegal street entertainment animals – the snakes, monkeys, bears, birds – are run by Muslims in India." (Vaughan, n.d.)

As Ashima Narain's short film shows, complex issues and messages can be communicated simply, intelligently and engagingly without compromising their importance. By addressing the viewers' emotional and intuitive intelligence, ideas and images may go beyond both politics and religion by drawing out and channelling the empathy of one sentient creature for another, sharing their experience of pain, suffering and hardship. This empathic experience is a pivotal point in the transformative learning of the viewer to become an engaged environmental citizen. Fortunately, in December 2009 International Animal Rescue announced the successful end of a seven-year campaign to rescue India's 600 dancing bears when the last dancing bear was given to a sanctuary, the 40-acre Banarghatta Biological Park near Bangalore, by its impoverished owner in return for compensation and retraining.

Turtles in the Soup, a film by Kalpan Subramanian and also produced through the British Council's UK Environmental Film Fellowship, explores the threat to the freshwater turtle by human development, poverty and poaching. Turtles are scavengers, and keep the waterways clean and this the film's narrator suggests is perhaps why they have been considered sacred. They too are a protected species. Nonetheless, poor communities hunt them as a source of cheap food, but the biggest threat to Indian fresh water turtles is from China, where an almost insatiable demand for their meat and cartilage in food and medicine is fuelling a lucrative and illegal trade. Subramanian uses footage taken with a hidden camera of turtles being weighed, killed, dismembered and boiled. These images are intercut with long takes of some small animals crawling slowly over heavily laden canvas sacks waiting to be shipped abroad. There are one or two shots of a turtle placed on it back, its underside exposed and its legs moving helplessly and forlornly. These images capture the viewers' attention through presenting a sense of vulnerability, fear, helplessness and incomprehension. *Turtles in the Soup* is just twelve minutes long, and tries to end on a positive note showing the work of conservationists, of turtles swimming serenely in a river and young ones crawling jerkily over the sand towards the freedom of the stream. The images and commentary play on each other and the emotional pull is strong, but Kalpan Subramanian recognised that to achieve this with an animal such as the turtle would not necessarily be straightforward. She said:

> Throughout the process of the making the film everybody kept saying, 'How are you going to get the viewers to relate to this animal, how are they going to feel for it?' They are reptiles. They are not cuddly or furry, they don't make cute noise, they don't even move. It is hard to express through its body language what it is going through. It was a visual challenge. In Indian culture there are polarities. People have always worshipped turtles and always exploited turtles. . . . Making them [the audience] feel is very important, but thinking and feeling is just one thing isn't it? One has to feel otherwise one is being selfish. . . . When you are out there filming with the animal in the wild you suddenly realise it's much bigger than anything. It's much bigger than the film you are making or the producer who has financed the film or the audience watching it. In the end you have this guilt tripping conscience . . . it's humbling. I know a lot of film-makers who are giving up making big budget films and are working to help grassroots agencies. (Kalpan Subramanian, interview 23rd October 2008)

The film has been shown in schools and at grassroots level as an education and training resource in India, but whether it or similar films could play sympathetically in China or other parts of south-east Asia is something that Kalpan Subramanian and many other wildlife film-makers seriously doubt:

> Somehow we always make films, even in India, to the lowest common denominator which would be the American audience, and we have to work to satisfy the American audience no matter where we are. This does influence the kind of film-making, and it would be interesting to see how the films would change if we started looking at Chinese audiences for example. I have a feeling that if

a Chinese audience was watching my film, they might be wondering 'I have not tried that one. I'd like to try it.' I would love to address the Chinese audience. I have shown it to Chinese friends and people I know. This type of film would not communicate to a Chinese audience in the way it would communicate to a Western audience. A different approach would be required. India has these eth-ical values and China has its own ethical values and its a question of cultural preference. (Kalpan Subramanian, interview 23rd October 2008)

To overcome this problem Kalpan Subramanian has suggested that a pos-sible experiment could involve the same conservation issue being addressed by film-makers from three different cultures. In this way, the cultural preferences and sensitivities of their specific audience could be built into the production from the earliest stages. Similar small-scale experiments have been conducted by both Wildscreen and the BBC, and they have indicated that different cul-tural inflections do manifest themselves in the mode of storytelling, sound design and in the visual aesthetic (Nimmo, 2009; Nightingale, 2009). Pro-ducer Robert Lamb, who initiated the long running *Earth Report* series for Television for the Environment, made sure that a number of these pro-grammes were translated into Chinese so they could be screened on Channels 10 and 11. However, during an interview (18.5.09) he admitted, "What impact they had, I just don't know."

Xi Zhinong is one of the few film-makers and photographers in China whose work focuses on conservation. His interest in wildlife photography came about when as a nineteen-year-old he was employed as an assistant on a film where the cinematographer tied the legs of newly hatch chicks to the nest in order to get a good shot. He didn't untie them, and a little later Xi found them all dead. This formative experience led Xi to form China's first – and so far only – wildlife film and photographic agency, Wild China Films. He and his wife have used their photographs and films of the endangered snub-nosed monkey in Yunnan province, an area subject to heavy tree felling and habitat clearance, to lobby for a ban on the logging of the old growth forest. He has also used his photographs to campaign against the large-scale poach-ing of antelopes in Tibet, and has been quoted by CCTV (2008) as saying:

I have long believed in the power of images. The expression in the eyes of the mother golden monkey when she looks at her baby is so touching. I believe images like this can inspire and move many people. And with such inspira-tion, people can take action to protect the wildlife and the environment. Sometimes you get the feeling you can't shoot pictures fast enough to keep up with the speed of species' extinction and environmental damage. The severe consequences of global warming, such as glacier melting and desertification, are fatal to wildlife.

His work on the golden monkey has been featured in a 2002 documentary commissioned by Chinese Television, *Searching for the Yunnan Snub-nosed Monkey*. The film documents researchers' long and patient search to locate and observe the elusive monkeys, whose slow reproductive cycle and limited lichen diet makes them highly vulnerable to habitat destruction.

China is a country not known for its sympathetic attitudes to wildlife, and economic development is placing serious strains on the ecosystems in many areas. Wildlife photography is also fairly undeveloped in China. Although China does show natural history programming from Animal Planet, Discovery and even some investigative environmental documentaries from Television for the Environment's *Earth Report* series, these are imported and few Chinese nature magazines are able to hire Chinese photographers. The question of culture is also extremely important. Animal welfare is not a high priority in China and many conservation and other organisations have attacked China for its appalling cruelty to animals, desperately inadequate conditions in many zoos, the use of parts from seriously endangered animals in traditional medicine and its heavy involvement in wildlife crime, poaching and trafficking in India and Africa as well as in China itself. The Chinese eat animals which are totally taboo in the West: cats are very popular, especially in southern China; dogs are a popular dish in many parts of China, and dog restaurants are very common in the capital city, Beijing. Many Chinese believe that eating dog helps to keeps the body warm in the cold winter months. Yang et al's (2007) attitude surveys in Hunan Province indicate a very low level of conservation awareness, although following the impact of the SARS virus and bird flu epidemics the authors detected some change in attitudes towards consuming wildlife. Animal welfare science has a very short history in China too, but there are other signs that at least among the younger generation of more affluent and educated Chinese more sympathetic attitudes to animal welfare are beginning to emerge (Davey & Higgins, 2005; Davey, 2006). In an interview with *New Scientist* magazine, conservation scientists and photographer Lu Zhi, Director of the Center for Nature and Society at Peking University, told Phil McKenna (2009) that as China develops economically two trends seem to be emerging as regards attitudes to the environment:

For instance, a group of young Chinese entrepreneurs [ALXA SEE Ecological Association] is calling for an end to the consumption of shark fin soup. But there is also a rise in the number of affluent people who want to show off their wealth. Eating wildlife is a part of Chinese culture, so when people get richer they eat more wildlife. They need something to persuade them. I think culture is the most effective tool. A respect for life is part of the Buddhist tradition, which has had a big influence on Chinese culture, though sometimes people forget it.

In September 2009 Chinese officials announced its first ever animal protection law had been drafted in order to deal with animal abuse and desertion. It led to considerable public discussion (Shigong, 2009).

Beyond the blue chip

Just as there is no single audience in India or anywhere else, there is also no single universal 'nature' of the type fictionalised in natural history blue chip films, nor any definitive evidence that they do anything other than provide modestly edifying entertainment. The Indian films attempt to reevaluate our assumptions about the overwhelming importance of human society by highlighting the significance of what economic development and urbanisation are doing to the environment. The conservationist message is often communicated as part of an overall approach that philosophically locates *homo sapiens* as one of many life forms inhabiting the planet, and only more important than others because of the damage it is doing. These film's are neither Darwinist nor teleological, pure spectacle or pure entertainment; neither are they doom-laden or depressing, and although certain religious references are sometimes used as a means of conveying a broader ecological sensitivity, information and data produced by scientists and NGOs are offered too. As Mike Pandey says, "Whatever religion we are, we all need the environment, we all need sustainability." It is this overarching need that comes through most strongly in both the individual films and when viewed within a series. Their aim is to nurture an ecological awareness and an ecological identity (Thomashow, 1996) within viewers by facilitating an identification with these other sentient creatures, their wants and needs, loves and fears, pain and hardships. The source of their fulfillment is ultimately the same as our own. Where those viewers are close to their local ecosystems, as are the Orissa fisherfolk, then an ecological identity may be retrieved. Where viewers are more distant, then the aim becomes one of fashioning new or alternative perspectives, meaning schemes and cognitive frameworks with which to interpret the world and so fashion an ecological identity for the first time. Either way, the aim is essentially educative, going beyond the attraction of seeing nature in slow motion but not discounting the power of film or television or imaging more generally as a way into people's hearts and minds.

Natural history films from other cultures add to the diversity and richness of what and how the environment and the creatures within it are seen and understood. Many of these are screened at film festivals and some find their way on to the internet, but relatively few find their way on to the mainstream commercial global media networks. This is a pity because such films say much about cultures that viewers in the West know little about – beyond the obvious and not necessarily accurate headlines. *Irani Wildlife*, made for Iranian public television and shown at peak time on Channel One in 2006-2007, where it became the channel's second most popular programme, attempts to do just this. The series was made by Mani Mirsadeghi, a film-maker, photographer and founder of the Iranian environmental NGO 'Blue Awareness'. He explores the lives and behaviours of Iranian wildlife with a visually poetic aesthetic using slow dissolves, plenty of sky shots, slow pans of landscapes and mountains, local music and many close-ups and tracking shots of birds and mammals. There are sequences without words and when the verse commentary comes in, phrases like the "magic of life" and "a sign and symbol to the eyes of the wise" shape the emotional texture and tone.

Irani Wildlife is the story of life itself, through which the viewer is invited to review the significance of having or lacking an ecological identity. Unlike many natural history films made in the West, the star of the show is not the presenter, a scientist, a conservationist-hero, the featured animal or perhaps most significantly the technical brilliance of the film-maker. The hero is the Iranian wildlife, and parts of Mirsadeghi's films have been seen by government officials and members of the Iranian Parliament to inform and raise awareness among decision-makers as to the importance of conservation. Sometimes he makes short specialist films for the Department of the Environment to develop conservation awareness and understanding that could inform appropriate policymaking on such issues as protected areas. Feedback on his films from the Iranian general public has been very positive, but his films – like so many other films made by film-makers in the developing world – are rarely seen outside their home countries. He says (interview 25th October 2008):

> I try to put my feelings in my art, inside my films, to try to open up the small windows to show something of Iran. International distributors say 'We have David Attenborough, we have Discovery Channel, National Geographic, we don't need your films.' They never see it, they never come to see my footage. It is very complicated, very hard. You can see my film at Wildscreen.

Chapter Five

Image, truth and the imagination

If you see an image of a single polar bear on an ice floe, it may simply show a bear stuck on an ice floe. Or, that bear may signify the endangered predicament of that particular species of which it is a member; or, the image as a whole may be a visual metaphor for global warming. Where and how that image is seen is important too: the visual coding, when resonating with context, offers a sharper meaning. Thus the way in which the photographic image is composed – its form, shape, colour, line, angle, focus, identifiable representations of the world outside itself – establishes a certain visual rhetoric that may in certain circumstances effectively guide the viewer's understanding of the meaning (Barthes, 1977). The still image invites exploration in a number of ways: as an image – and if encountered in a book, magazine or art gallery – as a material object. The image will in part be defined by what that book, newspaper or art gallery is purporting to do, is engaged with, is itself related to, as well as its relation to a range of other cultural artifacts, processes, ideas, feelings, discourses, institutions and meanings. The truth value of any particular image is therefore relational, which includes these other cultural artifacts as well as the manner in which the image was composed, created, framed or otherwise manipulated. In his discussion of photographic meaning, Allan Sekula (1982) likens a photograph to a type of utterance that carries or is actually a message. This message, however, depends on an external matrix of conditions and presuppositions for it to be understood or 'read'. In other words, the meaning of any photographic utterance is determined by its cultural context and its association with a range of linguistic propositions that turn images into words, arguments, suggestions, concepts or connotations. Visual literacy encompasses this range of cultural relationships, which means that there is no single, intrinsic or universal meaning to a photographic image. For Sekula, any meaningful encounter with a photograph inevitably occurs at the level of connotation – implication, intimation, association, suggestion and so on. Every photographic image is therefore a sign of something else, something that is in the photograph but not the photograph itself. Every photographic image is characterised by a certain visual rhetoric that organises these signs and suggests possible meanings and interpretations. Photography in the public sphere also tends to veer between two simultaneously opposing and complementary poles: between photography as witness, as reportage, as empirical truth, and photography as expression, as imagination, as art. A photographic image can also veer between metaphoric signification (a symbol of something else, or a transposition of qualities from one thing to another) and metonymic signification (where the part or a single example stands for the whole, the genus or species).

Any interpretation will depend on social and cultural values, but also the visual codes the viewer is familiar with. These codes may relate to style, a certain premise or an identifiable message. When Jane Goodall walks into the sunset in the final shot of *Miss Goodall and the Wild Chimpanzees*, or when the camera shows a lion baring its fangs, usually accompanied by suitable sound effects or music, the sense is generally clear: the end of a long and meaningful time in the forest and the power, majesty and ferocity of nature as symbolised by the 'king' of the beasts. It is also important to remember that photographs and moving images are usually two-dimensional. The animal depicted is rarely of the same size as it would be in actuality, or indeed the same colour. You certainly would be unable to smell it, although there could easily be visual hints in that direction. The Soviet film director Sergei Eisenstein, working in the silent era, developed an editing technique that suggested the aural. He spoke of visual sound. One of Picasso's patrons complained to the artist that his cubist portrait of his wife looked nothing like the woman in real life. "Well, what does she look like then?" The client pulled a photograph of the woman from his wallet. "Oh," said Picasso, "I didn't realise she was so small." What constitutes a realistic image for the viewer is a product of the set of visual codes which are generally agreed to represent the real, as well as the range of institutions that endorse them as being so, and may, in the process, reproduce or subtly alter them over time. National Geographic, for example, deploys a range of visual codes that combine ideas and presuppositions of 'photographic quality' with ideological assumptions of scientific and educative integrity. National Geographic's approach to nature and the developing world is now where the positive, the good, the beautiful tends to take precedence over the the ugly or the politically controversial (Lutz and Collins, 1993). Similarly, the Sierra Club series of coffee table nature/wildlife books comprising the Book of the Month Club, initiated by David Brower in 1960, posited consumption as a form of environmental politics and images of the sublime as a way of motivating action for environmental reform. Brower, founder of the Sierra Club and later Friends of the Earth and the Earth Island Institute, believed in the power of images to fashion awareness and attitudes to conservation that would in some way translate into action. With *This is the American Earth* exhibition and the spin-off Sierra Club book series, photographer Ansel Adams and his wife and picture editor Nancy Newhall produced awesome and fascinating black and white images of the natural world:

> . . . as emblems of memory, as reminders of primordial nature. Trying to remember, they also forgot; through words and images, they evoked the idea of a peopleless wilderness, an idea grounded in amnesia, in forgetting of human interaction with the land. . . . The book aimed to represent reality, to reveal an authentic world of wilderness. Displayed on coffee tables around the nation, it promised subversive elegance, tasteful dissent from a culture of artifice. (Dunaway, 2005: 147)

In some ways this approach is also enshrined in many highly expensive blue chip films and similar book projects today that are produced by conservation organisations and their sympathetic financial backers. Such images may be said to place an idealistic and ideological frame on the public's perception of what the natural world is 'really like'. There are certain truth claims inherent in the glossy image that are emotive and imaginary, but are also subject to challenge in what philosopher Michel Foucault termed the "general politics of truth". Media organisations, logging companies, NGOs, conservation activists, governments, TV viewers, bushmeat eaters, community groups and universities are all in some way embroiled in this politics that determines what words and images count as true or are believed to be such. Foucault (1980: 131) stated in an interview:

> The important thing here, I believe, is that truth isn't outside power, or lacking in power: contrary to a myth whose history and functions would repay further study, truth isn't the reward of free spirits, the child of protracted solitude, nor the privilege of those who have succeeded in liberating themselves. Truth is a thing of this world: it is produced only by virtue of multiple forms of constraint. And it induces regular effects of power. Each society has its regime of truth, its 'general politics' of truth: that is, the types of discourse which it accepts and makes function as true and false statements, the means by which each is sanctioned; the techniques and procedures accorded value in the acquisition of truth; the status of those who are charged with saying what counts as true.

As academic critic John Tagg (1982: 131) writes, "This takes us back to the nature and function of representation."

The truth about whaling

Many conservation and animal welfare issues revolve around truth claims, supposed scientific evidence or justification, and the emotive and intellectual power of still and moving images. The controversies surrounding the International Whaling Commission's (IWC) 1982 moratorium on the commercial hunting of whales illustrates how various discourses, policy proposals, moral philosophies and emotional appeals intersect with crude financial interest, concern over the future existence of a number of iconic and highly endangered species, and the actual welfare of those remaining. In the interests of 'scientific research' and human entertainment, Japan still hunts, captures and/or slaughters whales and dolphins in large numbers. Iceland and Norway are also ardent supporters of whaling. *Whale Hunters* (2002), an investigative documentary film made by Jeremy Bristow at the BBC Natural History Unit, focuses on how Japanese whaling interests have exploited a clause in the IWC's moratorium allowing the hunting of whales for scientific research purposes. Opponents suggest that this scientific research is largely bogus and that the hunting is designed purely to provide a lifeline to a threatened national industry which developed substantially in the years following World War Two. It was then imperative that sufficient protein could be made available to a devastated people, but outside a few small coastal areas whaling was before that time of only historical minor significance. Whaling is not, as such, part of Japan's national heritage. Today the meat of those whales killed for science is sold as food on the open market, and critics have suggested that the scientific research that is undertaken is designed to provide evidence that could be used to justify the resumption of commercial whaling (Hirata, 2005). Little of the research is aimed to help conserve existing stocks of minke, sperm and other whales, but like climate change the politics of whaling science is both highly important and politically contentious.

Some Japanese people, particularly in urban areas, no longer eat whale or dolphin meat (both cetaceans) and tend to agree with conservationists that these beautiful and intelligent creatures need protection. However, there are cultural factors that suggest the persistence of the Japanese pro-whaling position is less to do with finance and more to do with the perceive cultural imperialism of former whaling nations in the West attempting to impose their cultural norms on Japan. Japanese pro-whalers view whales as constituting part of their national cuisine, as part of their heritage and significant as a fish rather than as a mammal. The Japanese, like many Westerners, have less affection for fish than for warm-blooded creatures, and the Japanese national diet has traditionally been dominated by seafood. Anti-whaling campaigns in Japan are also quite mute and relatively small-scale as compared with those elsewhere, although aquaria and dolphinaria display captive cetaceans providing entertainments that have gone some way to enhance public appreciation and emotional attachment to these animals among some younger Japanese. Arne Kalland (1993), a Norwegian researcher, argues that anti-whaling campaigners have created a false understanding of whales, fashioning a popular notion of a 'superwhale' – a single animal that is a composite: one that nurtures, has a big brain, lives in human like societies, has language, nurtures its young, babysits, looks after its sick, has an ancient lineage and so on. Whales are 'like us' and so have become a modern urban totem, a metonym for nature, a political and ethical symbol, with whalers cast as enemies of the environment. Kalland concludes (1993: 6):

> The anti-whaling campaign is an ideal issue for national governments and polluting industries to support. Being of only marginal economic importance – and in most countries of no importance at all – whaling is a 'safe' issue and there is hardly anything to lose by joining the crowd. The rewards in terms of 'green images' are, on the other hand, substantial. The anti-whaling campaigns, therefore, offer governments and industries an opportunity to show their consideration for the environment, while at the same time they have proved excellent fund-raisers for the environmental and animal rights movements. By giving support to the super-whale myth, companies and governments have acquired 'green' legitimacy (and partial immunity) while the movements have got political legitimacy in return. It is, perhaps, not coincidental that some of the nations most vehemently opposed to whaling (and sealing and elephant hunting for that matter) are among the nations with the poorest records when it comes to international co-operation to combat acid rain, global heating and destruction of the ozone layer.

The public debates, discussions, books, articles, films, protests, cultural festivals around whales and whaling, heritage and myths have certainly kept the relationship between human beings and nature on the international agenda and have to some extent helped those promoting more ecocentric worldviews or "earth identity claims" (Stoett, 2005: 173). Indigenous peoples such as the Inuit are allowed to hunt because whaling is a historical part of their cultural identity. The 1960s US television series and feature film spin-off *Flipper* has also fed this attitude. The highly effective Save the Whale media campaign, waged by Greenpeace International in the 1980s and 1990s, fuelled both widespread disgust and disapproval of the cruel, violent and frequently bloody whaling practices and a demand, certainly among Western nations, for all whaling to be banned irrespective of whether stocks would permit 'sustainable harvesting' or not (Dale,1996; De Luca, 1999). The now classic, highly newsworthy and telegenic images of Greenpeace activists confronting and being attacked by Japanese whalers, of bloodied whales being harpooned and dragged into the bowels of factory ships or being cut into once on board have been used by many news agencies and documentary film-makers including Jeremy Bristow himself. In *Whale Hunters*, the provenance of still or moving images which have not been shot by the BBC crew are acknowledged with a caption: either as Greenpeace footage or that of the Institute of Cetacean Research. In this way the images are presented as being ideological, as derived from and used by campaigning bodies to promote a partial point of view. By contrast, Bristow's investigative telejournalism is structured in such a way as to offer a sense of balance, of objective analysis of differing perspectives and approaches to the controversial issues at hand.

Whale Hunters is not a campaigning film, nor does it present an authored or personal view. The narrator is anonymous (although named of course among the credits) and only rarely is an off-screen voice heard asking an interviewee a question or making an interjection. The issues discussed by many academic commentators are identified and explored during the programme's narrative journey – cultural tradition, national pride, vested commercial interests, conservationist tactics, the politics of the IWC, the influence of the media and public relations, bribery and so on. However this objectivity, like that of academic scientists, is only objective within a particular framework of values, principles or regime of truth. Immediately following some *vox pop* interviews in a restaurant serving whale, Bristow cuts to some Greenpeace footage of a dead or dying whale turning over in the ocean, about to be hoisted tail-first on to a whaling ship. The documentary then cuts to a publicity video produced by the pro-whaling Institute for Cetacean Research – whose research, the narrator notes, has been criticised as irrelevant and unnecessary. The narrator draws the viewer to attend closely to the nature of the images in the publicity film. The research is conducted "in meticulous detail, in entirely bloodless surroundings". The viewer is therefore lead to read the images and the truth claims of the Institute's major spokesman in the documentary, Dr Seiji Ohsumi, as essentially ideological, of serving a particular interest, of articulating a certain version of 'the truth'. Similarly, just as it may be difficult to deny that Greenpeace is taking and using images of whale slaughter to further its own campaigns, it is difficult to deny that these images are indeed true on at least one level. The whales are dead, or bleeding and they are clearly, and understandably, distressed if still alive. These whale images are not only metonyms for nature: they symbolise humanity's continuing cruelty and wanton destruction of both an important marine species and possibly whole marine ecosystems. In another sequence, Dr Ohsumi is seen showing photographs of the fish contents of whale stomachs to the BBC camera. The logical conclusion, based on the evidence of these images presented in Dr Ohsumi's well-designed Institute brochure, is that whale appetites are denuding important fish stocks necessary for the commercial and nutritional health of the Japanese nation. The *Whale Hunters* audience is now predisposed to question the truth claims of Dr Ohsumi's images – that is, Dr Ohsumi is indeed showing photographs of the contents of whale stomachs that are not in any way doctored or manipulated or enhanced and therefore questionable in that regard. However, they are presented as a constituent part of the pro-whaling discourse and PR campaign which is politically illegitimate and morally suspect as the intention is plainly to deceive. The narrator suggests, over images of whales swimming in the deep blue sea, that these animals actually tend to eat fish such as krill which humans do not, and the decline in fish stocks is not so much due to whale populations increasing but more to the human fishing industry extracting too much from the oceans. As Gerber et al (2009: 881) state in the journal *Science*:

> Today, the majority of fish stocks and many whale populations are seriously depleted, but most available evidence points toward human over-exploitation as the root of the problem. When developing tropical countries are encouraged to focus on the notion that 'whales eat fish,' they risk being diverted from addressing the real problems that their own fisheries face, primarily, over-exploitation of their marine resources by distant-water fleets.

The truth value of Bristow's own footage of the Institute's still-image-based evidence is not questioned by the narrative trajectory of the programme or the scientific evidence recited. What the film shows is real at the denotive level, but their meaning, what the images themselves connote, is not so simple. Consequently, the balance and objectivity of *Whale Hunters* is coded aesthetically rather than politically, and this could itself be challenged by viewers approaching the film from a pro-whaling interpretative framework. The evidential force of the image, as John Tagg (1993; 2009) has written, is a burden of representation and the meaning conveyed is subject to the violence of many potentially competing discourses and institutional power-plays – IWC, Greenpeace, Japanese Fisheries Agencies, academic researchers, BBC producers, pro-whaling and anti-whaling lobby groups as well as moral, scientific, financial and cultural interventions.

Another sequence towards the end of *Whale Hunters* shows Mr Masayuki Komatsu of the Japanese Fisheries Agency, Dr Ohsumi, the captain of the Institute's research/whaling vessel and some other pro-whaling people at a reception in Nagato celebrating a recent PR success. They are standing in a semi-circle facing the camera drinking beer and conversing unguardedly about the politics of whaling. Mr Komatsu asks the captain if he had seen much of Greenpeace this year. The weather had been good was the reply. "Let's get good equipment next year. When they approach," (the camera zooms into a head and shoulders shot as Mr Komatsu turns his gaze away from his companions to the film crew and producer) "blow them out of the water." He reaches up to his right, hits the off-screen microphone, and says jokingly, "That was one for the microphone." He continues suggesting that what would be good would be to use tear gas "because if they can't open their eyes, they can't do anything. They are wasting their money disturbing us. Why don't they count whales instead? . . . . they just want to make money." This candid moment is captured in one take with the camera jerkily zooming in and out, panning side to side, in one continuous sequence of nearly three minutes. The discussion then turns to the IWC negotiations where Mr Komatsu uses the following terms – "dummies", "stupid", "they don't really intend to negotiate", "don't understand the diversity of the world", "we just tell them what we are going to do". . . . This remarkably indiscreet conversation undermines whatever case the Japanese pro-whalers had presented to documentary film-makers, and its placing in the documentary effectively serves as the conclusion to Bristow's investigation. The veracity of this image event is not intended to be doubted by the viewer, as its preferred meaning is rooted in the crafted filmic discourse that is quite unsupportive of the Japanese position. As Jeremy Bristow said, the BBC has to be balanced and impartial over a period but it doesn't necessarily have to be within an individual programme. The interesting issue here is, as Bristow recalled (interview, 8.4.09):

> [*Whale Hunters*] tried to let the Japanese do most of the speaking, and I think I managed to have entirely Japanese speakers in the film. It was allowing the Japanese to try to explain themselves and to explain to us why they carry on whaling but they didn't put their best arguments forward. I kept feeding them questions, saying: 'We in Europe eat beef and look at how the cattle are kept. Is that any different or better? Whales are free range.' I gave them the opportunity . . . . This is where the current affairs documentary side comes up. They were just God's gift. They had those loudspeaker vans going round, like something out of George Orwell, and they sank themselves with spurious science. . . . My inclination because of my background is to find out who is the guilty party and why are they lying to us, whereas in natural history it is how do we get the animals, and never mind that nuclear power station that's being built next door.

Whale Hunters has not been shown in Japan, and the Japanese have continued to lobby for the abandoning of the moratorium. They have enlisted the support of other nations, often poor states from the developing world grateful for Japanese financial aid, to join the IWC and vote with them for a restoration of commercial whaling. *The Cove* (2009), directed by former National Geographic photographer Louie Psihoyos, addresses Japanese whaling practices from an animal welfare perspective, concentrating on the capture of dolphins for use in aquatic leisure complexes across the globe and the brutal slaughter of thousands of others for food. Screened at the Foreign Correspondents Club in Tokyo in September 2009 and the Tokyo International Film Festival in October, after initially rejecting it as too controversial, newspaper reports suggest many Japanese were astonished at what they saw (Tabuchi, 2009). *The Cove* won the 2010 Oscar for best documentary feature together with 46 other film awards which has enabled it to gain considerable publicity for the anti-whaling and marine conservation cause. Indeed *The Cove*, perhaps because of its Hollywood status and ability to tap into a range of cultural sensitivities, has done more to publicise the gruesome nature of Japanese drive hunts than ten years of campaigning by the WDCS (Whale and Dolphin Conservation Society), whose own short film *Driven by Demand* is both less exciting and visually less revealing. Like *Whale Hunters*, *The Cove* deals with truth claims, politics and the veracity of the image in a contested regime of truth, but opens out into a deeper contemplation of humanity's harmful effects on planetary ecosystems and a philosophical meditation on what it actually means to be human. Aesthetically, *The Cove* adopts the format of a Hollywood heist movie rather than of an abstracted essay-film that characterises many reflective art movies. The human-hero element is provided by Ric O'Barry, who in the early 1960s created the *Flipper* TV series. He trained the dolphins who 'played' Flipper to perform for the camera, and the popularity of the series, as the now quite elderly O'Barry says, led to the amazing growth of dolphinaria and other similar entertainments across the world. However, O'Barry's epiphany came when one of his dolphins died in his arms. He called it suicide, for dolphins are intelligent and sensitive mammals who cannot cope with the strict regimen, loud noises and physical restrictions imposed by captivity, the leisure business and the television production business: they become stressed, ulcerated and often simply die. Since that moment O'Barry has dedicated his life to freeing dolphins wherever he could and campaigning against their use as human entertainments, their capture for money and, more dramatically, their slaughter for human – largely Japanese – cuisine.

The Cove follows a highly expert team of activists enlisted to gain footage of the annual dolphin slaughter at Taiji on the coast of Japan. Taiji is a small town whose fishermen can earn up to $150,000 for a live dolphin for the entertainment business and around $600 for a dead one which goes to the food market. For 96 minutes the documentary film shows the team's preparation and planning, encounters with hostile Japanese fisherman and discussions with unhelpful, duplicitous officials. The slaughter of many hundreds of dolphins has never before been filmed, and O'Barry believes if images of this slaughter can be captured then they will undermine, and hopefully destroy, this cruel unnecessary practice. O'Barry and his team consequently invest great belief in the emotive power, persuasive charge and undeniable truth value of what will be covertly shot high-quality images of beautiful creatures being brutally killed in a secluded lagoon within an idyllic coastal environment. Apart from the ethical animal welfare and conservation issues, O'Barry reinforces his case by arguing that the dolphins themselves are contaminated with mercury and the meat sold openly in Japanese markets is harmful to human health. The memory of the Minimata mercury poisoning scandal in the 1950s and 1960s surrounding the Chisso Corporation's denial of wrongdoing is evoked. The documentary photographs of horrifically deformed children taken by W. Eugene Smith in 1971 and the attack on him by Chisso employees are a pre-echo of O'Barry's action and faith in the capacity of the image to reveal truth, change minds and affect positive change.

Digital moving image cameras are placed in the lagoon itself and around the cliffs, carefully camouflaged by a material that resembles the local rock. Thermal image cameras are used to shoot footage at night, and these black and white digital negatives add both aesthetic interest and dramatic tension to the narrative. The key scene is the slaughter itself, which occurs over an hour into the picture and lasts for only four minutes. The dolphins are driven by fishing boats, making for dolphins unbearably painful noises, from the open sea into a large bay where the healthiest animals are taken for sale to the global leisure industry. The rest are later corralled by nets into a smaller, very secluded lagoon to be harpooned or clubbed by fisherman standing in open boats. The underwater camera captures the blue water turning red as dolphin blood drifts down from the water's surface. The whole screen turns red. A baby dolphin is seen from a distance hurling itself against some rocks as its pod are systematically destroyed by fisherman who see the activity as just a job. They are, however, like many government and industry officials, acutely sensitive to how any image-based publicity could impact upon this highly lucrative income stream. The DVD commentary has the director and producer talking over the images – the slaughter is the 'money shot', but self-censorship and restraint is clearly evident in the selection and editing of this image sequence.

Compared with the footage not shown and the experience of bearing witness, the commentators refer to the slaughter montage as "like Disney", and like Disney the film immediately cuts to live dolphins swimming energetically and freely in the oceans. From this horror sequence the film transforms itself briefly into a dream-like fantasy as a way of reinforcing, of seeing and feeling, the moral message and as preparation for the next scenes, which see O'Barry entering the conference room of an IWC meeting with a flatscreen monitor fastened to his chest displaying images of the slaughter. Dolphins are not protected by the IWC, even though they are cetaceans and their slaughter is endangering their survival (Vail and Risch, 2006), with – the film-makers claim – up to 23,000 dolphins and porpoises being killed by Japan in 2007 alone. News cameras hone in immediately as the delegates glance as the screen. O'Barry is swiftly and firmly led out of the auditorium. Another scene shows O'Barry standing in a busy Tokyo street one evening, the neon lights a pointed contrast to the slaughter images being displayed on his chest. The time-lapse photography has the pedestrians whizz by but one, two and then a small group stop, form a semi-circle around him to look more closely at what is there. The group's stillness symbolises the frenetic nature of the city, which may perhaps be taken as an oblique comment on the dolphin slaughter itself. Who, and how many people, have the time, interest or inclination to know or to care? If many Japanese were unaware or cared little about both the dolphins' slaughter and 'dolphin sentience', then many people in Britain, France, USA and other nations feel the same about the slaughter of cows, chickens and pigs, as Tracy Worcester's *The Pig Business* (2009) demonstrates. The *New York Times* (Tabuchi, 2009) quotes Professor Tetsu Sato of Nagano University as saying, "The feeling here is that the world needs to respect cultural differences. Why should there even be a debate on this issue?" The same argument can be read in Komatsu and Misaki's *The Truth Behind the Whaling Dispute*, published in 2001 by the Japan Whaling Association. What *The Cove*, as a film, demonstrates is possibly two things. First, the meaning and impact of a film or indeed a photograph are dependent on context, including the discourses, public/media debates and political campaigning surrounding it; and secondly, the capacity of the image to directly and physically link what is seen and represented with what is in some ways actually out there. There has been no suggestion by anyone, anywhere, that the slaughter images were faked or manipulated except, as to be expected, temporally compressed through the editing process according to established cinematic and documentary conventions. As many image theorists and neuroscientists have suggested, knowledge is gained through vision and the image, the likeness, is apprehended by the brain at a preconscious or unconscious level and is affective, and effective, at that level. This can lead to an intuitive knowledge and understanding or as Michael Gazzinga (1998: 63) notes, "The brain knows before you do"; but the sense made of it is the product of social action, social constructions, of social sensitivities, of being in society. What is significant here is that these decisive images, like those of Mike Pandey's in *Vanishing Giants*, were suggestive of rather than a full exposition of what for many is an unjustifiable cruelty.

Saving Luna (2008) is the story of a young orca whale stranded in Nootka Sound, British Columbia, Western Canada. Luna has been separated from his pod, and is desperate for social interaction of any sort. The film is deeply moving and highly personal, being told through the experiential understandings of two journalists, Mike Parfit and Suzanne Chisholm, who went to the area to write a whale story for the Smithsonian magazine. They stayed with Luna for the four years he lived there. *Saving Luna* is a personal meditation on the meaning of being sentient and the meaning of being human in a complex world of competing knowledge claims and ethical perspectives. Consequently, a number of different discourses and world-views enter the film's narrative: of government scientists, who believe all contact with the whale is detrimental to its (and to human) safety and well-being; of local people, who enjoy touching and communicating with the whale; of a First Nation's tribe, who perceive the whale as the return of its recently deceased chief; and of those who just want the whale to be shot or sent to an aquarium because it is a nuisance or because its playfulness occasionally damages boats.

The story unfolds with a sense of inevitability that Luna will ultimately be killed despite the love and affection it and its human friends share. Parfit's narration speaks of an invisible wall between humankind and the animal world, and the ability of Luna, for a short time to breach that wall with his own peculiar sociability, intelligence, sense of fun and need for companionship. This is not a film that anthropomorphises an animal but one that articulates the intelligence of a being which is, once again, like us.

Video footage of Luna playfully approaching boats, being stroked, talked to and caressed is complemented by the verbal testimony, presented to camera, of all those involved who made sense of the experience in their own ways. The images of this essentially vulnerable creature being itself, at one with its environment, is contrasted with that of human beings searching for what they are and being unable either to find out or learn what that is, are the direct causes of Luna's death. It is the images that express both the similarity and difference confirming what many of the interviewees intuitively know and acknowledge. Luna is like us, and not like us. Luna, a whale, is in need of company (like us), is intelligent, responsive, social, experiences physical and emotional pleasure and pain, and has other capacities that far exceed our own. The images reveal the preciousness of this other life form. When an elder of the First Nation people comments, "When something happens that we don't understand, we should be respectful enough to allow it to happen", there is an ominous sense that this is the only thing that is not going to happen. After Luna's death he is referred to as "dancing in the sky with the stars", but the poetic wisdom of this First Nation worldview cannot be accommodated by the social, bureaucratic, scientific and political arrangements of the modern world. It is, perhaps, best captured in a freeze-frame Parfit selects from some video footage of Luna joyously dancing in the churning wake of his boat. Luna jumps through the white surf and the moving image stops, time stops, fixing this being digitally as a splendid constellation of colour, shape, energy and form. Jonathan Balcombe (2009; 2010) has written extensively on the sentience of animals and, like many others, argues that animals have lives that are intrinsically worth living which either give them interests that should be respected or rights that should be upheld. What the viewer is invited to see in *Saving Luna* is exactly this. The evidence is before the eyes, on the screen – the images triggering an emotional knowing that only conscious self-interest or willful ignorance can deny. Balcombe (2009: 213) writes:

> Very few investigators have addressed the pleasure of touch. In some cases, animals' liking of tactile contact may reveal itself by accident. For example, in a study in which dolphins could request rewards (pleasures) by pressing plastic symbols on a keyboard with the tips of their beaks, some animals favoured getting a rub to getting a fish. . . . In some locations, whale-watchers have gained the trust of gray whales, who ride up against the sides of boats to have their bodies stroked and patted. . . . These examples do not prove that cetaceans enjoy the feeling of touch, but they are consistent with it.

David Rothenberg is one of a small number of inter-species musicians – an academic who approaches other creatures from an arts rather than a scientific perspective. His *Thousand Mile Song* (Rothenberg, 2008) explores the musicality of whale song, recognising their sounds as a mode of non-linguistic communication which we too can share. As a jazz clarinettist he has played along with the song of an orca. An underwater speaker relayed the sound to the animal, and seemingly the whale responded changing his song in relation to that of Rothenberg's. The question of meaning is elusive, but the evidence that the whale was changing his song in relation to what he heard can be confirmed aurally and visually through sonograms (Rothenberg, 2007). The whale song is in fact music – and music, as the philosopher Susanne Langer argues, articulates feeling and as such is a form of non-linguistic communication. For the writer Lyall Watson, whales and elephants can communicate with each other, and his own lyrical book *Elephantoms* (Watson, 2002) is both an expression of wonder and a plea for human beings to move from centre stage, to understanding the lives of others and allowing space for these others to live. This is not to deny that orcas and dolphins are complex creatures, aggressive as well as playful, but it does indicate that when there are authentic human encounters with other creatures there is often a sense of being genuinely privileged in some way (Bulbeck, 2005). This is a privilege that is marketed and arguably degraded by the growing ecotourism business, aquaria, zoos and wildlife theme parks, but which can be revealed, if only incompletely, through still and moving images, television documentaries and feature films, art exhibitions, books and music. There are still lessons to be learnt. Mike Parfit (2006) writes:

> We can surely seek lessons . . . . And we have to accept that we all share responsibility here. We all cared, but we failed to find agreement, and we failed to learn what Luna really needed. We just failed. But we have to accept also that one of the costs of freedom is risk, and Luna was free and took risks. Could we have lessened those risks? Perhaps. But wherever he was we could not have eliminated them, even by taking away his freedom, where a different set of risks would have come into play. You can lock your child in the bedroom away from fast cars, but then he dies of loneliness or the flu you bring him.

Saving Luna won two Panda Awards at the 2008 Wildscreen Festival.

The journalistic voice in conservation

For film theorist Brian Winston (1993), in the digital age the image requires cultural agreement for it to retain a legitimate reference to what commonsensically is referred to as the real world. For Bill Nicholls, another who has written extensively on the non-fiction film, it is not only documentary but all forms of discourse that place the evidence for the legitimacy of their interpretation on the world outside itself. The evidence for the dolphin slaughter, Luna's social need and the dissimulation of the pro-whalers in Japan refers to something that comes alive through discourse, through the film. The evidence

Bristow, Psihoyos and Parfit cite is therefore both part of the discourse and external to it. In other words, writes Nicholls (2008: 29), "Facts become evidence when they are taken up in discourse; and that discourse gains the force to compel belief through its capacity to refer evidence to a domain outside itself." It is also the way this discourse is framed, presented, addresses the viewer, elicits questions and feelings, that at least in part determines its persuasive power. It is the rhetoric of sound and image, the way the ideas, values and facts are communicated through the editing, composition, tone, perspective, music and silences that gives a film its identifiable voice, its rhetoric and symbolic form. Voice is not to be confused with style, which tends to divert the viewer's attention towards the film-maker, but that which fastens the viewer's attention onto the film itself. Nicholls continues (2008: 35):

> Voice functions within an ideological, affective arena in which meaning is up for grabs rather than subject to final determination.

The voice with which an image or film speaks is capable, of course, of innumerable effects, many of which may well be ideological but not necessarily ideological in the sense of reinforcing the status quo. Speech and images may embody counter-ideologies designed to subvert or reject the status quo.

It is then the distinctiveness of the voice as well as the evidence incorporated within the filmic discourse that is important to any film-maker if he, or she, wishes 'to make a difference'. Clearly there are many constraints – finance, contract, copyright, material, equipment, medium, distribution outlet, audience expectations, time, luck, politics, skill, imagination and so on. Robert Lamb has made environmental documentaries for Television for the Environment, One Planet Pictures and DevTV which have been shown in half-hour slots on the BBC's commercial channel, BBC World, and Al Jazeera International. The multi-platform *The State of the Planet* and *Nature Inc.* series were first aired in 2007 and 2009. Each programme lasts twenty-two minutes, having gone down from twenty-seven and then twenty-four minutes. He said:

> The primary outlet for our programmes is BBC World News. The emphasis is on the word 'news'. All of the documentaries we are involved in are not airy-fairy things; they are all fact-checked through and I hope they all accord to the old principle of being new, true and interesting. . . . If I talk to documentary producers, especially the old-time ones who remember the 1980s, they will say: "My God, how can you possibly say anything in twenty-two minutes?" If you talk to the news people, they think it is just amazing you've got twenty-two minutes.

Lamb's programmes tend to cover four or more short stories within a particular theme. His audience research has indicated that viewers of the international news channels rarely stay tuned for the whole twenty-two minutes, hopping instead from channel to channel, to the internet and other things. An earlier series, the Shell-financed *World Challenge* included a series of vignettes lasting little over a minute which went out separately and could be incorporated into media releases to be picked up by news agencies such as Reuters or used within news programmes produced by other channels. Both series involve DVDs, programme downloads and occasionally the full interviews with people featured in the programmes being posted on YouTube. Lamb's programmes tend to rely heavily on spoken commentaries, which is partly due to time and financial constraints. One-person crews often have little opportunity to seek visual material that is more than purely illustrative.

Nature Inc. is a series of six programmes covering a range of themes relating to the increasing pressures on the world's ecosystem services. They have been broadcast by BBC World, but also in French on a French international channel and in Arabic on Al Jazeerah. Lamb emphasises the objectivity of good journalistic reporting, but recognises that 'there is only so much bad news people can take'. Examples of positive solutions are always sought, and sometimes this has meant reporting an issue that may antagonise the sponsor. In one episode, eco-tourism is presented as an ecologically sound economic solution to the progressive destruction of the Great Barrier Reef by fishing and industrial pollution in Australia, and to the unsustainable use of coral for building materials in the Maldives that has altered tidal currents, resulting in the need to build expensive concrete coastal walls. The rise in sea temperatures, a product of global warming, is only adding to the problems. However, there are times when 'telling the story' and finding a voice causes problems of its own. Lamb recalls:

> It is very difficult when you are on an international channel transmitter to come out with programmes that are investigative because there are lots of litigious people out there and it really get tough. For example I did a programme in Tasmania, and there was real balance in that programme but it fell foul of the Australian timber interests and for a year they pursued the BBC and us and it was a year before the old Ofcom came out and said it was a factually accurate programme and well balanced. They didn't sue us but it took about a year of my time, on and off, to give the stuff to the BBC to refute everything the Australian timber people were saying. It's a big pity we are all frightened of the big [legal] case and I don't think there is enough investigative stuff. It can be very dangerous. (Robert Lamb, interview, 18th May 2009)

Although natural history and environmental film, photography and television does incorporate investigative reporting, as has been discussed already in the work of Jeremy Bristow, television journalism is not readily associated with this field. The Kenyan journalist Aidan Hartley has produced *End of the Elephant?* (2010), an incisive documentary on Chinese and local government collusion in elephant poaching in Tanzania, as part of Channel Four's *Unreported World* series using covert camera techniques to gather visual evidence on the extent of this illegal trade. Dead and decomposing elephants riddled with rounds from AK47s, their trunks sawn off and their tusks hacked out are matched by shots of tonnes upon tonnes of confiscated ivory piled high in a Kenyan government establishment awaiting disposal. The images in Hartley's film serve the purpose of providing evidence – bullet holes are shown and maggots and flies are seen feasting on the decaying flesh, but there is again a restraint that prevents the visual depiction of these contexts being accused of perpetrating a pornography of violence. For Hartley, Chinese culture and Chinese capitalism is hollowing out Africa. There are two million Chinese in Africa working to extract the continent' oil and minerals, and towards the end of his report he is offered by one of his contacts 1,000 kilos of elephant ivory at £1,000 a tusk. He asks what hope there is, if buying a tonne of ivory is so easy? In an article accompanying the programme, Hartley writes (2010):

> But they are also eating Africa. At the camps for Chinese road gangs there are piles of empty tortoise shells. Locals say there is not a dog for miles around, nor many donkeys. Elephant carcasses are mysteriously shorn of their testicles. China is ripping out Africa's timber, the sandalwood, rhino horn, the fish, the seahorses, the sea slugs. Now Asia's tigers are almost gone, Africa's big cats are next: their claws and their vital organs being turned into medicines.

In 2008 IFAW published a report, *Killing with Keystrokes: An Investigation of the Illegal Wildlife Trade on the World Wide Web,* on how the internet in general and eBay in particular are fuelling the illegal trade in ivory, other wildlife products, live animals and endangered species. The images in the report are largely of healthy animals brought to the fore by cropping or the use of a narrow depth of field that places the background out of focus. The report relies on data gathering, tables and charts, facts and figures to make its case to its audience of government and business decision makers: reason is not to be clouded by distressing visual evidence of the real world process by which these animals are killed, captured or transported. The report clearly worked in one regard, for on 19th October 2008 eBay announced that from 1st January 2009 it would ban all trade in ivory products on all its websites worldwide, whether the trade was in compliance or contravention of the complex international and domestic laws governing the trade in CITES listed species. By contrast, WildlifeExtra.com welcomed this news with an image from the Kenyan and US conservation charity Wildlife Direct of a dead elephant with a large bloody space where its tusk had earlier been hacked out. The caption read "where ivory comes from". Not Kenya, not Tanzania, not Africa, but from the living, feeling, sentient animals themselves. Similarly, Swiss journalist and wildlife photographer Karl Amman, who has been based in Kenya for over 20 years, has not been shy of showing the full, often gruesome, details of the animal cruelty integral to the illegal trafficking in live animals or the trade in bushmeat or ivory.

Developing a voice in a multi–platform environment

Not only individual films or new reports can have a voice: conceivably NGO websites and web-based indymedia outlets like GreenTV and Earth-Touch.com can develop a voice too. GreenTV was the first broadband TV channel to bring together films from a range of sources: IUCN, Greenpeace, UNEP, Friends of the Earth, WaterAid, Stop Climate Chaos and many others. For Ade Thomas, its founder, Green TV is a "green Google" for environmental films, where from its separate channels documentary shorts, promos and news reports can be viewed and downloaded. It is a media space for any organisation wishing to communicate a clear pro-environmental message to reach a wide net-based audience and exploit the affordances of new media technologies that are increasing a trend towards platform and content convergence (Birchall, 2008). The internet is pushing the aesthetic boundaries of non-fiction film-making and seeing a return, reconfiguration and reappraisal of overtly propagandist products, verité films, talking heads, personal meditations, animation and eclectic modes of address that are polycentric, labyrinthine, intertextual and sometimes baroque (Ndalianis, 2005).

Earth-Touch.com is an award-winning documentary company founded by Richard Van Wyk and Brian Palmer in 2007. It makes nature films for broadcast on South African television, which is its major income stream, and more interestingly for narrowcasting on a number of new media distribution platforms including VUZE, YouTube and its own site. Highlights are made available via RSS though Apple iTunes, Miro (an open source video player) as well as the Earth-Touch site. It also has an HD version of this feed with (by early 2010) 6,000 subscribers. The company uses five film crews working in the field, marketing itself as having a production cycle, from raw filming in the bush to global distribution, of just 48 hours. The podcasts come with a commentary by the film-maker, recorded separately a little after the event, or with just ambient sound. This is one aspect of Earth-Touch's attempt to rework the wildlife non-fiction film in the "guerilla space that new media offers". Brian Palmer (interview 14th April 2009) continued:

> We didn't want to do what the others were doing. We were rebelling against what the traditional wildlife film-makers were doing. We know about all the horrible things that go on behind the scene, and it is a well known fact in wildlife that you never let reality get in the way of a good story. If the story isn't going where they want they'll get footage from wherever to get what they want. It was always really a lie. . . . Wildlife happens 24 hours a day and it isn't always exciting or high drama or high tension, but the reality is often more meaningful than the kind of fabricated reality that wildlife film-makers put together. We are trying to achieve a genuine experience. . . . We wanted to give the purest, purest experience we could. There is an element of translation in that people can't be in all those environments around the world themselves. we don't grade or colour our footage, we edit sequentially 99% of the time and we deliver the audio that's there. Most of the wildlife [films] you see have a 'buzz track' which is just an audio track they slap on as a piece of effects, whereas our audio is the actual audio in the field as if you were there. We are really reality television but there is an element of interpretation which we will never get around unless we run live cameras 24 hours day.

Similar to Robert Lamb and other journalists, Earth-Touch said Brian Palmer tries not to get too involved in the conservation issues but prefers to "get to the facts and allow people to make up their own minds". The aim is not to impose an ideological position on viewers but to show "the earth as it is", which could be considered, of course, an ideological position in its right. Not saying something can be eloquent and ostensibly quite democratic, enabling space for free and open discussion which through uploaded contributions and comments may reveal the ideological assumptions, discourses economic and power relationships at work in Africa, India and everywhere.

The Earth-Touch website does feature a number of endangered species on the IUCN's *Red List*: African wild dogs, the black rhino, the cheetah, the giant otter and the loggerhead turtle. This alone suggests the value base from which the site operates for these are creatures, the web text states "whose presence we can no longer take for granted" and are filmed carefully so as not to disturb or stress any of the subjects. Internal audience research has shown that Earth-Touch viewers share similar values to the film-makers. The audience is

68% male and 32% female, with ages ranging from 25 to roughly 55 and over. Over 70% are in professional occupations and 18% are students. Users are predominantly from English-speaking countries with broadband connectivity, and like most other wildlife viewers are attracted to the big iconic species but may also explore images of animals that rarely feature in conventional wildlife documentaries. Users tend to select the clips with the filmmaker's commentary rather than those with only the ambient sound, and although there is currently no space for user-generated content this possibility is being actively considered. The 'voice' of Earth-Touch is therefore one that attempts to connect the viewer to the animals in a quiet and thoughtful way. It attempts to break down the species wall through observation, through framing an experience and revealing the everydayness of animal activity – yawning, sleeping, scratching, ambling, playing, waiting, wallowing, drinking and just being. There are no cataclysmic climaxes, no musical crescendos and little melodrama, but an invitation to see great deal of beauty in the quotidian life of small (and big) things. Earth Touch's truth claims are rooted and contextualised in the animal everyday – a world beyond the four-minute clip that continues in much the same way every day. What makes these images function effectively as 'documentary' is that viewers can, and do, interrogate them for their truth but this, as Frank Kessler (2009) concludes in his discussion of digital images, requires a general level of media literacy. Viewers must have the skills and knowledge to assess why and how digital images can bear witness to what is real, what is true. Part of this knowledge would be an ability to recognise the motivation behind the framing and use of certain images. Martin Atkin, former Head of Creative Development at Greenpeace International and now Director of Media Relations at WWF-International, suggests that these motivations may be as complex and polysemic as the images themselves. He said (interview, 2nd June 2009):

> As you know WWF is trying to reposition itself – not just a wildlife protection organisation. We are doing a lot more work on things like climate change, food security, poverty issues and a whole range of broadly social issues. But if you look at WWF's fundraising material, it's nearly all based on sad tiger eyes and poor orangutans, cute and cuddly. . . . those type of iconic species that traditionally are used to tug at people's heart strings and therefore get them to give money. What works best in terms of fundraising are the traditional wildlife images. It's something we wrestle with actually. Greenpeace are emotional on a different level. Take the whaling campaign, hideous pictures of whales being harpooned and that type of stuff is about an emotion that stirs up anger.

Extinction Sucks is a WWF co-production with global internet TV company Babelgum which provides free on-demand professionally made TV content and is supported by advertising. The series involves six thirty-minute programmes made by Amsterdam-based production company Off The Fence, aimed predominantly at a youth and young person's market. It communicates very a strong conservation message. Two young female presenters, conservationists Aleisha Caruso and Ashleigh Young, go to WWF conservation projects for Asian elephants, sea turtles, Tasmanian Devils, Hectors dolphins, Asiatic black bears and Indian rhinos. They observe what the projects are doing, mount exhibitions and raise money for them in rather unusual ways. They dress up in gorilla and polar bear costumes to work as squeegee merchants, enlist a cook to make biscuits, scour their neighbourhood for junk to sell, organise 'hot guys' to dress as devils, sell kisses and so on. Martin Atkin suggests this would possibly be far more difficult on conventional broadcast television although BBC Three, a relatively new digital channel aimed at young persons, and some children's programming has used similar types of programme formats to engage younger audiences (Buckingham, 2000). The films are fast-paced, energetically cut with a soundtrack designed to appeal to a clubbing audience. Martin Atkin continued:

> The reason why it was an interesting project for me was because I could try and reach younger web-savvy audiences which WWF, with a more staid middle-class middle-aged audience, has not tried to reach or not been successful at reaching in the past. It raised a lot of eyebrows within the organisation because it takes a rather irreverent approach to the subject. . . . Two wacky Australians girls rushing frantically around the planet – not really WWF, but that was the interesting part about it. . . . Maybe because it is online perhaps they [WWF] feel they can push those boundaries a bit more.

Launched in February 2009, the series is linked to a number of social media sites – My Space, Facebook and Twitter – as well as to the WWF and Free the Bears. Ellen Windemuth (Off the Fence CEO) and series producer Deborah Kidd told the online new media business hub NMK (NMK, 2008):

> The series aims to take the conservative out of conservation, and give viewers much more of an experience. Ultimately the goal is to encourage viewers to not only care about the plight of these species, but to get involved in any way they can with helping ensure their survival. This is done through showing how easy and enjoyable it is to organise fund-raising events to buy vital equipment for these groups – equipment that may not cost an enormous amount of money, but that can make a very real difference to these animals.

The social media aspects of *Extinction Sucks* will encourage the creation of community through the sharing of ideas and stories, the pooling of knowledge and the incentive to get together.

In July 2009 Babelgum claimed two million unique viewers and by early 2010 *Extinction Sucks* had 3,280 fans on Facebook, with a very engaged set of comments and uploads ranging from the sentimental to the seriously political. On My Space there were 4,668 friends and 686 comments, many of which are brief and consisting of little more than an uploaded image – a cuddly panda, a photograph of a Canadian cull of baby seals, a campaign video from PETA, an animated baby leopard waving hello, a home video of pets and the like. Social media enables a global connectivity of like-minded persons who communicate through words and symbolic images by cutting out items from their own mediated lifeworlds, networks and experiences. These communications are quite small and in many ways quite trivial, but they are rooted in the everyday and articulated in relation to the possibilities new media offers. This décollage is a vibrant expression and extension of feeling, emotion and belief. It is a public cultural politics that lies beyond but is nevertheless dependent on and determined by the hard material realities of human economic development. The pressure and depth of concern that new media is able to collect and organise generates a force that sometimes compels traditional media to catch up even if, or perhaps because, the conservation problems identified seem so familiar. It is perhaps this familiarity that makes them so urgent. In 2010 Australia's Channel 10 and the Discovery Channel announced they would screen *Extinction Sucks* later in the year.

Wildscreen's ARKive project is another new media intervention, but of a very different sort. Originally conceived as something akin to an electronic zoo, ARKive is now the flagship initiative of an organisation that has developed considerably over the years. Comprising donated photographs and film/video footage of a wide range of species, ARKive provides both text-based information in the form of downloadable briefing or fact sheets with images that reveal a range of animal behaviours and in some cases offer opportunities of seeing creatures that have rarely and sometimes never before been photographed or filmed. Many images have been donated by the BBC Natural History Unit, Granada Wild, National Geographic Digital Motion, Discovery Communications Inc, other mainstream media organisations and around 3,500 film-makers and photographers. These still images and moving image clips are downloaded for use in education and conservation projects, and the provenance of each image or clip is clearly displayed. The film clips include location-recorded (ambient) sound, so that when the viewer accesses footage of bottle-nose dolphins their calls and sound of the water on the microphone can clearly be heard. Like Earth-Touch, these ARKive clips have not been forced into a narrative, although occasionally the longer extracts are edited sequentially and do tell a story – an African rhino kicking out his back legs to disturb the ground which the viewer soon learns becomes a latrine. In Rebecca Hoskins' *Hawaii: message in the waves* there is one shot of a seal caught in some rope. It struggles to raise its head above the waves to breathe. No help is in site. The shot lasts for just a few seconds. This same shot is available on ARKive but the whole take is available. One of the film crew moves in front of the camera to cut the seal free, allowing it to swim away unharmed. Both the edited shot in the film and the extended take on ARKive are full of educational potential and emotive impact. Viewing context is important, but then so is (showing) the act of cutting free. Media and conservation literacy become one and the same, for although Wildscreen is ostensibly politically neutral, all its activities and initiatives are focussed on promoting conservation, awareness, education and action. ARKive users may sign in and produce their own scrapbook of images, linked to the IUCN *Red List* species of the day, send an e-card, spread the world about Wildscreen and ARKive on the major social media sites, become active conservationists to help save the world's endangered species or give money to help with Wildscreen's ongoing work. The user interface is colourful and intuitively navigable, and unlike E.O. Wilson's Encyclopedia of Life web project, is less concerned with rigorous scientific classification than with direct public engagement. Wildscreen's ARKive is therefore a far cry from being an electronic zoo, although the Enclycopeadia of Life is quite close to being an electronic natural history museum cataloguing the whole of the planet's biota and providing a searchable scientific database for researchers and conservationists. As Wilson has written (2003):

> Only with such encyclopedic knowledge can ecology mature as a science and acquire predictive power species by species, and from those, ecosystem by ecosystem.

Funded principally by the Environment Agency of Abu Dhabi, ARKive is promoted as the ultimate multi-media guide to endangered species. It is a free choice multi-media learning environment. The user selects what is of interest to him or her and develops that interest according to the various opportunities and affordances the site offers (Falk and Dierking, 2002). There are educational resources for schoolteachers and schoolchildren, including audio-visual modules or integrated multi-media presentations on topics such as ecology, habitat-human and predator-prey relationships. There are short video games, some of which are at first glance simply fun although all convey a clear education or conservation message: such as that being a wildlife photographer requires a quickness of the eye as well as profound patience, or that designing a wildlife habitat for endangered animals involves dealing with a range of interlinked and complex variables. It is easy to become quickly immersed and as many games, media and educational analysts have suggested, interaction and immersion in a game can develop skills, knowledge and understanding in a way that is often missing in the conventional classroom (Gee, 2005; Shaffer, 2005; Michael and Chen, 2006; Raessens, 2009; Chatfield, 2010). Some researchers have argued that time is sometimes required to reflect and distance oneself from the activity in order to learn (Pelletier, 2005), but the multi-functionality and non-linearity of much internet use continually requires the user to oscillate between immersion and reflection as part of the overall flow.

ARKive also offers the capacity to virtually travel round the planet via Google Earth by clicking on layered place marks that identify threatened marine species that link to an impressive range of textual and image-based information. These place marks are doorways into the lifeworlds of other species which human beings all too frequently aggravate or destroy. The constant reminder that the animals depicted and made available as image downloads are endangered is itself a distancing device, inviting the learner to be mindful of what is being seen, read and heard. Whether the internet, with its array of social media sites and virtual constructions, can facilitate a more ecocentric as oppose to a more technocentric, mediated and self-referential worldview, has yet to be seen. What is apparent, though, is that new media technologies have the potential to open out the public sphere, facilitate social organisation and political action, initiate new forms of collective intelligence, creativity and knowledge and connect people and peoples to each other and indeed to other sentient creatures (Jenkins, 2006; Boler, 2008; Leadbeater, 2009). The human can use the web to see the image of an animal, the image of an eye which when locked on to may offer the sense of reciprocal interaction, of reciprocal knowing. Luna's gaze can fix you and you can feel his warmth through the cold water – or at least imagine you can by looking into rather than at the screen. It is this sensuous experience of seeing and of being seen that gives screen-based media both its emancipatory and repressive power, as well as its capacity to simultaneously recognise similarity in difference, as evident in *Saving Luna*. In 2009 around 20,000 people were accessing ARKive every day, but as Harriet Nimmo, Wildscreen CEO, said (interview, 9th March 2009), "The big drive is to create a regular community, not just users flitting in, and be more interactive." It is hoped that eventually ARKive will be multilingual. Some research for this book invited responses from a number of ARKive users, many of whom were professionally engaged with wildlife conservation, education and communication and all of whom could be categorised unsurprisingly as deeply concerned about the future of the planet's flora and fauna. The extended quotations below are indicative of a small group of users, but not necessarily representative of all of the site's users. Nonetheless, their comments show how the site's usage integrates personal and professional values and predispositions, and how its accessibility stimulates return visits. Thus the ARKive is more than an archive. For some people, the value of ARKive's images lie in their capacity to foster concern and interest in the natural world. (The names of contributors below are pseudonyms for individuals who participated in the internet-based ARKive research).

> The ARKive website is most valuable for the consistent high-quality images of life on earth. Limiting the photography to professional photographers means that the images are always clear and easy to see. The images are beautiful and the more people see this website the more people will be excited about conserving and protecting our earth. (Simon)

> It is important to create a powerful resource of information about wildlife that is open to everyone. Many people are ready to help but they don't know how. It would be good to translate this site to other languages. It would be also good to expand information on environmental conservation issues about every specific species and let people know how to contribute. (Geoff)

> I guess anything that captures children young so they grow up valuing these creatures in the ecosystem has to be good but it seems pretty well covered already especially with the resource modules – anything to make teachers more likely to take up the material is also good. As a child growing up in Kent in England I learnt to love 'nature walks' and can't walk in a natural area (62 now) without being aware of the unseen populations of creatures. Now in the Australian bush and vegetated urban areas around Brisbane I love to e.g. encounter a wedge-tail soaring in the afternoon sky or find (as I once did) a carpet python in my Tuckeroo tree in the front garden! This is why I think the secret is 'catch 'em young' and I have tried to teach my children etc by example to wonder and inquire. (Jenny)

ARKive is a member of the Institutional Council of the Encyclopedia of Life and is a key content provider. Not surprisingly, some people used the ARKive site for professional purposes and valued it for that reason:

When I'm editing someone else's text I may want to check the author's information, or write up picture captions if they have not been supplied. For example, I often freelance at BBC Wildlife and frequently use ARKive when I'm there. The site is most useful to me for species I'm less familiar with, especially extra-European species. Sometimes I'm after no more than an IUCN rating, and I confess that I use ARKive because the site is faster than the IUCN itself. I like the fact that the information is clearly footnoted and checked, which is quite rare in websites. I feel that the info is more reliable. Sometimes I go straight to the sources quoted in the footnotes and that is a major motivation for visiting the site in the first place. ARKive is one of a fairly small number of general-purpose natural history sites that I can trust. (Celia)

Since my work involves working with animal species in the wild, I need to collect as much information as I can. This information helps me to produce scientific reports which I need to build out the management plans for our protected areas in Jordan. More literature will enrich the text and supports our conservation work. Also I can obtain information about researchers in the field of conservation from the literature provided at the information page and in consequence have wider contacts. In Jordan, we have a scarcity of wildlife photos, and in order to prepare a presentation about animal species in Jordan for educational purposes, I am using the Arkive photo database. Photos are a very good tool: "A single photo is worth a thousand words" for awareness, education and public support, especially as people know so little about other species. Moreover, it is a good tool for new researchers hired to recognise species' morphological characteristics for further identification in the field. . . . Sometimes, I am using videos in my presentation to attract audience more. Because when people see these animals, how they act and how they behave, they will start to respect them and this is a great awareness technique. (Catherine)

[I am a] building surveyor undertaking bat surveys and designing mitigation schemes to accommodate bats and development. Alongside this is training of new bat licence holders, both volunteers and consultants. Stills in Powerpoint presentations of the more unusual bats of the world. Also stills of insects that are bat prey. The ARKive is an excellent source of material on worldwide bats, insects throughout this country and bat images to supplement those already in my collection from my own photographs, Bat Conservation Trust records and Natural England sources. (Ken)

The professional interests of many users married closely with their personal beliefs and feelings. They believed that ARKive could, when applied in a wide variety of contexts and situations, raise awareness and develop a disposition to think and act differently:

> It is an excellent website to allow children to roam around, looking up either animals we have directed them to look up or just following their own interests. We are trying to interest children in their environment, so they will be more inclined to value and protect it as adults. This fits in with developing a wildlife garden and encouraging recycling within school. (Sasha)

> I look at it for general interest. It is an excellent website to allow children to roam around, looking up either animals we have directed them to look up or just following their own interests. We are trying to interest children in their environment, so they will be more inclined to value and protect it as adults. This fits in with developing a wildlife garden and encouraging recycling within school. (Janet)

For some creative workers, ARKive provides accurate and useful information which when articulated in other forms or when resonating with cultural or religious experiences can stimulate further learning:

> I used ARKive to enhance a novel I wrote and that I was publishing in my blog. Each time I spoke of a different animal, I linked the word to its profile on your wonderful site. Many of my readers told me they loved learning new things about animals and watching their marvellous photos. I am a bird maniac. I am collecting, as a hobby for my own personal use, photos of all the world's birds and ARKive has been of great use – even though I do feel it's short on many of the world's bird species – as a very important source of information about different animals for my writings. (David)

> I am working with an NGO as material development supervisor and our work is on street children [in Pakistan]. But I want to do something for environment conservation. I also lead a group and we are trying to make the school children aware about environment pollution but we are limited in a specific area. I try to start a programme to complete a food chain in the nearest forest but I have limited sources and we still achieve this goal. If we try to make some effort to create an ideal environment then this will help the wildlife. If environment will be safe and healthy then all types of life can survive healthily. As we know, the population of the world is increasing rapidly and forest land is declining. This means that much wildlife and many species will die. We all are responsible for all of these because we want a luxury life and we are not thinking about these God's creatures. (Mohamed)

When film-makers, teachers and campaigners use images in their own specific campaigning or educational activities they learn that some images have a greater impact than others, although much depends, as always, on context and audience. Mary Colwall, an independent media producer who formerly worked at the BBC's NHU, is concerned to persuade Catholic lay people, the Church hierarchy and other faith groups in Britain and elsewhere to give greater prominence in their work to wildlife conservation and the environment. For Colwall this is simply a matter of living one's faith, and as deforestation in the Amazon and many other environmental and wildlife issues are occurring in Catholic countries, or in other nations which express a strong commitment to a religious faith, linking key images and stories with faith can, as Mike Pandey also suggests, can be most effective.

> I use a section from *Deep Trouble* on the fishing industry, and every time I use that it gets people really worked up. I use stuff on deforestation, stuff on palm oil but I also use stuff from *Planet Earth: the Future* – the intercut of beautiful images with people talking about the importance of the natural world for our spiritual and emotional well-being. I use my documentary-making skills and put it into a presentation. Using moving images puts it [the illustrated lecture] on another level. I spent the whole of last weekend with the Methodist Women's Network – fantastic group of feisty ladies, 120 of them – and they were absolutely thrilled by it. (Mary Colwall, interview 23rd April 2009)

The ready availability of still images and film/video clips on ARKive means that the internet provides many people with access to a large and growing web-based repository of material that only a few years ago could be only accessed by a few professionals in the media or in education. These images can be used by many groups in all manner of conservation campaigns and activities. If the medium is the message, then it is that one's voice can be found through the technological and content opportunities afforded by the new media.

Chapter Six

A mirror to nature

Karl Ammann

Later that same day, while they were still hanging around Mambele Junction and hoping for a ride, someone else mentioned that a hunter in a nearby settlement had just killed a gorilla. The settlement, known as Lepondji, was within walking distance, so Gary and Karl headed off and located the hunter at his house. He told them he had been sent a gun by the Mouloundou Chief of Police with a specific order for gorilla meat. So he shot a gorilla and sent the best of the meat and the gun by bush taxi back to the police chief; since he had made the kill, the hunter kept the head and an arm. In his small kitchen, the hunter lifted up a woven basket that had been placed over the gorilla's head to keep the flies away. The head was in a shallow bowl next to a bunch of bananas.

With a basket behind and the bananas beside it, the big ape's head was momentarily brightened by a flash from Karl's Nikon F4. (Peterson, 2003: 46-47)

Peterson thus tells the story of one of the most well circulated and iconic photographs documenting Africa's illegal trade in bushmeat. The photograph, taken in south-east Cameroon in 1994, can be seen all over the web, in books and magazines and occasionally in educational materials produced by zoos. *Eating Apes* is a powerful book exploring the various nuances of the trade, and in particular award-winning photographer Karl Amman's hard struggle to get his stories and his images published in conservation and nature magazines. In the 1990s he consistently demonstrated the link between the bushmeat trade and logging concessions, warned of the dangers to human health relating to the spread of viruses carried by primates, and recognised that although eating bushmeat was indeed sanctified by some cultures within Africa this was not universally the case. Karl Amman is a powerful and tenacious campaigner who has produced images that shock and are genuinely distressing to many Western audiences. His images of the trade, of dismembered apes or deer at food markets, of chimps chained to rusting cars, of gorillas being hacked apart with blood collecting in their chest cavities, of baked gorilla hands and bones in plastic bowls, of an emaciated baby chimp lying against red meat packed in a suitcase, of another chimp reaching out pathetically from a crack in a wall, of dead baboons tied to the back of a human hunter, of a hunter lifting up the head of a dead gorilla so the camera has a clear shot, a row of primate skulls at a market, a young boy carrying a gorilla head on his own, a mass of smoked primate corpses reminiscent of a human genocide, and of course the gorilla head sitting in a bowl next to a bunch of unripe bananas on a shelf in someone's hut. The head is in a shallow metal container, with a small pool of fresh blood collecting at the bottom. The face is at an angle, looking down, and a small wicker basket can be seen to the right, behind the fruit. It looks like a gruesome still life – a scene an artist had spent ages trying to arrange for maximum effect in a middle class urban gallery. However, this is not the case. It is actually one of those decisive historical moments in photojournalism that deserves its place among the other key images of the twentieth century that periodically do adorn gallery retrospectives.

> That one iconic image of the gorilla head sitting next to the bananas which I have lost total control over. I've seen it ten or twenty times without me actually giving permission to anybody to use it. Everybody assumes it is in the public domain and use it one way or the other. That's fine, you know, so long as the background story is halfway correct. (Karl Ammann, interview 1st June 2009)

These images have not been digitally enhanced nor are they distressing to those who eat or trade in bushmeat, but the fact remains that these creatures are genetically close to humans, they are endangered and the trade is illegal. The way the images were captured and presented clearly conform to the ethical norms outlined by Dona Schwartz (2003) in her perceptive discussion of the credibility of photojournalism: only photographs that depict the subject as the camera sees it should be published; only photographs that depict the subject as as someone present at the scene would have seen it; and, photographs should only be produced which are consistent with prevailing norms governing journalistic representations, that is, to establish and maintain accuracy and the trust of the public there should be no touching up or enhancing that undermines the integrity of the image as a record. Similarly, organisations such as PETA will use harrowing still and moving images in their campaigns against the fur trade and for animal welfare. Covert video footage of live animals being skinned in Chinese fur farms generate media attention and public anger even if part of the surrounding publicity is about the ethics of making these distressing sights available to a wide public. There is no watershed on the internet, and as Poorva Joshipura, PETA's European Director, has said, a raccoon dog being skinned alive is far more distressing to the animal than it can possibly be to a anyone watching low-resolution images on their computer. For PETA, just as for Karl Ammann, the general public and influential decision-makers need to be confronted with these harsh and sometimes unbearable realities whether they like it or not.

Karl Amman's career has developed from being a wildlife photographer to that of a photojournalist and now to predominantly that of an activist. Many of his conventional wildlife photographs are still with agents and they continue to sell, but what they sell is a very different image of the natural world than the ones Karl Ammann himself sees as being more expressive of contemporary reality. But even those which do not depict the horrors of bushmeat or habitat destruction have an edge that goes beyond the clichéd big cat silhouetted against an ochre sunset or zebras jousting in the dust of the open plain. The other reality, the reality of commerce, of making a living, means some of these images can be found in Ammann's portfolio too. His career trajectory, though, has followed a clear and consistent path leading to a position that is perhaps as logical as it is clearly reasoned: to remain predominantly a wildlife photographer documenting the beauty of the world would be, in large part, to deny or to discount the destructive things that are occurring on the planet.

> At some point you have to decide can you live with documenting the beauty world, which is much easier to sell in terms of photographs and films, and ignore all that goes on around it. I have decided I can no longer afford to ignore it. The more I keep my eyes open the more distressed I get about the state the natural world is in. I feel that should be documented, taken to the public and the policymaker, but it is not easy because people don't want to hear bad news. (Karl Ammann, interview 1st June 2009)

Ammann's work has been published in *National Geographic*, *BBC Wildlife* magazine, *Time* magazine, the *New York Times*, *Asia Geographic* and in many other outlets. He has made short documentaries on bushmeat, development and corporate PR *(Blood Timber* and *Blood Timber Two)* for TVE's *Earth Report* series and a number of other films on the wild animal trade including *The Kinshasa Connection*, focusing on the trade in monkeys with six American zoos; *Boten* about a bear bile farm in Laos; *The Mong Lah Connection*, about the supply of bear meat for banquets in China; *The Bangui Connection*, about the killing of elephants for their meat as well as ivory; and *The Cairo Connection*, about the role of Egypt as a focal point for illegal trading in wildlife. These films have all been used by Karl Ammann as evidence in his campaigns against what he sees as the timid and ineffectual approach of the CITES Standing Committee to enforce the treaty outlawing the trade. Confronting government officials and decision-makers on camera with the evidence produced by his investigative report is a tactic Ammann regularly uses. When officials are not perceived to be telling the whole truth his aim, like many other activist photographers, journalists and film-makers, is to reach decision-makers directly, and if unsuccessful, through their publics. As a member of the accredited Speigel TV (Germany) media team attending the CITES Standing Committee Meeting in Geneva (SC 58) in July 2009, Karl Ammann attempted to interview the Chinese delegation on the active wildlife trade occurring at border posts between China and Myanmar. The request for an interview was filmed and this led to the expulsion of the Spiegel team from the meeting, with the Secretary General of the CITES personally and physically intervening. The Chinese delegation were then approached in the street and the film crew were once more physically manhandled. The Chinese delegation filed a complaint, and the Secretary General announced at a full plenary session the total expulsion of Karl Ammann and the Speigel team from the convention. In discussions with delegates Karl Amman says he was told that a more diplomatic approach to non-compliance would have been more successful. But Amman disagrees and has the evidence to prove it.

His film work has been broadcast extensively in Switzerland, Scandinavia, South Africa and Germany, and clips and podcasts may be found on YouTube, Lemondreamz and other internet channels. He is unsurprisingly quite critical of mainstream magazines, TV networks and their advertisers who, he believes, shy away from presenting too much bad news, preferring instead to commission films that have heroes and happy endings. However, news channels sometimes do offer a great opportunity to get a story aired, although achieving this too is by no means easy or straightforward. He said:

The major news outlets don't have the resources anymore to send correspondents out to do an environmental news story in Africa. They rely on feedback from people like myself, and if my stories are negative they will pick up the phone and call WWF or WCS or Greenpeace or somebody and they will told that basically I'm a radical extremist, but yes there might be a problem, but that someone is going to solve it one way or the other. If you are a journalist sitting at a desk in London and you get those two different versions you are going to balance the story and balance has very little to do with the reality which is on the ground now. The few times I've managed to get journalists to travel with me . . . The bushmeat story only started being published after I had travelled with the correspondent from New York Times magazine into central Africa. Nobody was willing to run my story. I was accused by the

WWF of creating the bushmeat crisis so I could sell my photographs, but after the *New York Times* magazine ran it then everybody accepted may be there is an issue with bushmeat and everybody was ready to run with it. But those were strokes of luck and they had the money to send a correspondent to Africa. (Karl Ammann interview, 1st June 2009)

He is also an informed critic of conservation NGOs, whose approach he calls in his Afterword to *Eating Apes*, "feelgood conservation":

I have a very serious problem with the way conservation organisations present themselves. If you go to any major conservation organisation they are all advertising success in one form or another, or they have found a new problem and they are just about to solve it if you write them a cheque. In my opinion that is all pretty much feelgood conservation, which practically nobody ever audits – no independent third party auditing of these projects take place. We never know what works and what doesn't work, and based on my personal experience 99% of the projects that advertise success are actually failures. (Karl Ammann interview, 1st June 2009)

In *The Gombe Connection* (2009) his investigations extended to the work of Jane Goodall, whose work is rarely, if ever, publicly questioned. He offers an audit of the Gombe reserve and the Jane Goodall Institute by asking a series of questions designed to assess the various claims and strategies adopted to protect the chimps in this one small but very famous reserve and others which have been modelled on it. The Gombe chimp population is now too small to be genetically sustainable and living in effect on a tiny island of forest surrounded by farmland, roads, poaching and plenty of desolate open space where logging companies have cleared away the natural vegetation. Amman assesses Jane Goodall's work to improve the area in and around Gombe according to four categories derived from the Institute's own funded activities: reforestation, marketing of fair trade speciality coffee to improve the economic livelihood of local people, control of local human populations through family planning and the creation of 'chimpanzee corridors' to break the physical and genetic isolation of the Gombe chimps. Ammann concludes that the first two projects have yet to show their worth and the final two have clearly failed. Jane Goodall herself is interviewed and comes across as dedicated, honest, well-meaning but perhaps a little naive. The film ends with Ammann stating to an off-screen interviewer that people need to be confronted with the harsh realities, and that selling easy solutions is no longer the answer. This is not a comfortable message for governments, NGOs or their corporate sponsors whose corporate responsibility strategies could consequently come under more serious public scrutiny.

The materiality of the image

Another approach, which Karl Ammann and other photographers who are members of the non-profit organisation The International League of Conservation Photographers (ILCP) have adopted, is the publication and targeted distribution of high-quality books of environmental and wildlife photographs. These books have an accompanying text written by respected academic experts, who add status and kudos to the issue and to the recipient as a result of their very materiality and luxurious format. *Consuming Nature* is a coffee-table book very expensively produced by Conservation International and published in 2004 by Altisima Press. It is a powerful photo-essay by a group of conservation scientists and anthropologists about the exploitation of the African rainforest, with pictures by Karl Ammann, which aimed to appeal and perhaps flatter those in decision-making roles; 1,000 copies were sent to the European Union Parliament and other key figures in Europe and Africa, and 1,000 were sent to government and financial leaders in North America. Like David Brower before him, Karl Amman and his colleagues Anthony Rose, Russell Mittermeier, Olivier Langrand, Okyeame Ampadu-Agyel and Thomas Burtynski believe that a material artifact can add literal and metaphorical weight, context and persuasive power to an image which may certainly work on the emotion but often benefits from further informed, discursive, reflection and subsequent action.

> I feel if I can get to the policymakers in one way or the other which they can't ignore that would be the best bet, but that's hard to do. That's why we gave *Consuming Nature* to the European Parliament and to every member of the Parliament in the Congo Republic. We did get a reaction from the French president when we didn't even know he had received a copy of the book. It was a strong reaction which we had never asked for. We never knew he had the book. It shows that policymakers can be effected if the right kind of imagery is used. To get to them is the hard part. (Karl Ammann interview, 1st June 2009)

Although at the time of writing the book is out of print, a selection of photographs from *Consuming Nature* can be seen on Karl Ammann's own and the National Geographic News website. In a letter written on 10 February 2004, President Chirac wrote:

> The information that I gathered from this high-quality book provoked a great dismay. The ecological disaster that this book illustrates and the crude reality that it describes reinforce the idea that I have had that African countries need urgent help to rapidly develop active policies to conserve and carefully and sustainably manage tropical forests. It is about the preservation of

an irreplaceable natural heritage. It is also about a certain idea on humankind, his rights and obligations *vis à vis* nature, without which man is nothing. As you know, this constitutes one of the directions of the policy of France that I have been promoting in Africa and is part of the dialogue that I keep maintaining with African heads of state.

Photographic books do have an important quality which film, video, TV and the web-sourced digital image lacks. They are physical objects, existing in three dimensions, in time and space and their very materiality means they become enmeshed into sensuous and embodied experiences. The fact they have been designed, manufactured, distributed, consumed, shelved, left in waiting rooms or lent to others imbues them with a direct intentionality that is perhaps absent in an abstracted digital image. The materiality of the photographs in *Consuming Nature* takes two forms: first, the paper used to print the pages, the toning and surface variations; second, the presentational forms, book design, physical relationship to written text, etc. The viewer can literally feel the image, weigh it, even smell it. Indeed these books, these objects, can be considered to be social actors whose meaning is derived from their social effects and the way they help construct and influence social, environmental and political action. Even if only for a short while they have a social life (Appadurai, 1986) encompassing various aspects such as their production, exchange, usage, loss or disposal. These books may be sold to libraries and borrowed, bought and added to private collections, displayed in the press as part of a promotional campaign and may ultimately be thrown away or simply lost. The books as well as the images residing within them therefore have a currency. As Elizabeth Edwards and Janice Hart write, the eye is an organ operating within a biological context which implies specific relations and responses to the object and to the materiality of the images. They continue (2004: 6): "Material forms create very different embodied experiences of images and very different affective tones or theatres of consumption."

Cristina Mittermeier, President of the ILCP, is very conscious of these theatres and the possible effects of making the image a material object. Photographs are powerful ways of conveying complex messages about conservation and environment, but on their own they rarely work unless they have that iconic status and impact that the most well-known journalistic or documentary images have gathered around them. Karl Ammann's gorilla head, the clubbing of a Canadian seal pup and the hoisting of a bloody whale into a factory ship are some images that no longer require explanation. She speaks of the need for images to have a physical footprint:

We publish one book every year with CEMEX [a global building materials company], and now we are expanding into our own editorial line called Urgent Focus Editions, and with Urgent Focus we want to turn every book into a campaign that has a multi-media component for a website, the whole social networking groundswell component and a physical footprint where we travel, exhibit and have our photographers speak. For us we are trying to create a different kind of product and tell a different kind of story. Having editorial control is really important. . . . I want to make sure we tell the story that really needs to be told, not the one that is going to generate dollars. That is why having these sponsored publications is really important because they give you that freedom.

Although the books retail at $58, their purpose is not to make money for the ILCP but to raise public awareness and directly educate decision makers. The CEMEX series, first started in 1993, often involves other conservation bodies in their production and includes the following titles: *A Climate for Life: meeting the global challenge*, *The Human Footprint: Challenges for Wilderness and Biodiversity*, *Transboundary Conservation: A New Vision for Protected Areas*, *The Red Book* and *Hotspots*. In 2010 *The Wealth of Nature* was launched in London by both CEMEX and the IUCN as a contribution to the International Year of Biodiversity. The book was presented to Members of the UK Parliament, civil servants, community partners, environmentalists and commercial guests at a reception at the House of Lords. Each book is accompanied by a travelling exhibition which is free to the general public and at which some of the photographers may be scheduled to speak. But more importantly perhaps, says Mittermeier:

We give them away. We send them to influential people, to the ministers of the environment, to the press and to the owners of companies – to whoever are the people who are making the decisions. They are education tools for a different type of audience. . . . These are books to educate the decision-makers on conservation strategies that matter.

The problem inevitably is being able to accurately assess and evaluate their impact, and the ILCP does not have the resources to do this. However, Cristina Mittermeier tells one story that she believes is indicative of both her hopes and the possibilities for a book to change the world.

We have some evidence that a former President of Madagascar had never seen his own country until he was able to see it through the coffee-table books of the CEMEX series, and based largely on the recommendations of that book he tripled the protected area system of that country. This is not just anecdotal information. He used the book as a blueprint for conservation in his own country. That's the type of effect we try to get. The books are not just sent with a thank you note. They are sometimes delivered by conservation leaders and we use them as a presentation car and say, "Here, Mr Minister, is a book that might help in your decision-making."

The ILCP started a photo-documentary initiative called RAVE (Rapid Assessment Visual Expedition) in 2007, whereby members employ their photographic skills to produce significant images on specific conservation areas in targeted locations. RAVEs undertaken in Africa, Canada, Patagonia, Mexico and the United States have generated both money and media interest. In 2008 a RAVE was conducted in the Wyoming's Upper Green River Valley to document the area's natural beauty and the effects of local gas exploration and industrial development on local animal populations, water resources and habitats. Twelve photographers were involved in an expedition that lasted three days. In 2010 the ILCP started to plan a Great Bear RAVE in western Canada to visually explore the impact of a proposed 2,000-mile oil pipeline from the tar sands exploration sites in northern Alberta to the coast. Without this pipeline and without a lifting of the moratorium on tanker traffic along the coast of British Columbia, the tar sands project cannot expand. However, as the ILCP suggest, recalling the ecological disaster in Prince William Sound following the grounding of the *Exxon Valdez* in 1989, such action could seriously endanger marine and other life in the region, including that in the Great Bear Rainforest. The project partners are the conservation NGOs Pacific Wild, Save Our Seas Foundation and the Gitgaat Nation. For Cristina Mittermeier, ILCP photographers are primarily journalists who make their photographs available to others involved in specific campaigns because decision-makers, particularly in the extractive industries, she says, rarely present all the relevant information to the public for they tend to concentrate mainly on the economic benefits. The photographs produced by the RAVE illustrate and present evidence of what will be lost in order to secure these economic benefits. She continued (interview 15th June 2009):

> RAVE is something we do to raise awareness either locally or internationally about an issue that requires immediate attention. It is a very targeted activity to try to influence decision-making if there is legislation that is going to be passed, or a decision that is going to made on a protected area, a concession that is going to lead to destructive activity. . . . You can use the presence of the photographers, as some of these are well-known, influential and charismatic, to have a series of press conferences and press releases to make a per-

sonal statement about why these things matter. This creates a media buzz, newspapers and television channels pay attention and this helps inform the decision-making process. . . . [RAVE] only works when there is a local conservation initiative or a group of scientists who need this help. It never works when you employ photographers on their own to take a bunch of pictures because you need that presence on the ground and the political process that is happening sustained by the people who are there.

The photographic eye

Film and photography can therefore be instrumental in shaping and maintaining public understanding of nature, of the environment and of wildlife. Photographers need originality to get noticed and published. Yann Arthus-Bertrand pioneered aerial photography and outdoor photographic exhibitions in a quest to convey a deep sensuous understanding of environment, development and ecosystem destruction. His approach has influenced many other photographers and film-makers, and offered viewers a visual sense of the planet from a vantage point that enhances the beauty and wonder of what is before the camera with, what Karl Amman would say, are 'the realities on the ground'. His book *Earth from Above* (Arthus-Bertrand, 2005) and his three-hour documentary series *The Fragile Earth*, made for French television, have attempted to tell the conservation story in a new and different way. Similarly Daniel Beltra's photographs of the Amazon, the Congo and Indonesia, taken from the ground and from the air, present deforestation in a way that intentionally aims to jar the consciousness and motivate people to action. Some of his images show islands of forest in a sea of desert, others grey logging camps, timber burning and forest inhabitants, people and chimps attempting to get on with what is left of their everyday lives. The most interesting and affecting wildlife and nature photography is often produced with the specific purpose of generating a critical apprehension of our relationships with animals and the environment. This is often done by presenting a mirror to nature that denaturalises the animal image that is so often seen in more commercial wildlife photography, challenging the arrogant assumption that human society is of paramount significance. The images that puncture the viewer's expectations reveal the mediated and constructed nature of what is being seen in and by the photography. It attempts to offer the opposite to what Matthew Brower (2005) sees as the success and intention of nineteenth-century animal photographs, that is, the illusion of an unmediated encounter through nature photography that offers the viewer transparent access to the animal while denying any appropriate relation to or understanding of it. Beltra works as a freelance, and has Greenpeace as a main client. In 2009 he won the Prince's Rainforest Award at the Sony World Photography Awards, and his exhibition 'Focus on the Rainforest' opened at the Nash Conservatory, Kew Gardens, in London the same year.

Michael 'Nick' Nichols, a photographer with *National Geographic*, is often referred to as the Indiana Jones of wildlife photography. He has been a member of the ILCP for a number of years, and has been actively using his photography to save habitats and to illustrate the mediated nature of human relations to wild animals and the environment. His photography invites us to re-appropriate these relationships for the benefit of all living creatures. One way he has done this is by explicitly linking conservation with animal rights or animal welfare issues, which in many academic and policy discourses are kept analytically separate. His photographic work on elephants in Kenya is about, he says, the soul of the elephant. The more people who care about the well-being of the elephant as an individual, the less the killing of elephants for their ivory can be allowed. This may cause problems of course, because conservation is usually concerned with whole species rather than individuals, although there is always a concern for humane treatment or humane killing if culling is seen as a desirable management solution. Thus conservationists will care for individual animals, as has been frequently been documented, and for the species as a whole. Conservation scientists and managers often refuse to see or prevent themselves from seeing or recognising an animal's individuality as in need of protection, when arguably it would be quite possible to acknowledge its significance. As philosopher Peter Singer (1993) says, many animals are intelligent and sentient creatures, and some such as the elephant, the whale and the higher primates are also, like human beings, self-aware. They are 'non-human persons', so approaching animals as such is neither anthropomorphising or sentimentalising but itself rational, scientifically verifiable and humane. It also presents a serious moral dilemma. A cull means the killing of individuals, whether it be for the greater good of the species or not. There may be too many elephants, too many humans, too many individuals. What then?

In 2005 Nick Nichols worked with Jane Goodall to produce *Brutal Kinship*, a book about human beings' relationships with chimps. Published by Aperture, the images are printed on high-quality gloss paper in deep colours that, when combined with Goodall's prose and her facial expressions seen in some of the images, eloquently express Nichols' philosophy. The photographs present details of the everydayness of the chimp's lives – grooming, feeding, fighting, playing, hunting, huddling in the rain, using tools, baring teeth, sleeping and so on. The deep green of the jungle foliage is contrasted with the bright shafts of sunlight piercing the treetop canopy and the inky darkness of the chimps' fur. Sometimes the foreground is out of focus or the image deliberately blurred to convey movement or energy. Frequently there is a sense that Nichols, and the viewer, are peering in or eavesdropping on another world. This is a type of photographic seeing that offers a sense of another world while acknowledging only a dubious right to be there. It is perhaps a confrontation of consciousness with nature. There are some close-up portraits of a chimp looking intently out at something beyond the edge of the picture. A chimps rests his chin on the back of his hand and strikes the pose of a thinking person. A baby looks blankly towards the camera lens with his finger touching his tooth. There is a full-page photo of Jane Goodall, slightly out of focus, sitting cross-legged in a cell with Gregoire, an old virtually hairless chimp who is partially sighted and malnourished. He can be seen with great optical clarity, standing and looking past Goodall. His left forefinger is gently scratching his chin. The photograph's dominant colour is brown, with only Goodall's white slacks, blue shirt, grey hair and pink flesh tones brightening an image which is emotionally and visually dark. An familiar shot (a Jane Goodall visual theme tune) is the hand a full grown male, Jou Jou, reaching out from the bottom right of the frame to gently touch Goodall's forehead which appears face down in the top left. The background shows no detail at all; it is as if it were a colour wash, an abstract mass of graded sepia colours. Jou Jou's fingers move through some wispy strands of grey hair made golden by the bright sunshine lighting the subjects from behind. Jou Jou had, like Gregoire, been caged in a zoo for many years and this yearning for contact is contextualised and prompted by an explanatory caption. It is another Goodall image that leaves itself open to a religious or spiritual interpretation.

The second half of *Brutal Kinship* includes black and white and colour photos of chimps exploited for human purposes: chimps being used for medical experiments in NASA laboratories; chimps kept in small cages as part of the wildlife, pet or bushmeat trade; a chimp chained round the neck or huddled in a white wheelbarrow displaying a red cross for use in HIV AIDs research in Liberia. There are images of other individuals in language research centres in US universities. Others have been photographed while starring in entertainment TV shows, performing at gala dinners or even smoking a cigarette in a chimp retirement home. There is an image of a playful 54-four-year-old Cheetah, retired star of the *Tarzan* films, living with his retired trainer in California. The book ends with a series of images of orphaned chimps now living in sanctuaries. These images are playful. The chimps are displaying their sociability and their affection for each other and for their human carers. *Brutal Kinship*, writes Nichols in his brief Afterword, is about creating an awareness of human myopia. It is not so much conscious wrongdoing that sees the chimps treated as they are, but one of moral blindness, ignorance and even misguided love. There is a need for restitution and change, of taking responsibility and of learning about ourselves as much as there is about these other creatures. He writes (Nichols and Goodall, 2005: 126):

> If we can see that our treatment of chimpanzees has been and is wrong, then we will have truly evolved.

A strong ethical code is the key to Nichols' work: it encompasses his relationships with his employer, other photographers, his human or animal subjects and his prospective or intended audience. He is wary of transgressing on the private space of others, of pressurising his animal subjects in the interest of securing a cool image. His website is full of advice and tips on the do and don'ts of being a professional wildlife or nature photographer. For Nichols (2001), authenticity is most important:

> Where ethics really play in, is whether you set up a picture or not. I want people to trust my photographs, so I try to do them as realistically as possible. But setting up a picture is not a horrible thing if that's what it requires. The important question is: is it misleading? If it is, then it starts to cross a boundary. I can't stand a photograph that I've made, no matter how cool it is, that I set up. It's dismissed. It's one that you will not see. The pictures that I care about the most are real moments, not cropped, not set up, and that have kind of an energy.

This position is echoed within the ILCP, whose statement of ethical principles emphases respect, honesty and care. The ILCP's code of ethics states that captions must never deceive. Animals photographed in captivity at game ranches must never be presented as having been taken in the wild, and digital image manipulation must never alter essential content in such a way that it either misrepresents actual events or deceives the intended audience in any context in which the truth of the image is assumed. When creative manipulation has been used, it must be declared. As former editor of *BBC Wildlife* magazine, content organiser of WildPhotos (Wildscreen's annual photographic symposium) and ILCP affiliate Roz Kidman Cox said (interview 7.5.09):

> You might feel it is perfectly OK to keep wolves in dog kennels, release them so they run in the snow towards the photographers and then charge for that. The trouble is most photographers who pay to take those sort of pictures,

including pumas airlifted to the top of a mountain in the US, or even snow leopards – virtually every image of a snow leopard has been taken in captivity – never divulge how their shots were taken or even lie about the behaviour they show. And on the publishing side, very few publications even know that game farms exist, let alone think about the truthfulness of the images or the welfare of those wild animals. What matters to both is that photographs of big cats sell.

Redefining the 'creative treatment of actuality'

Niall Benvie (2001) has castigated "fantasy photography", which at one moment came dangerously close to defining what was generally considered to define wildlife photography. In book and magazine publishing the editorial process does inevitably include the processes of selection, placing, cropping and captioning photographs. *National Geographic* editors will look through all the photographs a photographer takes on an assignment to check for authenticity and to understand how the image was achieved. However, as editor and writer Nancy Newhall wrote in *Aperture* in 1953, the layout and slant given to the story is that of the editor, while the photographer is trusted as a sort of "remote controlled eye" (Newhall, 1999). Digital photography has enabled photographic images to be manipulated and altered with a high degree of subtlety and precision. The technology has perhaps changed the game somewhat, as can be seen in the various arguments and debates that photographic theorists have had over whether digital manipulation is more or less significant than in the days of chemical processing and the creation of negative originals. As in other photographic fields, there have been a few controversial instances of wildlife photographers faking it – that is, altering images digitally or using captive animals without having declared they have done so. Steve Bloom's coffee table book *Untamed* and some other work has been criticised for including digitally manipulated (or enhanced) images and composites. The photographic blogosphere includes a wide range of comments, ranging from outright disapproval through to a recognition that enhancement or manipulation is common practice. One blogger on Safaritalk.net wrote an entry in 2008:

> I once had a chat with Steve Bloom on this. I asked him about the ways he improved his images. Well, he was 100% open on this. He took a pic in his book *Animals* (you know, the big, 5kg 'should be considered a potential murder weapon' one), and showed it to me. It was a dolphin, jumping out of the ocean. He asked me what manipulation I saw. I could not find anything. Well

. . . it seems a whole team worked on that pic for quite some time. Every spat of water flying in the air was digitally altered in some way (to make it stand out more).

He said to me straight away: "Be very wary of photographers that tell you that they do not do this."

Rob Gray, photographer and writer, quoted Bloom as stating digital manipulation is acceptable so long as the basic integrity of the picture is retained and that the animals are not presented as doing something they would otherwise not have done. In an essay first published in *Better Digital Camera* magazine he writes (Gray, nd):

Let's take the case of Steve Bloom's polar bear cubs playing on their mother.

My initial response was 'what a great shot', but then I looked closer. There was something not quite right about the image, and eventually I realised what it was. The light source is different for one of the cubs than for its sibling and mother. It appears to be a fabricated image; the animals are not 'in the wrong environment' or 'doing something completely out of character', and I'm sure that the cubs were indeed playing on their mother at the time, but this scene was almost certainly never captured by the photographer in one decisive moment.

Steve Bloom is without doubt one of the world's finest nature photographers, but I now find myself wondering about his images.

In commenting on his other work including his 2006 book *Elephant*, bloggers have suggested a shot of a swimming elephant was presented as wild when it was not, that an image of elephants near Mount Kilimanjaro had a different light falling on the elephants than on the land, that the same tusks can be seen on different elephants, broken tusks have been replaced with complete ones and travelling elephant herds have increased in number, but there is no acknowledgement in the captions or introduction that the photos have been digitally altered. Art Wolfe, an American photographer whose work is presented as combining art with nature photography has also been subject to much critical scrutiny, particularly since the controversy surrounding his book *Migrations*. In that book, visual forms and shapes created by flocks of birds or swarms of bees were sometimes adjusted and gaps filled in order to complete a perfect pattern. For art theorist W.J.T. Mitchell (1992), digital imaging is blurring the boundaries between painting and photography, and for Rudolf Arnheim (1993) there is danger that this enhanced formative power of the image-maker may lead to a lack of trust in both the still and moving image. However, *Migrations* is not a piece of photojournalism or a documentary project. It is as much about design as nature, and Wolfe (2010) himself applies the term 'digital illustrations' to those images in the text that have been altered digitally. Additionally, as Wolfe has stated a number of times, photographers have always sought to control their images by changing exposure, lens or shutter speed. Photography is no different from any other artistic medium. Wolfe (2010) continues:

> I think that people have this perception and certainly within the bastions of nature photographers, there's this perception that photography is real, and that whatever you aim the camera at is a pure recording of reality and I've never maintained that. I've never maintained that whatever I was photographing was absolutely real. I could alter its content by compression through the use of telephoto lenses, I could conversely distort the angles by using wide angles, I could change the colour depending on the film I chose, I could change the reality of the image by what I chose to include in the composition and exclude in the composition.

Steve Bloom's photographs are certainly powerful and artistic. Whether they document what is 'real' or not is another matter, for a number are digital composites. But just as blue chip documentaries may not be real in some ways but convey the wonder and beauty of nature, then so do Steve Bloom's images, books and outdoor exhibitions. No more so perhaps than *Spirit of the Wild* (Bloom, 2008), where in the Introduction he writes that the camera may be viewed as an extension of the heart, that the creative objective remains paramount, and that as an artist the role of the photographer is to fashion a wider intuitive awareness of the natural world. It can be argued that many of Bloom's images are far more spectacular and affecting than may have possibly been taken by adopting the principles of straight photography and this, together with the controversy surrounding changes in established techniques and technologies, could stimulate photographers to think, conceive images and messages in ways they would not otherwise have done. Thus, as Niall Benvie has suggested (interview 13th May 2009), it is possible to see the work of Steve Bloom and Art Wolfe in quite a positive way.

Like other photographers and like Godfrey Reggio, director of *Anima Mundi*, Bloom often concentrates on the eye of the animal. It is offered to the viewer as a window to its soul, a means of apprehending its sentience and intelligence. He also attempts to reinforce this notion by using a selection of quotations on natural history derived from a variety of famous authors, song writers and philosophers. There is a sentimentality in some of this that seems to mirror the striving towards ART, being an artist and being accepted as such. For instance, adjacent to an aerial shot of three African elephants crossing a dusty plain:

> Non violence leads to the highest ethics, which is the goal of all evolution. Until we stop harming all other living beings, we are still savages (Edison).

Adjacent to dancing red crowned cranes:

> O Lyric Love, half angel and half bird. All all a wonder and a wild desire (Browning).

For Newhall, the caption is important to help the viewer find meaning in the picture. It may be little more than a title or the date and place of when the image was taken. An additive caption is one where words and image interrelate to produce meaning together. For Newhall, photographs are not to be mere illustrations and the words are not there to describe what can be seen. Neither are they to seem trite or contrived. Newhall (1999: 135) understands the art of the photographer as the art of connotation, of multi-layered significance whose power "springs from a deeper source than words – the same deep source as music". This art of connotation has to cut through the visual noise created by all the other images circulating in society. The problem perhaps with perfect, digitally enhanced artistic images is that they are contrived, sentimental, sometimes trite . . . and look like it.

More about photography than nature

The Wildlife Photographer of the Year competition is one of the most prestigious of a growing number of wildlife and nature photographic competitions. It is owned by two institutions: *BBC Wildlife magazine* and the Natural History Museum in London, where the first of the annual travelling exhibitions are held. There are usually at least 30,000 entries every year, competing in a range of categories, covering every aspect of nature, including animal behaviour, underwater life, plants, wild places and environmental reportage. The Competition's stated aims are as follows (Kidman Cox, 2008: 8):

- to use its collection of inspirational photographs to make people worldwide wonder at the splendour, drama and variety of life on Earth
- to be the world's most respected forum for wildlife photographic art, showcasing the very best photographic images of nature to a worldwide audience

- to inspire a new generation of photographic artists to produce visionary and expressive interpretations of nature
- to raise the status of wildlife photography into that of mainstream art.

For Roz Kidman Cox, a judge of the Wildlife Photographer of the Year competition, such competitions stretch the talents of the photographer and display ways of seeing that can be deeply evocative, reflective and spiritually engaging. She notes (interview, 7.5.09):

> The now-classic bushmeat image by Karl Ammann won the World in our Hands category in 1995, and as a result of being exhibited and published worldwide, it drew attention to the bushmeat trade at a time when it was little known about. But a simple portrait that is special enough to achieve an emotional response can also be incredibly powerful. And a particularly evocative picture of a landscape or underwater seascape can definitely help to persuade politicians to consider an area worth safeguarding.

The entries to Wildlife Photographer of the Year attempt to realise this idea but their technical sophistication, supreme artistry and generic similarity has occasionally led critics to suggest such images and such competitions are far more about photography than they are about nature, conservation or the environment. The beautiful image becomes an end and a thing in itself. The picturesque nature of some of them conveys an idealised rather than idyllic construct which in its ideological and cultural coding is alternately beautiful, sublime and hyperreal. Very occasionally, some dispute occurs over the truthfulness of a particular constructed image. In 2009 the Competition's overall winner, Jose Luis Rodriguez, was disqualified after the reconvened judges concluded the photographer who had taken "the shot of his dreams – one that he had even sketched on paper" (*BBC Wildlife Magazine*, 2009: 6) had used a model animal to get his perfect shot. In other words, the technically complex photograph of a rare Iberian wolf jumping over a fence, a perfectly lit nighttime image, was set up (Edwards, 2009). Even for professional photographers and the highly experienced judging panel it was difficult to verify that this actually was the case, and given that many other competition entries exhibited a technical and aesthetic – albeit contrived – brilliance, a question must remain as to whether a photograph can do anything other than convey a sense of an image of naturalness or an image of reality. If competition images are intended to be largely symbolic, artistic or evocative of feelings rather than examples of the photojournalist's intention to document a state of affairs as seen, then the issue of photographic ethics as enshrined in Rule 8, which was deemed to have been breached, is one that requires further reflection.

> Rule 8: Only pictures of wild animals and plants and landscapes are eligible subjects. Images of domestic animals (cats, dogs, farm animals, etc) and cultivated plants (species or hybrids grown in a cultivated setting) do not count as wildlife. Pictures of captive animals (animals that do not live a free and wild existence) or involving baiting using live bait are not eligible, and any other baiting must be declared. Pictures of animal models or any other animals being exploited for profit may not be entered.

Is an Iberian wolf kept in a zoological park no longer a wild animal? Is the commercial photographic exploitation of a tame animal any different from the commercial exploitation of one that is not tame, that does not live in a captive environment, that goes through the bars of a gate rather than over it? Is reality as much in the imagination as outside it? Possibly more so? Many competition images are self-referential, not so much conditioning a way of seeing the natural world but of diverting attention from it to something more controllable and more enticing – the hyperreal rather than the real. What comes first? What happens when the the picture is itself the story? Or the image is neither real nor fake but something in between? Paula McCartney's *Bird Watching* (McCartney, Himes and Irvine, 2010) is a book and exhibition of photographs of beautiful birds sitting in trees: the Blue Jay, American Gold Finches, the Spotted Back Thrush and others. The point for McCartney is that these pictures are too beautiful, too perfect – no blur, no motion and perfect positioning. For McCartney, many people look at images to recognise, name and see, but not to look deeply into. The Spotted Back Thrush doesn't exist, or at least it only exists in the photograph as a carefully painted styrofoam model fixed to the branches of a tree like all her other birds. The birds are real, like the landscape and trees, and were actually photographed but are themselves fake birds. As McCartney has explained, what you see in the photographs is true and cannot be true. Not everything is fake. Things are changed but not 'after the event'. There is no digital manipulation making the photographs 'real fakes'. "It is a bird, after all," she says, "so what is the reality?" (McCartney, 2010). Even David Maitland's winning entry in the 2008 Wildlife Photographer of the Year Competition One Earth Award category of a dead monkey lying on a griddle over a fire having its fur singed off has a terrible hyperreal beauty about it. The staring dead eyes looking upwards into the camera's wide angle lens, the image's foreshortened perspective, the gap from a missing tooth visible in the animal's partially opened mouth, may also be read as offering a too perfect rendition of the macabre and the horrific.

Art and ecology

By contrast, the photos in James Mollison's book of chimp portraits, taken in extreme close-up, have just the name – Wendy, Gregoire, Matoko, Liana – next to the image. People have names, and so do chimps. There is a brief biography of each animal at the back – an orphan, rescued from a zoo and so on – but the meaning of the photographs extends beyond that. The intention behind *James and other Apes* (2005) is to show that each chimp face is unique in some way, and like a human face expressive of an individual personality which can be known through the eyes that look directly out of the page into those of the viewer. The images are disturbing in their very familiarity, for the clear intention on Mollison's part is to remind us, of us. As a photographer who has worked with Benetton and other major image-conscious companies, James Mollison is not known as a nature or wildlife photographer, and his techniques, particularly those employed to take these images, are a far cry from those of Nick Nichols and others like him. The images do however have a documentary purpose because of the way they have been contrived, for they suggest a reality that only an artistic intervention can make apparent. After watching a David Attenborough documentary on primates, Mollison recognised that chimp faces have a similar structure to those of humans, and that humans tend to think of animals as generic – 'like a banana' – indistinguishable one from another. He then considered the format used in passport photographs, which is intended and accepted as conveying a true image of an individual's identity. As Mollison said in an interview he didn't want to use a long lens. He wanted to get up close to the animal and for the animal to look into the lens, to initiate a relationship with the viewer. Many conservation bodies and sanctuaries were reluctant to allow James to realise these ideas, but he eventually succeeded, got the necessary medical clearance to ensure no diseases could be passed on, and then proceeded to take a series of striking images of bonobos, chimps, gorillas and orangutans.

> I was always in with the animals about 70-75 centimetres away from them. I found that it was incredibly hard to get them to look into camera and when they had the distraction of something going on behind them it meant they were constantly turning round. I also found that a tighter crop, rather than doing the passport photo that includes shoulders and ears, worked visually and had a directness to it and you really felt the animals were looking at you. Looking through the book doesn't give you any sense of the moment of taking the picture which was a moment of complete pandemonium and chaos. (James Mollison, interview 30th May 2010)

The portraits have been exhibited in Arles, in London at the Natural History Museum and at the National Media Museum in Bradford. For James, exhibition spaces create a greater visual impact than when seen on a website or in a book because of the sheer size of the photographs, but a public exhibition also occurs in a particular place and inevitably engages with the local culture, values and belief systems. Exhibitions can therefore be very educational and very challenging because their own peculiar materiality and presence makes tangible what may otherwise be an artistic or philosophical construct. James Mollison continued:

> I have been trying, and I haven't succeeded yet, in doing the show in middle America or in the southern states. I read about a poll recently which said that still only about 15% of Americans agree with the theory that humans have evolved over millions of years. For me there are those interesting readings to do with who sees the pictures. I did a job in the Appalachians, very conservation, very religious, and one woman was absolutely fascinated with the book. It was quite a revelation. "I had never thought of the connection like that," she said, and that for me is exactly the type of reaction I want to have. For me what's really interesting is that grey area between humans and animals.

When part of the *Animalism* exhibition at the National Media Museum in Bradford in 2009, Mollison's images appeared with photographs and video art, including those from Keith Arnatt's 1976-79 *Walking the Dog* series, Albrecht Tubke's 2008 *Donna* series, Michael Stevenson's 2007 series from Nigeria, Brent Stirton's images from the Virunga National Park of the gruesome effects of gorilla poaching, and Los Angeles-based Sam Easterson's video art. The short videos and photographic images in this exhibition yet again explored human beings' relationships to animals and to nature. There are photographs of a dog licking a face, a baboon on a motor cycle sitting in front of his human companions, a woman in a full-length fur coat cuddling her tiny pet dog, and videos taken from an animal's point of view. With small cameras strapped to the heads and bodies of live animals, Sam Easterson invites the viewer to see the world as an animal – an alligator, duck, buffalo, tarantula or wolf. The video film is taken from the height and travels at the speed of the animals but the lens remains these same. There is no attempt to mimic how the physical structure of an animal's eye actually sees, which is likely to be very different from that of a human. Many of the other senses an animal has are also very different, There are different smells, different sounds and different physical sensations. Therefore what the viewer sees is something clumsy, amusing and a little confusing, but there is a serious purpose for this imaging, for Easterson's eco-sensing animal-cams have helped scientists learn about the behaviour and habitats of some animals.

It is not unusual for artists to argue that art should have a purpose beyond itself, and this is certainly the case with *Animalism* and the 1999 exhibition *The New Natural History* which was also held at the National Media Museum (then called The National Museum of Photography, Film and Television). Its starting point was the ubiquity of animal imagery in contemporary culture – Disney movies, dog training books, zoos, natural history documentaries and 'the high gloss and unreality' of the Wildlife Photographer of the Year competition (Williams, 1999: 14). Included in the exhibition were romaticised portraits of dogs set against wild natural settings or the abstracted space of a studio, elephant foot umbrella stands, caterpillars eating a tomato, a stuffed bear fastened securely in his traveling crate standing erect and staring out with dead glass eyes, black and white images of an overweight security guard pressing a puppy against the wall of a stairwell, and a scrap metal worker sitting on a dirty mattress holding a goose by its neck. This exhibition presented images that depicted more than what they actually showed. There was an invitation to imagine a form of seeing that goes beyond the light and shade, line and form of the photographs' formal aesthetic structure, inviting a questioning of the apparent and the obvious. Some detective work needed to be done (Maynard, 1997).

A 1994 exhibition at the Barbican in London called *Who's Looking at the Family?* included some black-and-white images of visitors peering into the primate cages at London Zoo. The photos were taken by the primates themselves, reversing the usual specular relationship and challenging the viewer of the photographs to see themselves as perhaps they are seen by these non-human others. The images are portraits, and portraiture is a medium of communication often seen as conveying, or at least claiming to convey, the essence of personality. There is no vanity to be seen in faces and demeanours of the human visitors, just as there was no vanity in Mollison's photographs of his apes. Both sets of images suggest an equality or at least an equalising set of photographic possibilities. As Lippincott and Bluhm (2005: 29) write in their introduction to *Fierce Friends: artists and animals, 1750-1900*:

> It seems to us as art historians, however, that there is still one more mirror. This would be a mirror that, when held up to nature, shows us not ourselves, but how the rest of creation looks at us. Then, perhaps, we might truly understand what it means to belong to the animal kingdom.

Other artists such as Mark Dion, whose work also appeared in *The New Natural History*, examine the role of the popular media, science and the conservation and heritage industries. One of his exhibitions, *Natural History and Other Fictions* (1997) included an installation featuring an extinct member of the zebra family, the Quagga, last seen alive at Amsterdam's Artis Zoo in 1883. Dion wanted to make a point about the vulnerability of life on this planet and the problems scientific knowledge raises as well as solves. He works in visual metaphors that are simultaneously complex and direct, pointing to a reality that is unseen, denied or ignored.

Two other image-makers are worth considering in this context of helping the viewer to see. German-born Britta Jaschinski's claustrophobic and uneasy photographs of zoo animals, *Zoo* (1996), convey through their darkness, off-centred composition and occasional absurdity the existential pressures of being incarcerated. It is sometimes difficult to express in words what is best expressed in other ways, and Jaschinski is able show feeling and empathy imagistically. They have significant and signifying form: the images are composed specifically and intentionally to have an impact on the viewer. The book is small – the pages are not much larger than those of a postcard. The viewer steps into a relationship with the images that are consequently confining in their very materiality and physical shape and size. Jaschinski's zoo animals are abstractions from their natural world, positing a series of questions about the purpose and possible justification of zoos in the 21st century. The pictures are not designed to be entertaining although zoos, despite their scientific and conservation work, basically still are. *Wild Things* (2003), a companion work, develops this theme with a combination of black-and-white and colour images of various animals, landscapes and captions which collectively form an open letter to the reader about the animals threatened by human existence and the responsibilities of human readers to nature as a whole. The texture of the book and the graininess of many of the images seem to create echos in a void that will soon be created by the rhinos when their existence is confined to the pictures in a book, the images in a documentary or a sad survivor or two in a zoo. In a large font, reminiscent of that of a manual typewriter, part of the letter reads, "I hope you don't mind me telling you that your strength and craving for an unrestricted existence make you quite anachronistic; maybe that is why people consider you incompatible with modern times." Jaschinski's photographic style has influenced other photographers who have adapted her approach to spread a similar conservation message. Art, she says, can do this very well – more so than a straight documentary. She was awarded a 'Highly Commended' in the 2009 Wildlife Photographer of the Year for an image of a lone lion walking through the Serengeti National Park. Addressing Wildscreen's WildPhotos conference in 2009, she spoke on the subject of animal captivity and "how wrong zoos are". These values have raised her public profile and further influenced her professional work, which can be seen clearly in her latest photographic project DARK. For Jaschinski, though, the art work and the need to preserve natural habitats for the remaining 'anachronistic' creatures are one and the same. In an interview for the Captive Animal Protection Society (Jaschinski, 2009) she said:

> It's up to the public to decide whether my zoo images are art or documentation. Personally, I prefer not to be put into any drawer. When I worked on the Zoo project, people called me a photojournalist, then with *Wild Things* they referred to me as a wildlife photographer and suddenly, through DARK, I am an artist. None of this is important to me because what counts is the message. I am not creating anything to please anyone or to find success or to stimulate my ego, I just say through my images how I feel about the state of this planet. If I had to give up on photography, I would find different ways to raise my concerns. It is a bit like being on a mission, whatever it takes. Even if I have to do a handstand and balance the last surviving panda bear on my little toe in Trafalgar Square . . . or whatever. I have picked photography as my tool to communicate because it is something I can do.

> The balancing act would be harder for me.

American academic and photographer Frank Noelker has also presented images of animals in captivity. His zoo pictures are sometimes surreal and figuratively rather than literally dark. His images in *Captive Beauty* (Noelker, 2004) depict the solitary nature of many zoo animals' lives, and despite their vibrant colours they show the emptiness of the animals' existence. Some photographs have the animal subjects placed against an artificial, sometimes painted, backdrop of what purports to be a natural habitat. This technique was often employed by zoos in the 20th century to enhance the visual pleasure of the human visitor. The backdrops resembled those of a film set, and the tourists' gaze resembled that of a movie-going audience. Zoo visitors gained pleasure from the act of seeing, and colourful or exotic replica habitats added to the attractiveness of zoos as tourist destinations, boosted civic pride for those cities which had zoos and enabled the institutions to claim the status of being educational and scientific (Hanson, 2002). Today, modern zoos look to creating landscape immersion exhibits of threatened habitats. As Elizabeth Hanson said (2002: 161):

> The new exhibits are monuments to habitats and animals facing destruction and extinction. The threats to their existence make their accessibility in the zoo that much more spectacular.

Not surprisingly perhaps, the faces and demeanor of many of Noelker's animals suggest the experience of being a captive has not altered significantly. Despite the zoo designers' skills and imagination, captivity has not become any more fulfilling or meaningful, as may be seen in one image of a giraffe photographed in New York in 1997. He is standing against a wall which has painted on it an African landscape – a dusty plain, scattered trees, scudding clouds and a blue sky. Three sharp lines cut across the backdrop and the image of the giraffe itself. It looks as if the giraffe could be part of the painted backdrop or of a mural composed of three horizontal panels. Only the slight shadow of the giraffe against the painted wall shows the viewer that this is not the case and the lines are in fact the wires of a fence. This photograph is an imprint of a moment in time, of an actual life lived, captured for display, and similar to 'The Nubian Giraffe' exhibited in Paris and painted by Jacques-Laurent Agasse in 1827. But what was exotic in the early 19th century has become pathetic in the 21st. The roles have been reversed and art, photography and film are facilitating this process of seeing, perceiving and understanding differently.

Award-winning National Geographic photographer Jim Brandenberg, whose images of the American prairies, or of cuddly wolf pups who find themselves in the Defenders of Wildlife calendar, falls into a different category. In 1999 he and his wife Judy set up the Brandenburg Prairie Foundation to promote, preserve and expand the native prairie in south-west Minnesota. His many photographs of this area have been used extensively and successfully to educate decision-makers and others to value and conserve this landscape and its songbirds, flora and wildlife. Together with the US Fish and Wildlife Service the Foundation purchased over 800 acres of untilled prairie land, which was then named the 'Touch the Sky Northern Tallgrass Prairie National Wildlife Refuge' after one keynote image. In the lower half of Brandenburg's photograph 'Touch the Sky', light green prairie grass and tall purple flowers can be seen. In the top half is blue sky, and an ephemeral cloud formation is taking the shape of a bird of prey spreading out its wings as far as they can go. The image is at once intensely personal and symbolic of a world which has been lost – and of a world Brandenburg is seeking to recover. In 2006 he told Minnesota Public Radio:

> I suppose when I make a picture it's almost like I'm dreaming. It's like a prayer in a sense, not in a church-like prayer; maybe it is. But I get into kind of a zone and I'm trying to reach out and beg for something like to bring back a type of feeling of what it was like before we came and changed the landscape so much that it's hardly recognisable.

The deep spirituality of many of Jim Brandenburg's images is in some ways a visual articulation of the deep ecology of Aldo Leopold, Arne Naess and Thomas Berry and the early pioneers of the American conservation movement in whose footsteps he treads. Something is right when it tends to preserve the integrity, beauty and stability of the biotic community and wrong when it does otherwise. For Brandenburg, the experience of nature and the images that convey a sense of that experience are the educational tools that can turn values into action, appreciation into deep commitment, seeing into imagining and action into deeds. Environmental philosopher Thomas Berry (1990: 11) has written:

> If we have powers of imagination, these are activated by the magic display of color and sound, of form and movement, such as we observe in the clouds of the sky, the trees and bushes and flowers, the waters and the wind, the singing birds, and the movement of the great blue whale through the sea. If we have words with which to speak and think and commune, words for the inner experience of the divine, words for the intimacies of life, if we have words for telling stories to our children, words with which we can sing, it is again because of the impressions we have received from the variety of beings about us.

Working as a commercial photographer, taking hundreds of reels of film and many thousands of images per assignment led Brandenburg in the late 1990s to pause and meditate deeply on his art. The result was a self-directed personal project, *Chased by the Light*, in which Brandenburg resolved to explore his Minnesota surroundings during the period between the autumnal equinox and the winter solstice. His self-imposed task was to take just one image a day in which he would distill and express both his feelings of the landscape and the nature of the landscape itself. These pictures reveal a Zen-like intensity through which he went to the edge finding that significant form expressive of emotion, feeling and life in one split second. *Chased by the Light* is a visual art work in a particular key. It is the ocular equivalent of music, of no discursive meaning, of knowledge as a way of seeing. Many of the images distill nature into a detail such as a leaf, a pattern, a shaft of light, a footprint, an eye or a ripple. Many of the images dissolve into an abstraction of colour, shape, texture then transports the viewer, as it possibly did the photographer to a world beyond but within that we inhabit. An inner sense of presence is revealed, which at times seems to be almost an intrusion but which also focuses a reverence for nature into a single image.

All of the ninety images are made rather than taken. They are created by Brandenburg's deep engagement with and rootedness in place. He knows his world and is able to visually articulate this embodied knowing, this feeling. A spark of light (life?) is seen fading from the eye of a dear killed by a poacher. A waterfall is just a mass of colour which can be heard and felt. Back lighting creates a luminosity that brings to the fore a temporal continuity transcending day and night. This picture, number 36/day 36, is of the night-time. The light is artificial, provided by a torch held by Jim Brandenburg's wife. As the photographer says while explaining the provenance of the image on the film about the project, does it matter whether the picture was 'made' by the artist rather than simply 'taken' or 'shot'? Does it add or take away from the picture knowing that the light was not natural? On November 13th Jim Brandenburg created an image of a moss-covered 350-year-old cedar tree fallen to the ground within a small glade. The light is diffused, the image sharp in places and soft in others. The colours are an array of whites, yellows and greens. The exposure was fifteen seconds. Half-way through, Brandenburg lifted his tripod and moved towards the log, creating the mysterious and mystical sense of being simultaneously here and not here. The complete image is a symbol not a representation, a significant form not a document. The final photograph was made at 1.40 a.m. on day ninety, 21st December. The moonlight was natural but the exposure lasted 50 seconds. The image reveals a beauty that the naked eye finds hard to see but one which the mind's eye can readily create. And that is the essence of the image, of the beauty of Brandenburg's natural world. *Chased by the Light* is a collection of sensuous images that have inspired and motivated many people to care for and preserve this Minnesota prairie land. On US National Public Radio Brandenburg (21st December 1998) explained his approach:

> My experience of photography is that it is the light that makes the photograph. It's not just the subject matter. I can be in this most beautiful, beautiful land and if the light is poor, blue dark light, you just don't see a photograph. I finally had to take a picture. The sun was down and I knew I had to take off the tripod with a long exposure. It was that last two or three minutes when the light collapses. I looked out at my feet at this tiny little pool and saw this beautiful red floating leaf and a reflection of some grass in the water. I thought 'well', out of desperation, 'I have to shoot something; I'll shoot this'. I composed and shot much faster than I usually do. I was quite down, quite depressed. . . . When the film came back, it was one of the first frames that I saw and there was something there that I didn't see, something shows up that you can't quite explain.

There is beauty in the music of small things and meaning in the world that can only be captured through image, through seeing, through revisiting memory and understanding feeling. Some of the 90 images Brandenburg took in that quarter were published in *National Geographic Magazine,* and the whole set in a book. A documentary film was also made a little later, in which Brandenburg presents his relationship to the land, to photography and to the process of making sense of the environment through its artistic capabilities.

Images at the edge

Benvie (2001) defines images at the edge as a zone of transition in space, being or time to which our visual systems willingly respond. Photos taken at dawn or dusk are more interesting than those taken at mid-day. Young and old animals are more interesting than those who are simply mature. They are photos that depict danger or reveal the struggle between culture and wildness, anarchy and control. He writes (2001):

> It seems to me that in this country there is a cultural determination to infantilise our relationship with wild nature, to cosset and protect us from it, to make it safe and palatable. The need to take responsibility for our actions therefore diminishes and with it our appreciation of the power of nature unmediated by man.

One image emblematic of his approach has a hedgehog half-way across a road. In the distance, out of focus, is a car en route to another road kill. That photo has an edge, although not all of Benvie's have one. His conservation message and his respect for locality, whether it be his native Scotland (Benvie, 2004) or elsewhere, is always apparent; for Niall Benvie is extremely interested in the formal qualities within a picture that have the capacity to attract attention and make a difference.

> The edge of life also has an appeal. If an animal appears in a hostile environment, whether it is a naturally occurring one or one with the last tree standing in the rainforest, people understand the message. . . . The way I approach the landscape is, yes I want to make beautiful images, but very often it is with quite a critical mindset. So whereas one person might look at a scene in the Scottish Highlands and say 'what a wonderful view you've got there, you can see such a long way', I'm looking at it very often in terms of 'this is a really devastated landscape – we've lost natural vegetation, tree cover and all the animals that go with it. I am now going to employ a set of techniques through which I hope the viewer will get a less positive impression of this place than

they would if I was photographing this place, idealising it with beautiful light and a deer moving across the frame. (Niall Benvie interview, 13th May 2009)

For Benvie, these images that come from the edge need not be of the big disappearing iconic species enclosed with increasingly insecure national parks but can, and should, be of where people are living in their own neighbourhoods and communities. For Pete Cairns, another photographer based in the Scottish Highlands, telling the stories from his locality is also integral to his photographic practice. Red deer management, for instance, is a key issue and Cairns' often themed galleries will attempt to depict the story from a variety of perspectives: from a stalker's and wildlife watcher's point of view, to the meat arriving on the dinner table. Influenced by Richard Louv's *Last Child in the Woods* (2005), Benvie is also keen on 'rewilding childhood'. This media project recognises that the majority of the world's population now live in urban areas, making rewilding more necessary and possibly more difficult than ever. Access to unmanaged urban green space is of utmost importance, but these spaces are becoming increasingly rare because of housing and other developments. However, some post-industrial cities such as Detroit in the US and to a lesser extent Birmingham in the UK have opportunities to allow some unmanaged green space to become small oases of urban biodiversity. Photography can be used as a vehicle for enticing children out of doors to seek out local flora and fauna, to create images of their home areas, fashion visual memories and experiences and perhaps to feel the aesthetic delight of what surrounds them and what they physically sense when the sun shines, the wind blows or the rain falls. Photography and digital video offer the opportunity to see and to feel, to merge art with nature and through that to learn and simply to be.

There can be art without artifice, for feeling and authenticity is compromised when the image becomes the most important thing. With a digital camera and internet access, images of vulnerable areas and of creatures endangered by development can be instantly communicated to elected representatives, government officials, NGOs, journalists and others. In this way wildlife photography becomes democratised and an aspect of a wider more ecologically focussed democracy and public sphere. These images, says Benvie (2005), need not be issue-led but could be conceived as a form of localised place-marketing, of getting into, of dwelling in and of valuing a specific place-based experience. He links some of these ideas to the concept of photo-lobbying, which with the ease of creating and disseminating digital images via the internet is a practice that has yet to realise its full potential.

What triggered the idea for me originally was the Net and the unimaginable number of photographs people are taking of natural subjects. Presumably some interest or empathy is there for people to take that picture in the first place, and the pictures never go anywhere. Maybe they are not seen by anybody other than the photographer himself, the immediate family or maybe some web forums. So I thought: is there not some way of harnessing that interest and that visual resource and if you put it in front of the people who make decisions they'll think there are people out there who care about this? A picture is more immediate and understandable for a politician or councillor who is not necessarily engaged in the issues. Put a picture in front to them and it has more chance of registering if they see it and if enough people do it (Niall Benvie, interview 13th May 2009).

Many participants on social media sites and people making commentaries on blogs frequently include uploaded photos, and chain emails addressing specific issues are frequently illustrated with a range of word- and image-based content. As one researcher has discussed in relation to photoblogs, new media technology enables disparate elements that would otherwise remain separate to come together through a common causal process or motivation (Cohen, 2005). Photoblogs incorporate, and themselves become part of, four distinct activities: the self of the photoblogger, the potential audience, the practice of image-making/photo-taking and the technologies around these actions and activities. Photographs, movies, music, books and holiday destinations can become social objects around which subscribers to new media social networks affiliate, organise or otherwise share information and concerns (Dempsey, 2008). Additionally, Benvie suggests that many people's personal image archives of the natural world are often comprised of very positive pictures expressive of love, admiration and hope rather than bleakness or despair. These images and these feelings can be extremely useful and effective in showing what could be threatened or what, when too late, was lost. The images could also be highly motivating.

The *Shame on You Denmark* chain email, which addresses the bloody slaughter of blue fin pilot whales and bottle-nosed dolphins by predominantly young men in Dantesque in the Faroe Islands, has been circulating for some years and is an example of photoblogging and of images as a call to action. The still images in this mail are of a blood-red bay with dolphins having been hacked into and partially disemboweled and carcasses lying on the harbour front. The Faroese do not recognise the authority of the International Whaling Commission as a body competent to regulate the hunting of small cetaceans, and claim that whale and dolphin hunting is a part of their ancient culture and diet. It is this which justifies and explains the continuation of the practice, as a sympathetic 2007 Front Line report, *The Faroe Islands: Message from the Sea*, broadcast on America's PBS television station suggested. About 1,000 whales are killed every year around the Faroes, and PBS was very discrete in its presentation of the dolphin slaughter – a few seconds of video footage, a few still images, and an explanation that the animals are killed swiftly by the severing of a key artery to the brain which accounts for so much blood. However, as in Japan there are fears, as expressed by the chief medical officers in the Faroes, that whale and dolphin meat carry high levels of mercury and other toxins including PCB and DDT derivatives (Mackenzie, 2008). As in Japan, despite a campaign lasting over twenty years, the hunting continues. The email images, like many of those associated with Karl Ammann, are taken from 'the edge'.

Time to see, time to be

Video artist Bill Viola has explored the natural world and the place of human beings in it. His video/film *I Do Not Know What It Is I Am Like* (1986) is structured in five parts, has no voice-over, only ambient sound, and involves seemingly unconnected images of bison, birds, animal behaviour of various kinds, shots of the artists at work and what is assumed to be their home, and scenes of Fijian firewalkers who (like Viola attempts to do) through their actions seek a transcendent knowledge and wisdom. As Marjorie Perloff writes, *I Do Not Know What It Is I Am Like* foregrounds what may be termed a fractal sense of reality, the reality of nature composed of complex irregular fragments presented slowly and patiently to the viewers in the manner of an unfolding. The middle sequence shows the artist at his table. The main light source is a reading lamp. The artist reads, turns the pages of a book, and a drawing depicting the stimulus-response process is seen over the artist's shoulder. A small golden vessel in the shape of a Renaissance ship has a snail for its sail. There are cuts to more mundane things. A tap. A glass of water clearing to reveal a miniature bonsai type tree. A close-up of a cooked fish on a silver platter. An extreme close-up of a knife and fork cutting away some of its flesh. A cut to a clock reveals the time as 3.30, presumably a.m.. There is a cut to a close-up of an egg placed on the table. The snail slowly emerges from his shell and slithers from his golden craft. The egg is pictured once again. It rocks. The shell cracks. A series of cuts compress time as the crack in the shell grows. Behind the membrane is a life, pulsating. A faint chirping can be heard. The egg rocks again, finally cracks open and a small chick pushes its way out. It lies on its back, chirping, dazed and no doubt exhausted from its efforts. The beauty and wonder is of the life emerging and the fact that moments before such a relatively large and awkward creature could have been confined within the highly limited internal space of an egg. There is an abrupt cut revealing an empty space where the egg once was. A steaming white mug is placed in its former place. Round, hard, manufactured, inanimate. Another cut reveals the artist at his table. The reading lamp is the sole illumination. The mug is still on the table. The artist leaves, and the camera slowly tracks towards the mug. Then inexplicably and surprisingly the tip of an elephant's trunk wraps itself round the object and lifts it from the table. A fraction later the camera reveals an adult elephant in the room. A surreal intervention, a symbol, a visual rendition of a commonplace figure of speech. What is this elephant doing in the room that everyone is not talking about? Viola's video camera bears witness to something more than can be empirically verified. There is a poetic truth here which could not be shown by either television or film or science. The aim of Viola's video art is, as Perloff (1998) observes, "to slow down the viewer's attention and witness what has always already been there but never quite seen".

The same can be said for the films and installations of Slovenian artist Andrej Zdravic. His most famous film *Riverglass: A River Ballet in Four Seasons* (1973) has been screened continuously in art galleries, museums and art schools throughout the world. Using natural sounds and a pace that makes the viewer aware of time passing, Zdravic offers an opportunity to find one's own response to not only what is seen on the screen but to nature itself. At a conference on cinema and ecology held in Bristol in 2005 Zdravic said,

> . . . the whole thing is just to immerse yourself, and I often say to people 'try to see my film as you would listen to a piece of music in a theatre hall'. Meaning that you just sit there and listen and don't expect anything to be told, what to think, just experience it as music. Then see what happens.

What music is there in an image of a gorilla's head next to a bunch of bananas?

Coda

All professional photographers need to make a living, and very few are able to concentrate exclusively on conservation or animal welfare. They have to produce images that sell, and much time and money is being spent on sophisticated websites that promote their work, their skill, their philosophy and the precariousness of the Earth's ecosystems. The still and moving image is as good a way as any of conveying this core message. If images work best emotively and intuitively, if they imprint themselves on the memory of the viewer and help bridge the gap between passive spectatorship and action, then there is clearly hope for the future – not least because photography and increasingly digital video are democratic and popular arts. Many people have an urge to capture, to snap, to create images of this world, just as they have an urge to live and be in it. The world is now a much smaller place. A global village, perhaps, with new media technologies connecting peoples and continents in ways that were impossible just a few decades ago. Images and ideas circulate globally and in a matter of seconds. The politics of the image is intimately bound up with the politics of conservation and the politics of truth. The two are inseparable. If an image is worth a thousand words what can a thousand images be worth? Hopefully, more than just words.

The problem is that the reality of species extinction and habitat destruction is too grim and as such seemingly unsuitable for commercial or family viewing. Audiences shy away from hard truths and major media companies will do so too, relying on comforting images and the 'love of nature' argument to do the necessary conservation work. Without such images and without the blue chip documentaries, it could be argued that people would care even less, but as many of the film-makers and photographers discussed in this book would argue, even caring more is not enough. Without action, images remain simply images – colours, shapes, lines, dreams, memories, hopes, desires and perhaps denials. With action, images are a tangible force to be reckoned with, giving hope and possibility to all of us, for ultimately we are all animals whose habitats and futures are in danger. The surrealist artist Rene Magritte once painted a picture of a briar pipe with the caption 'ceci n'est pas une pipe' (this is not a pipe). It is as well to remember that, for when you see a photograph of a beautiful tiger, it is not the tiger you are seeing but its image. If you want to have real tigers, or at least know that there will be real tigers to see in generations to come, it is important the tiger has a future beyond that of being a screen saver, a calendar or a TV documentary. For Karl Ammann, Nick Nichols, Mike Pandey and others, it is also important that the image of the tiger is not just an image, but actually a just image. It must tell truth to power, and so must we.

References

Acampora, R. (2005) 'Zoos and Eyes: Contesting Captivity and Seeking Successor Practices' in *Society and Animals*, Vol. 13 No. 1, pp.69-88.

Adorno, T.W. (1991) *The Culture Industry: Selected Essays on Mass Culture*. London, Routledge.

Anderson, K. 2008. 'Understanding Green Audiences' in *Realscreen, 17 September*. Available at: www.realscreen.com/articles/news/20080917/psychographics.html.

Anonymous Daily Mail Reporter (2009) 'You cheeky monkeys: Safari park baboons ransack cars after learning to break into luggage boxes'. *Mail Online*, 20 July. Available at: www.dailymail.co.uk/news/article-1200917/.

Apel, D. (2009) 'Just Joking? Chimps, Obama and Racial Stereotype' in *Journal of Visual Culture*, Vol. 8 No. 2, pp.134-142.

Appadurai, A. (Ed.) (1986) *The Social Life of Things: commodities in cultural perspective*. Cambridge, Cambridge University Press.

Arluke, A. and Sanders, C.R. (1996) *Regarding Animals*. Philadelphia, Temple University Press.

Arluke, A. (2006) *Just a Dog: Understanding Animal Cruelty and Ourselves*. Philadelphia, Temple University Press.

Arnheim, R. (1993) The Two Authenticities of the Photographic Media. *The Journal of Aesthetics and Art Criticism*, Vol. 51 No. 4, pp.537-540.

Arthus-Bertrand, Y. (2005) *Earth from Above*. New York, Abrams.

Attenborough, D. (2003) *Life on Air*. London, BBC Books.

Bagust, P. (2008) ' "Screen Natures": special effects and edutainment in "new" hybrid wildlife documentary.' *Continuum*, 22.2; pp.213-226.

Baker, S. (2001) *Picturing the Beast: animals, identity and representation*. Urbana, University of Illinois Press.

Bal, M. (2003) 'Visual essentialism and the object of visual culture' in *Journal of Visual Culture*, Vol. 2 No. 1, pp.5-32.

Balcombe, J. (2009) Animal pleasure and its moral significance. *Applied Animal Behaviour Science*, Vol. 118, pp.208–216.

Balcombe, J. (2010) *Second Nature: the inner lives of animals*. London, Palgrave Macmillan.

Barclay, P. D.(2002) 'A "Curious and Grim Testimony to a Persistent Human Blindness": Wolf Bounties in North America, 1630-1752' in *Ethics, Place & Environment*, Vol. 5 No. 1, pp.25-34.

Barry, A.M. (1997) *Visual Intelligence: perception, image and manipulation in visual communication*. New York, SUNY.

Barry, A. M. (2006) 'Perceptual Aesthetics: Transcendent Emotion, Neurological Image' in *Visual Communication Quarterly*, Vol. 13 No. 3, pp.134-151.

Barthes, R. (1977) *Image Music Text*. New York, Hill and Wang.

Baudrillard, J. (1988) *Jean Baudrillard: Selected Writings*. Edited by Mark Poster. Cambridge, Polity Press.

BBC Wildlife Magazine (2009) 'Veolia Environment Wildlife Photographer of the Year Portfolio' in *Supplement*, November. London.

BBC News (2009) 'Polar bear unveiled at new home'. BBC News Channel, 22 October, available at: http://news.bbc.co.uk/1/hi/scotland/highlands_and_islands/8318276.stm.

Beardsworth, A. and Bryman, A. (2001) 'The wild animal in late modernity: the case of the Disneyization of zoos' in *Tourist Studies*, Vol. 1 No. 1, pp.83-104.

Beder, S. (2006) 'The Changing Face of Conservation: commodification, privatisation and the free market' in Lavigne, D. (Ed.) *Gaining Ground: in pursuit of ecological sustainability*. Guelph, IFAW.

Benvie, N. (2001) 'The Edge Concept'. Available at: http://niallbenvie.churchilljohnson.co.uk/blog/?page_id=211

Benvie, N. (2004) *Scotland's Wildlife*. London, Aurum Press.

Berger, J. (1972) *Ways of Seeing*. London, BBC and Penguin Books.

Berger, J (1991) 'Why Look at Animals?' in *About Looking*. New York, Vintage Books.

Bergmann, I. (1997). 'Visual Imagery for Environmental Concept Formation'. Paper presented at the Annual Conference of the Australian Association for Research in Education: Researching Education in New Times, Brisbane, Australia.

Berry, T. (1990) *The Dream of the Earth*. San Francisco, Sierra Club Books.

Birchall, D. (2008) 'Online Documentary' in Austin, T. and de Jong W. (Eds.) *Rethinking Documentary: new perspectives, new practices*. Maidenhead, McGraw Hill/Open University Press.

Blewitt, J. (2004) 'The Eden Project: Making a Connection' in *Museum and Society*. Vol. 2 No. 3.

Blewitt, J. (2006) *The Ecology of Learning: sustainability, lifelong learning and everyday life*. London, Earthscan.

Bloch, M. (2005) *Essays on Cultural Transmission*. Oxford, Berg.

Bloom, S. (2004) *Untamed*. New York, Abrams.

Bloom, S. (2005) *Elephant*. New York, Abrams.

Bloom, S. (2008) *Spirit of the Wild*. London, Thames and Hudson.

Boler, M. Ed (2008) *Digital Media and Democracy*. Cambridge Mass., MIT Press.

Boorstein, D. (1961) *The Image: a guide to pseudo events in America*. New York, Basic Books.

Bouse, D. (2000) *Wildlife Films*. Philadelphia, University of Pennsylvania Press.

Bouse, D. (2003) 'False Intimacy: close-ups and viewer involvement in wildlife films' in *Visual Studies*, Vol. 18 No. 2, pp.123-132.

Brandenburg, J. (2001) *Chased by the Light: Revisited After the Storm*. Lanham, Northword.

Bristow, M. (2010) 'Eleven rare Siberian tigers die at Chinese zoo'. BBC News, 12 March. Available at: http://news.bbc.co.uk/1/hi/world/asia-pacific/8563673.stm.

Brock, R. (2007) Interview (with Miranda Krestovnikoff). Wildscreen/WildFilmHistory. Available at: www.wildfilmhistory.org/oh/29/Richard+Brock.html.

Brockington, D. (2008) 'Celebrity Conservation: interpreting the Irwins' in *Media International Australia*, No. 127, pp.96-107.

Brockington, D. (2009) *Celebrity and the Environment: fame, wealth and power in conservation*. London, Zed Books.

Brower, M. (2005) ' "Take Only Photographs": Animal Photography's Construction of Nature Love' in *Invisible Culture*, Issue 9, pp.1-27. Available at: www.rochester.edu/in_visible_culture/Issue_9/brower.html.

Bryant, C.D. (1979) 'The Zoological Connection: Animal-related human behavior' in *Social Forces*, Vol. 58 No. 2, pp.399-421.

Buchen, L. (2008) 'Could Pandas be an Evolutionary Mistake – or Proof of an Intelligent Designer?' *Discover*, 5 August. Available at: http://discovermagazine.com/2008/aug/05-could-pandas-be-an-evolutionary-mistake2014or-proof-of-an-intelligent-designer/.

Buckingham, D. (2000) *After the Death of Childhood: growing up in the age of electronic media*. Cambridge, Polity.

Bulbeck, C. (2005) *Facing the Wild: ecotourism, conservation and animal encounters*. London, Earthscan.

Burt, J. (2002) *Animals in Film*. London, Reaktion Books.

CCTV (2008) Special report: Seeking harmony between man and nature. China Live, 11 March. Available at: www.cctv.com/english/20080311/103539.shtml

Chalfen, R. (2003) 'Celebrating life after death: the appearance of snapshots in Japanese pet gravesites.' *Visual Studies*, Vol. 18 No. 2, pp.144-156.

Chatfield, T. (2010) *FUN Inc.: why games are the 21st century's most serious business*. London, Virgin Books.

Chawla, L. (1998) 'Significant Life Experiences Revisited: a review of research on sources of environmental sensitivity' in *Environmental Education Research*, Vol. 4 No. 4, pp.369-382.

Chris, C. (2002) 'All Documentary, All the Time?' *Television and New Media*, Vol. 3 No. 1, pp.7-23.

Chris, C. (2006) *Watching Wildlife*. Minneapolis, University of Minnesota Press.

Christophers, B. (2006) 'Visions of Nature, Spaces of Empire: Framing natural history programming within geometries of power' in *Geoforum*, Vol. 37, pp.973-985.

Clutton-Brock, T. (2007) *Meerkat Manor: Flower of the Kalahari*. London, Weidenfeld and Nicolson.

Cohen, K.R. (2005) 'What Does the Photoblog Want?' *Media Culture & Society*, Vol. 27 No. 6, pp.883-901.

Cohen. S. (2001) *States of Denial*. Cambridge, Polity Press.

Conservation International (2004) *Final Project Completion Report: Awareness Campaign on the Bushmeat Crisis*. Available at: www.cepf.net/Documents/Final.Awareness.Bushmeat.Crisis.pdf.

Cottle, S. (2004) 'Producing nature(s): on the changing production ecology of natural history TV.' *Media, Culture & Society*, Vol. 26 No. 1, pp.81–101.

Cubitt, S. *EcoMedia*. New York, Rodopi.

Dale, S. (1996) *McLuhan's Children: the Greenpeace message in the media*. Toronto, Between the Lines.

Davey, G., and Higgins, L. (2005). 'Fear in China' in *China Review*, Summer, pp.30–33.

Davey, G. (2006) 'Chinese University Students' Attitudes Toward the Ethical Treatment and Welfare of Animals' in *Journal of Applied Animal Welfare Science*, Vol. 9 No. 4, pp.289-297.

Davies, G. (2000) 'Virtual animals in electronic zoos: the changing geographies of animal capture and display' in Philo, C. and Wilbert, C. *Animal Spaces, Beastly Places*. London, Routledge.

Davies, G. (1999) 'Exploiting the Archive: and the animals came in two by two', 16mm, CD-ROM and BetaSp. *AREA*, Vol. 31 No. 1 pp.49-58.

Davies, G. (2000) 'Narrating the Natural History Unit: institutional orderings and spatial strategies' in *Geoforum*, Vol 31, pp.539-551.

Davis, S.G. (1997) *Spectacular Nature: corporate culture and the Sea World experience*. Berkeley, University of California Press.

DCMS (2006) *A Public Service for All: the BBC in the Digital Age*. London, TSO.

De Zengotita, T. (2005) *Mediated: how the media shape your world*. London, Bloomsbury.

Debord, G. (1995) *The Society of the Spectacle*. New York, Zone Books.

DeLuca, K.M. (1999) *Image Politics: the new rhetoric of environmental activism*. Mahwah NJ, Lawrence Erlbaum.

Dempsey, L. (2008) 'Some thoughts about egos, objects, and social networks. . . .' Lorcan Dempsey's Weblog, available at: http://orweblog.oclc.org/archives/001601.html

Dingwall, R. and Aldridge, M. (2006) 'Television Wildlife Programming as a Source of Popular Scientific Information: a case study of evolution' in *Public Understanding Of Science*, 15, pp.131-152.

Dowie, M. (2009) *Conservation Refugees: the hundred year conflict between global conservation and native peoples*. Cambridge Mass., MIT Press.

Dunaway, F. (2005) *Natural Visions: the power of images in American environmental reform*. Chicago, University of Chicago Press.

Eco, U. (1987) *Travels in Hyper-Reality*. London, Picador.

Edwards, E. and Hart, J. (Eds.) (2004) *Photographs Objects Histories: on the materiality of images*. London, Routledge.

Edwards, T. (2009) 'Storybook Wolf a fantasy, say wildlife photographers' in *The First Post*, 22 December. Available at: www.thefirstpost.co.uk/57730,news-comment,news-politics,storybook-wolf-a-fantasy-say-wildlife-photographers.

Elkins, J. (2003) *Visual Studies: a skeptical introduction*. London, Routledge.

Elkins, J. (2008) *Six Stories from the End of Representation*. Stanford, Stanford Univ. Press.

Evans, M. (2009) 'Inside Nature's Giants'. Available at: www.markevans.co.uk/mark-evans-television-inside-natures-giants.php.

Falk, J. H. and Dierking, L. N. (2002) *Lessons Without Limit: how free-choice learning is transforming education*. New York, Altamira Press.

Finlay, James and Maple (1988) 'People's Perceptions of Animals: The Influence of Zoo Environment' in *Environment and Behavior*, Vol. 20 No. 4, pp.508-528.

Fossey, D, (1985) *Gorillas in the Mist*. London, Penguin.

Foucault, M. (1980) 'Truth and Power' in Gordon, G. Ed. *Michel Foucault: Power/ Knowledge (selected interviews and other writings)*. Sussex, Harvester Press.

Franklin, A. (1999) *Animals and Modern Culture: a sociology of human-animal relations in modernity*. London, Sage.

Frosh, P. (2003) *The Image Factory: consumer culture, photography and the visual content industry*. Oxford, Berg Publishers.

Gadgil, M. and Guha, R. (1992) *This Fissured Land: an ecological history of India*. New Delhi, Oxford University Press.

Gadgil, M. and Guha, R. (1995) *Ecology and Equity*. New Delhi, Oxford University Press.

Gamson, W.A., Croteau, D., Hoynes, W. and Sasson, T. (1992) 'Media Images and the Social Construction of Reality' in *Annual Review of Sociology*, Vol. 18, pp.373-93.

Garnham, N. (1996) 'The Media and the Public Sphere' in Calhoun, C. (Ed.) *Habermas and the Public Sphere*. Cambridge, Mass., MIT Press.

Garnham, N. 2003 'A Response to Elizabeth Jacka's "Democracy as Defeat"' in *Television and New Media*, Vol. 4 No. 2, pp.193-200.

Gazzinga, M.S. (1998) *The Mind's Past*. Berkeley, University of California Press.

Gee, J. P. (2005) 'What would a state of the art instructional video game look like?' Innovate 1 (6). Available at: www.innovateonline.info/index.php?view=article&id=80

Gerbner, G., Gross, L., Morgan, M., and Signorielli, N. (1986) 'Living with television: The dynamics of the cultivation process' in Bryant, J. and Zillman, D (Eds.) *Perspectives on media effects*. New Jersey, Lawrence Erlbaum Associates.

Gerbner, G. et al (2002) 'Growing up with television: cultivation processes' in Bryant, J. and Zillmann (Eds.) *Media Effects: Advances in Theory and Research*. Mahwah NJ, Lawrence Erlbaum.

Gerber, L.R., Morissette, L., Kaschner, K. and Paul, D. (2009) 'Should Whales Be Culled to Increase Fishery Yield?' *Science*, 13 Feb, Vol. 323, pp.880-881.

Goodall, J. and Berman, P. (2000) *Reason for Hope: an extraordinary life*. London, Thorsons.

Gosling, D.L. (2001) *Religion and Ecology in India and South-East Asia*. London, Routledge.

Grandin, T. and Johnson, C. (2006) *Animals in Translation*. London, Bloomsbury.

Grandin, T. (2009) 'How does visual thinking work in the mind of a person with autism? A personal account' in *Philosophical Transactions of the Royal Society B*, Vol. 364, Issue 1522, pp.1437–1442.

Gray, R. (nd) 'Digital manipulation'. Available at: www.robgray.com.au/grayoutdoors/essays/manipulation/index.php.

Grierson, J. (1930/1979) 'First Principles of Documentary' in Hardy, F. (Ed.) (1979) *Grierson on Documentary*. London, Faber.

Griffin, M. (2008) 'Visual Competence and Media Literacy: can one exist without the other?' *Visual Studies*, Vol. 23 No. 2, pp.113-129.

Gunning, T. (1990) 'The Cinema of Attractions: Early Film, its Spectator and the Avant-Garde', in Elsaesser, T. (Ed.) *Early Cinema: Space Frame Narrative*. London, British Film Institute, pp.56-62.

Guthrie, S.E. (1997) 'Anthropomorphism: a definition and a theory' in Mitchell, R.W., Thompson, N. S. and Miles, H.L. (Eds.) *Anthropomorphism: Anecdotes and Animals*. Albany, State University of New York Press.

Hale, B. (2009) 'Meet Spud, the bald hedgehog whose spines are making a dramatic comeback'. *Mail Online*, 14 July. Available at: www.dailymail.co.uk/news/article-1199477.

Hancocks, D. (2001) *A Different Nature: the paradoxical world of zoos and their uncertain future*. Berkeley, University of California Press.

Hanson, E. (2002) *Animal Attractions: nature on display in American zoos*. Princeton, Princeton University Press.

Haraway, D. (1989) *Primate Visions*. London, Routledge.

Hargrove, E. (1995) 'The Role of Zoos in the Twenty First Century' in Norton, B.G., Hutchins, M., Stevens, E.A. and Maple, T.L. (Eds.) *Ethics of the Ark: zoos, animal welfare and wildlife conservation*. Washington, Smithsonian Institution Press.

Hartley, A. (2010) 'Will China kill all Africa's elephants?' *The Spectator*, 24 March. Available at: www.spectator.co.uk/essays/all/5863872/will-china-kill-all-africas-elephants.thtml

Hartley, J. (1999) *The Uses of Television*. London, Routledge.

Hirata, K. (2005) 'Why Japan Supports Whaling' in *Journal of International Wildlife Law & Policy*, Vol. 8 No. 2, pp.129-149.

Holbert, R. L., Kwak, N. and Shah, D. V. (2003) 'Environmental Concern, Patterns of Television Viewing, and Pro-Environmental Behaviors: Integrating Models of Media Consumption and Effects' in *Journal of Broadcasting & Electronic Media*, Vol. 47 No. 2, pp.177-196.

IFAW (2008) *Killing with Keystrokes: An Investigation of the Illegal Wildlife Trade on the World Wide Web*. Available at: www.ifaw.org/Publications/Program_Publications/Wildlife_Trade/Campaign_Scientific_Publications/asset_upload_file848_49629.pdf.

Ingold, T. (2000) *The Perception of the Environment: essays in livelihood, dwelling and skill*. London, RoutledgeFalmer.

ILCP (nd) Ethical Standards. Available at: www.ilcp.com/?cid=58.

Isenberg, A.C. (2002) 'The Wild and the Tamed: Indians, Euroamericans, and the destruction of the bison' in Henninger-Voss, M. (Ed.) *Animals in Human History*. New York, University of Rochester Press.

Ito, M. (2008) 'Seeing Animals, Speaking of Nature: Visual Culture and the Question of the Animal' in *Theory, Culture & Society*, Vol. 25 No. 4, pp.119–137.

IUCN (1980) *World Conservation Strategy*. Gland, IUCN. Available at: http://data.iucn.org/dbtw-wpd/edocs/WCS-004.pdf.

IUCN (2009) *IUCN Red List of Threatened Species*. Version 2009.2. Available at www.iucnredlist.org. Downloaded on 3rd November 2009.

Jacka, E. (2003) ' "Democracy as Defeat": The Impotence of Arguments for Public Service Television' in *Television and New Media*, Vol. 4 No. 2, pp.177-192.

Jaschinski, B. (1996) *Zoo*. London, Phaidon.

Jaschinski, B. (2003) *Wild Things*. London, Thames and Hudson.

Jaschinski, B. (2009) Britta Jaschinki Interview. *CAPS News*, Winter. Available at www.captiveanimals.org/images/Britta_interview_CAPS.pdf.

Jeffries, M. (2000) 'Niche Broadcasting' in *Ecos*, 3/4, pp.70-76.

Jeffries, M. (2003) 'BBC Natural History Versus Science Paradigms' in *Science as Culture*, Vol. 12 No. 4, pp.527-545.

Jenkins, H. (2006) *Convergence Culture: where old and new media collide*. New York, New York University Press.

Jones, R. (2008) *Nano Nature: nature's spectacular hidden world*. London, Collins.

Jowit, J. (2010) 'Economic report into biodiversity crisis reveals price of consuming the planet.' *The Guardian*, 22 May. Available at: www.guardian.co.uk/environment/2010/may/21/biodiversity-un-report.

Kalland, A. (1993) 'Whale politics and green legitimacy: a critique of the anti-whaling campaign.' *Anthropology Today*, Vol. 9 No. 6, pp.3-7.

Kellert, S. R. (1979). *Public attitudes toward critical wildlife and natural habitat issues, phase I*. United States Department of the Interior Fish and Wildlife Service.

Kellert, S. R. (1980). *Phase II: Activities of the American public relating to animals*. United States Department of the Interior Fish and Wildlife Service.

Kessler, F. (2009) 'What You Get Is What You See: digital images and the claim on the real' in van den Boomen, M., Lammes, S., Lehmann, A-S., Raessens, J. and Schafer, M. T. (Eds.) *Digital Material: Tracing new media in everyday life and technology*. Amsterdam, Amsterdam University Press.

Kidman Cox, R. (2008) *Wildlife Photographer of the Year: Portfolio 18*. London, BBC Books.

King, L.E., Douglas-Hamilton, I. and Vollrath, F. (2007) 'African Elephants Run from the Sound of Disturbed Bees' in *Current Biology*, Vol. 17 No. 19, pp.832-833.

Komatsu, M. and Misaki, S. (2001) *The Truth Behind the Whaling Dispute*. Tokyo, Institute of Cetacean Research.

Lancendorfer K, M., Atkin, J.L., and Reece, B.B. (2008) 'Animals in advertising: Love dogs? Love the ad!' *Journal of Business Research*, 61, pp.384-391.

Lakoff, G. and Johnson, M. (1980) *Metaphors We Live By*. Chicago Il, University of Chicago Press.

Langer, S. (1942) *Philosophy in a New Key*. Harvard University Press.

Leadbeater, C. (2009) *We-Think: mass innovation, not mass production*. London, Profile Books.

Lekotjolo, N. (2010) 'Plan to kill elephants stirs outrage' in *Times Live*, 7 March. Available at: www.timeslive.co.za/local/article342977.ece

Lerner, J.E. and Kalof, L. (1999) 'The Animal Text: Message and Meaning in Television Advertisements' in *The Sociological Quarterly*, Vol. 40 No. 4, pp.565-586.

Lewis, M. (2005) Director Interview. BBC. Available at: www.bbc.co.uk/print/bbcfour/documentaries/storyville/mark-lewis.shtml.

Lewis-Williams, J.D. (2002) *The Mind in the Cave*. London, Thames and Hudson.

Lewis-Williams, J.D. and Dowson, T.A. (1988) 'The Signs of All Times: entoptic phenomena in Upper Palaeolithic Art' in *Current Anthropology*, Vol. 39 No. 2, pp.201-245.

Lippincott, L. and Bluhm, A. (2005) *Fierce Friends: artists and animals, 1750-1900*. London, Merrell.

Louv, R. (2006) *Last Child in the Woods: Saving Our Children from Nature-Deficit Disorder*. Chapel Hill, Algonquin Books.

Lovelock, J. (2006) *The Revenge of Gaia*. London, Penguin.

Lu Zhi (2002) *Giant Pandas in the Wild: saving an endangered species*. New York, Aperture.

Lutz, C.A. and Collins, J.L. (1993) *Reading National Geographic*. Chicago University of Chicago Press.

Machin. D. (2004) 'Building the World's Visual Language: The Increasing Global Importance of Image Banks in Corporate Media' in *Visual Communication*, 3, pp.316-336.

Maynard, P. (1997) *The Engine of Visualization: thinking through photography*. Ithaca, Cornell University Press.

McCartney, P., Himes, D. and Irvine, K. (2010) *Bird Watching*. Princeton, Princeton Univ. Press.

McCartney, P. (2010) 'Too Much Information with Benjamen Walker'. WFMU, 15.3.10. Available at: http://wfmu.org/playlists/shows/35063

MacIntyre, R. (1995) *War Against the Wolf: America's Campaign to Exterminate the Wolf*. Osceola, Voyageur Press.

McKenna, P. (2009) 'Eating Wildlife is Part of Chinese Culture' in *New Scientist*, 22 July, Issue 2717. Available at: www.newscientist.com/article/mg20327176.900-interview-saving-wild-china.html.

MacKenzie, D. (2008) 'Faroe islanders told to stop eating 'toxic' whales' in *New Scientist*, 28 November. Available at: www.newscientist.com/article/dn16159-faroe-islanders-told-to-stop-eating-toxic-whales.html.

McLuhan, M. (1964) *Understanding Media: the extensions of man*. Cambridge, Mass., MIT Press.

Messaris, P. (1998) Visual Aspects of Media Literacy. *Journal of Communication*, Vol. 48 No. 1, pp.70-80.

Messaris, P. (1994) *Visual Literacy: image, mind and reality*. Boulder, Westview Press.

Meyrowitz, J. (1998) 'Multiple Media Literacies' in *Journal of Communication*, Vol. 48 No. 1, pp.96-108.

Michael, D. and Chen, S. (2006) *Serious Games: Games that educate, train and inform*. Boston MA, Thomson.

Miles, H. (2006) Interview (by Mike Salisbury) *Wildscreen/WildFilmHistory*. Available at: www.wildfilmhistory.org/oh/18/Hugh+Miles.html.

Mitchell, W.J.T. (1987) *Iconology: Image, Text, Ideology*. Chicago, University of Chicago Press.

Mitchell, W.J.T. (1992) *The Reconfigured Eye*. Cambridge, Mass., MIT Press.

Mitchell, W.J.T. (2002) 'Showing Seeing' in *Journal of Visual Culture*, Vol 1 No. 2, pp.165-181.

Mitman, G. (1999) *Reel Nature: America's romance with wildlife on film*. Cambridge Mass., Harvard University Press.

Mollison, J. (2005) *James and Other Apes*. London, Boot.

Monbiot, G. (2002) 'Planet of the Fakes'. Available at www.monbiot.com/archives/2002/12/17/planet-of-the-fakes/.

Montgomery, S. (1992) *Walking with the Great Apes: Jane Goodall, Dian Fossey, Birute Galdikas*. Houghton Mifflin.

Moorehead, A. (1968) *The Fatal Impact*. London, Penguin Books.

Moores, S. (2000) *Media and Everyday Life in Modern Society*. Edinburgh, University of Edinburgh Press.

Morey, S. (2009) ' A Rhetorical Look at Ecosee' in Dobrin, S.I. and Morey, S. (Eds.) *Ecosee: image, rhetoric, nature*. Albany, SUNY Press.

Morris, B. (2000) *Animals and Ancestors: an ethnography*. Oxford, Berg.

Morris, D. (1979) *Animal Days*. London, Jonathan Cape.

Morris, D. (2000) Interview (with Christopher Parsons). Wildscreen/WildFilmHistory. Available at: www.wildfilmhistory.org/oh/19/clip/307/section/115/Desmond+Morris:+The+first+Zoo+Time+and+bringi....html

Ndalianis, A. (2005) *Neo-Baroque Aesthetics and Contemporary Entertainment*. Cambridge Mass., MIT Press.

Nelson, R.K. (1983) *Make Prayers to the Raven*. Chicago, University of Chicago Press.

Newhall, N. (1999) *From Adams to Stieglitz*. New York, Aperture.

Newton, J. (2001) *The Burden of Visual Truth: the role of photojournalism in mediating reality*. New York, Routledge.

Nicholls, B. (2008) 'The Question of Evidence, the Power of Rhetoric and the Documentary Film' in Austin, T. and de Jong W. (Eds.) *Rethinking Documentary: new perspectives, new practices*. Maidenhead, McGraw Hill/Open University Press.

Nicholls, H. (2007) *Lonesome George: the lives and loves of the world's most famous tortoise*. London, Pan Books.

Nichols, M. (2001) 'Nick's Take on Photographic Ethics'. Available at: http://michaelnicknichols.com/article/ethics/.

Nichols, M. and Goodall, J. (2005) *Brutal Kinship*. New York, Aperture.

Nightingale, N. (2009) Personal communication.

Nimmo, H. (2009) Personal communication.

NMK (2008) 'Conservationists Embrace Social Media'. 24 November. Available at: www.nmk.co.uk/article/2008/11/24/conservationists-embrace-social-media.

Noelker, F. (2004) *Captive Beauty*. Urbana, University of Illinois Press.

Norton, B.G. (1995) 'Caring for Nature: a broader look at animal stewardship' in Norton, B.G., Hutchins, M., Stevens, E.A. and Maple, T.L. (Eds.) *Ethics of the Ark: zoos, animal welfare and wildlife conservation*. Washington, Smithsonian Institution Press.

Nystrom, C. L. (2000) 'Symbols, Thought, and Reality: the contributions of Benjamin Lee Whorf and Susanne K. Langer to media ecology' in *Atlantic Journal of Communication*, Vol. 8 No. 1, pp.8-33.

Olson, R. J. M. and Hulser, K. (2003) 'Petropolis: a social history of urban animal companions' in *Visual Studies*, Vol. 18 No. 2, pp.133-143.

Orwell, G. (1957) 'Shooting an Elephant' in *Inside the Whale and Other Essays*. Harmondsworth, Penguin.

Papacharissi, Z. (2002) 'The Virtual Sphere: the internet as a public sphere' in *New Media and Society*, Vol. 4 No. 1, pp.9-27.

Palmer, C. (2010) *Shooting in the Wild: An Insider's Account of Making Movies in the Animal Kingdom*. San Francisco, Sierra Club Books.

Palmer, J.A. (1993) 'Development of concern for the environment and formative experiences of educators' in *Journal of Environmental Education*, Vol. 24 No. 3, pp.26-30.

Parfit, M. (2006) Report from Nootka Sound, March 14, 2006. Available at: www.reuniteluna.com/news_release.php?id=841.

Parsons, C. (2001) Interview with David Attenborough. *WildFilmHistory*. Available at: www.wildfilmhistory.org/oh/2/Christopher+Parsons.html.

Paterson, M. (2007) *The Senses of Touch*. Oxford, Berg Publishers.

Pelletier, C. (2005) 'Reconfiguring Interactivity, Agency and Pleasure in the Education and Computer Games Debate – using Žižek's concept of interpassivity to analyse educational play' in *E–Learning*, Vol. 2 No. 4, pp.317-326.

Perloff, M. (1998) 'The Morphology of the Amorphous: Bill Viola's Videoscapes'. Available at: http://wings.buffalo.edu/epc/authors/perloff/viola.html.

Peterson, D. (2003) *Eating Apes*. Berkeley, University of California Press.

Pettie, A. (2008) 'Animals in the Womb' in *Daily Telegraph*, 15 October. Available at: www.telegraph.co.uk/culture/tvandradio/3 562165/Animals-in-the-Womb.html.

Philo, C. (1995) Animals, geography, and the city: notes on inclusions and exclusions. *Environment and Planning D: Society and Space*, Vol. 13, pp.655-681.

Philo, G. and Henderson, L. (1998) *What the Audience Thinks: focus group research into the likes and dislikes of UK wildlife viewers.* Unpublished GUMG report for Wildscreen.

Pocius, G.L. (2001) *A Place to Belong: Community Order and Everyday Space in Calvert, Newfoundland.* St Johns, Institute for Research on Public Policy.

Pollo, S. Graziano, M. and Giacoma, C. (2009) 'The Ethics of Natural History Documentaries' in *Animal Behaviour*, Vol. 77, pp.1357-1360.

Postman, N. (1986) *Amusing Ourselves to Death.* London, Methuen.

Raessens, J. (2009) 'Serious Games from an Apparatus Perspective' in van den Boomen, M., Lammes, S., Lehmann, A-S., Raessens, J. and Schafer, M. T (Eds.) *Digital Material: Tracing new media in everyday life and technology.* Amsterdam, Amsterdam University Press.

Rey-Lopez, M., Diaz-Redondo, R.P., Fernandez-Vilas, Pazos-Arias, J.J. (2007) 'Entercation: engaging viewers in education through TV' in *Computers in Education*, Vol. 5 No. 2.

Reynolds, M. (2008) 'Animal Planet Show Has Whale Of A Season' in *Multichannel News*, December 23. Available at: www.multichannel.com/article/print/161230-Animal_Planet_Show_Has_Whale_Of_A_Seaso n.php.

Rich, B. (2008) *To Uphold the World: the message of Ashoka and Kautilya for the 21st century.* Delhi, Penguin/Viking.

Ritvo, H. (1989) *The Animal Estate: The English and Other Creatures in the Victorian Age.* Cambridge, Mass., Harvard University Press.

Rizzo, T. (2008) 'YouTube: the New Cinema of Attractions' in *Scan*, Vol. 5 No. 1. Available at: http://scan.net.au/scan/journal/ display.php?journal_id=109.

Rothenberg, D. (2007) 'To Wail With a Whale: Anatomy of an Interspecies Duet'. Available at: http://thousandmilesong.com/images/ wail_with_whale.pdf

Rothenberg, D. (2008) *Thousand Mile Song.* New York, Basic Books.

Rowlands, M. (2002) *Animals Like Us.* London, Verso.

Rowlands, M. (2009) *The Philosopher and the World: lessons from the wild on love, death and happiness.* London, Granta.

Sabloff, A. (2001) *Reordering the Natural World: humans and animals in the city.* Toronto, University of Toronto Press.

Schwartz, D. (2003) 'Professional Oversight: policing the credibility of photojournalism' in Gross, L., Katz, J.S. and Ruby, J. (Eds.) *Image Ethics in the Digital Age.* Minneapolis, University of Minnesota Press.

Scott, K.D. (2003) 'Popularizing Science and Nature Programming: the role of 'spectacle' in contemporary wildlife documentary' in *Journal of Popular Film and Television*, Vol. 31 No. 1, pp.29-35.

Sekula, A. (1982) 'On the Invention of Photographic Meaning' in Burgin, V. (Ed.) *Thinking Photography.* London, MacMillan.

Shaffer, D.W. (2005) 'Epistemic Games' in *Innovate*, Vol. 1 No. 6. Available at: http://innovateonline.info/pdf/ vol1_issue6/Epistemic_Games.pdf

Sharp, P. (2008) 'China's Zoos: "Asylums For Animals"'. Sky News, 27 February. Available at: http://news.sky.com/skynews/Home/Sky-News-Archive/Article/20080641266775.

Shigong, L. (2009) Does China Need an Animal Protection Law? *Beijing Review*, 22 October. Available at: www.bjreview.com.cn/forum/ txt/2009-10/17/content_224366.htm.

Singer, P. (1993) *Practical Ethics.* Cambridge, Cambridge University Press.

Singhal, A. and Rogers, E.M. (1999) *Entertainment-Education: a communication strategy for social change.* Mahwah NJ, Lawrence Erlbaum.

Singhal, A., Cody, M.J., Rogers, E.M. and Sabido, M. (Eds.) (2004) *Entertainment-Education and Social Change: history, research and practice.* Mahwah NJ, Lawrence Erlbaum.

Sobchack, V. (1992) *The Address of the Eye: a phenomenology of film experience*. Princeton NJ, Princeton University Press.

Sontag, S. (1979) *On Photography*. Harmmondsworth, Penguin Books.

Spamer, T. and Thorburn, G. (2007) *Animal Spy: animal welfare behind enemy lines*. London, Vision.

Spears, N. and Germain, R. (2007) '1900-2000 in Review: the shifting role and face of animals in print advertisements in the twentieth century' in *Journal of Advertising*, Vol. 36, No. 3, pp.19-33.

Spears, N.E., Mowen, J.C. and Chakraborty, G. (1996) 'Symbolic Role of Animals in Print Advertising: Content Analysis and Conceptual Development' in *Journal of Business Research*, 37, pp.87-95.

Steenkampf, W.S. (2008) *The Contribution of Wildlife and Environmental Television Programming to Conservation and Environmental Awareness*. Unpublished MSc Thesis. University of the Free State, SA.

Stelter, B. (2008) 'You've Seen the YouTube Video; Now Try the Documentary' in *New York Times*, 10 May. Available at: www.nytimes.com/2008/05/10/arts/television/10kruger.html.

Stibbe, A. (2007) 'Zen and the Art of Environmental Education in the Japanese Animated Film *Tonari no Totoro*' in *Journal for the Study of Religion, Nature and Culture*, Vol. 1 No. 4, pp.468-488.

Stoett, P. J. (2005) 'Of Whales and People: Normative Theory, Symbolism, and the IWC' in *Journal of International Wildlife Law and Policy*, Vol. 8 No. 2, pp.151-175.

Stuart, T. (2006) *The Bloodless Revolution: radical vegetarians and the discovery of India*. London, HarperCollins.

Tabuchi, H. (2009) 'Film on the Dolphin Hunt Stirs Outrage in Japan' in *New York Times*, 22 October. Available at: www.nytimes.com/2009/10/23/world/asia/23dolphin.html.

Tagg, J. (1982) 'The Currency of the Photograph' in Burgin, V. (Ed.) *Thinking Photography*. London, MacMillan.

Tagg, J. (1993) *The Burden of Representation*. Minneapolis, University of Minnesota Press.

Tagg, J. (2009) *The Disciplinary Frame*. Minneapolis, University of Minnesota Press.

TEEB (2009) *The Economics of Ecosystems and Biodiversity for National and International Policy Makers – Summary: Responding to the Value of Nature 2009*. UNEP. Available at: www.teebweb.org/LinkClick.aspx?fileticket=I4Y2nqqIiCg%3D.

Tester, K. (1991) *Animals and Society: the humanity of animal rights*. London, Routledge.

Thomas, K. (1984) *Man and the Natural World*. London, Penguin Books.

Thomashow, M. (1996) *Ecological Identity: Becoming a Reflective Environmentalist*. MIT Press.

Trumbo, J. (1998) 'Visual Literacy and Science Communication' in *Science Communication*, Vol 20 No. 4, pp.409-425.

Tryhorn, C. (2009) 'Fans go ape as Five axes Monkey Life' in *The Guardian*, 5 November. Available at: www.guardian.co.uk/media/2009/nov/05/channel-five-monkey-life.

Ulmer, G.L. (2004) *Teletheory*. New York, Atropos Press.

Ulmer, G.L. (2005) *Internet Invention: From Literacy to Electracy*. New York, Longman.

Vail, C.S. and Risch, D. (2006) *Driven By Demand: Dolphin drive hunts in Japan and the involvement of the aquarium industry*. WDCS. Available at: www.wdcs.org/submissions_bin/drivenbydemand.pdf.

van Stipriaan and Kearns, R.A. (2009) 'Bitching about a billboard: Advertising, gender and canine (re)presentations' in *New Zealand Geographer*, 65, pp.126–138.

Vaughan, C. (n.d.) 'Flying Solo – The Maneka Gandhi Interview'. First published in *Vegan Voice*. Available at: http://animal-lib.org.au/get-active/activists/86-gandhi-maneka.html.

Vidal, J. (2007) 'Welcome to Modbury. Just don't ask for a plastic bag' in *The Guardian*, 28 April. Available at: www.guardian.co.uk/environment/2007/apr/28/plasticbags.frontpage news

Vivanco. L.A. (2004) 'The Work of Environmentalism in an Age of Televisual Adventures' in *Cultural Dynamics*, Vol. 16 No. 1, pp.5-27.

Walker, A. (1991) *The Culture of Nature: North American Landscape from Disney to the Exxon Valdez*. Toronto, Between the Lines.

Watson, L. (2002) *Elephantoms: tracking the elephant*. New York, W.W. Norton.

Welling, B. H. (2009) ' Ecoporn: on the limits of visualising the nonhuman' in Dobrin. S.I. and Morey, S. (Eds.) *Ecosee: image, rhetoric, nature*. New York, SUNY Press.

Wells, P. (2009) *The Animated Bestiary: animals, cartoons, and culture*. New Brunswick, Rutgers University Press.

Wexler, R. (2008) 'Onward, Christian penguins: wildlife film and the image of scientific authority' in *Studies in History and Philosophy of Biological and Biomedical Sciences*, Vol. 39, pp.273-279.

Wheatley, H. (2004) 'The Limits of Television?: Natural History Programming and the Transformation of Public Service Broadcasting' in *European Journal of Cultural Studies*, Vol. 7 No. 3, pp.325-339.

Williams, P. (2009) 'Presenter Interview: Dr Charlotte Uhlenbroek' in *The NatureWatch*, available at: www.thenaturewatch.com/2009/01/presenter-interview-dr-charlotte.html.

Williams, R. and Newton, J. (2007) *Visual Communication: integrating media, art and science*. New York, Lawrence Erlbaum Assocs.

Williams, R. (1999) 'Beyond Visual Literacy: Omniphasism, a theory of balance (Part One)' in *Journal of Visual Literacy*, Vol. 19 No. 2, pp.159-178.

Williams, R. (2000) 'Beyond Visual Literacy: visual illiteracy and intuitive visual persuasion (Part Two)' in *Journal of Visual Literacy*, Vol. 20 No. 1, pp.111-124.

Williams, R. (2000) 'Beyond Visual Literacy: Omniphasism in the classroom (Part Three)' in *Journal of Visual Literacy*, Vol. 20 No. 2, pp.219-242.

Williams, R. (2003) 'Transforming intuitive illiteracy: understanding the effects of the unconscious mind on image meaning, image consumption and behavior' in *Explorations in Media Ecology*, Vol. 2, pp.119-134.

Williams, V. (1999) *New Natural History*. Bradford, National Museum of Photography, Film and Television.

Wilson, A. (1991) *The Culture of Nature: North American landscape from Disney to the Exxon Valdez*. Toronto, Between the Lines.

Wilson, E.O. (1984) *Biophilia*. Cambridge Mass., Harvard University Press.

Wilson, E.O. (2001) *The Diversity of Life*. London, Penguin Books.

Wilson, E. O. (2003) 'The encyclopedia of life' in *Trends in Ecology and Evolution* Vol. 18 No. 2, pp.77-80. Available from www.sciencedirect.com/science/article/B6VJ1-47C8RDN-3/2/befac60e32dd59 e55ff8bfc75f9848c6.

Winston, B. (1993) 'The Documentary Film as Scientific Inscription' in Renov, M. Ed *Theorizing Documentary*. London, Routledge.

Wolfe, A. (2001) *Migrations: wildlife in motion*. Hillsboro, Beyond Words Publishing.

Wolfe, A. (2010) 'Jim Goldstein interviews Art about the Age of Digital'. Available at: http://blog.artwolfe.com/2010/03/jim-goldstein-interviews-art-about-the-age-of-digital/.

Wright, J.H. (2007) *Can Wildlife Documentaries Change Attitudes?* GAFI unpublished report.

Wright, J.H. (2009) 'Use of Film for Community Conservation Education in Primate Habitat Countries' in *American Journal of Primatology* 71, pp.1–5.

Yang, D., Dai, X., Deng, Y., Lu,W. and Jiang, Z. (2007) 'Changes in attitudes toward wildlife and wildlife meats in Hunan Province, central China, before and after the severe acute respiratory syndrome outbreak' in *Integrative Zoology*, Vol. 2 No. 1, pp.19-25.

Zdravic, A. (2005) Discussion at Towards an Eco-Cinema. RSA Conference, Bristol 29.9.05. Available at: www.artsandecolgy.org.uk/__data/assets/pdf_file/0020/152732/Eco-Cinema_Transcripts.pdf.

Zinsser, H. (2000) *Rats, Lice and History*. London, Penguin Books.

Index